1987

THEATRE CRAFTS

HOW-TO

VOLUME ONE

GLUES • ADHESIVES • WOOD •
METALWORKING • PLASTICS •
PLASTIC SAFETY • PLASTIC-WORK-
ING TOOLS • CARPENTRY TIPS
AND TRICKS • PYLONS • DOOR
UNITS • BOARD STRETCHERS •
MODULAR SCENERY SYSTEMS •
SPATTERING • PLUMBING • PAINT-
ING • LIFT JACKS • HANGING
IRONS • SWIVEL BRAKE CASTERS •

FROM THE EDITORS OF THEATRE CRAFTS MAGAZINE

A THEATRE CRAFTS BOOK/DISTRIBUTED BY DRAMA BOOK PUBLISHERS, NEW YORK

Distributed by Drama Book Publishers, 821 Broadway, New York, New York 10003.
Published by Theatre Crafts Books, a division of Theatre Crafts Associates, 135 Fifth Avenue, New York, New York 10010

Cover and book design: Sally Blakemore

ISBN: 0-916477-01-0

HOW-TO

VOLUME ONE

INTRODUCTION

Trying to create an earthquake on stage? Looking for a way to actor-proof stage furniture? Searching for a solution to on-stage plumbing? Meet Theatre Crafts' HOW-TO, VOLUME ONE—an anthology of technical theatre problems and solutions from the pages of Theatre Crafts magazine.

Over the years Theatre Crafts has regularly published how-to articles. These articles and letters to the editor—submitted by our readers—are a combination of tips, tricks and techniques from theatres across the country. They are a combination of casebooks on how problems were solved for a given production as well as solutions for making life in the shop or back stage generally easier. The solutions run the gamut from the high tech and super sophisticated to low tech gizmos. Some may appear to be reinventing the wheel. Others might provoke the "that's nothing new" response. Theatre Crafts' has always taken the position that if it's news to them—it's probably news to someone else in the performing arts community. And still others are truly ground breaking solutions.

And, in fact the phone at Theatre Crafts rings most frequently with reader inquiries that go something like this," I remember that Theatre Crafts ran an article on how to fake etched glass—but I can't find it. Could you send me a copy? Or tell me which issue to look it up in?"

No problem. HOW-TO, VOLUME ONE puts together—in one book —a selected group of articles covering: 1. Basics: adhesives, plastics, wood and steel; 2. Platforms, flooring, escapes, and revolves; 3. Scenic construction: tricks and techniques; 4. Rigging and roll drops; 5. Uncle Dunc's column (one of our regular contributors) and scenic artists techniques; 6. Shop built hardware and more pneumatic solutions; and 7. Robert Scales' Lab Theatre on hydraulics and pneumatics (another regular contributor).

None of these categories is meant to be a definitive look at all you need to know about these subjects —but rather a collection of helpful, hands-on, how-to information from users and practioners in the field.

Each article—reproduced here from the actual pages of the magazine—indicates its date of original publication. We did not attempt to update budgets or material costs so dollar figures are as of the original publication date. And, in the back of the book we have tried to track down current biographical information on the contributors.

Stay tuned for HOW-TO, VOLUME TWO—scheduled to be out later in 1984. Number Two will include articles on shop built special effects machines, Garrit Lydecker's Prop Shop Power series, Frank Whaley's Prop Master's Notebook, a host of special prop and production solutions for specific shows and much more.

The Editors

CONTENTS

Basics: Adhesives, Plastics, Wood, and Steel

GLUE AND YOU
by Daniel Koetting   2

ADHESIVE FORMULATION
by Thomas J. Corbett   4

GARBAGE TO GRANDEUR
by James R. Bakkom   7

SAND DUNES THAT TRAVEL
by William Daniel File   16

POOR MAN'S VACUUM-FORM
MACHINE
by Michael Hottois   19

LATHING FOAM SPINDLES
by Thomas J. Corbett   20

WHAT—MORE WIRE CUTTERS?
by Thomas J. Corbett   24

TEMPLATE-SPUN POLYSTYRENE FOAM
FOR STAGE FURNITURE
by Richard H. Chapman   27

A PVC GAZEBO
By Raynette Halvorsen Smith   29

WELDING BASICS FOR STRENGTH
AND DESIGN FLEXIBILITY
by David Sealy   32

STEEL TUBING
by Richard W. Durst   35

WOOD WORDS
by Daniel Koetting   38

Platforms, Flooring, Escapes, and Revolves

SPIRAL STAIR DESIGN AND
CONSTRUCTION
by Jeffrey Sultan   42

ROTA-LOCK STAIRS
by William Anderson   44

IMPROVED STEP UNITS
by A. Evan Haag   45

A PORTABLE DANCE SUB-FLOOR
by Charles Purchase   46

SOLVE THE FLOORING
by Charles L. Riccillo   48

FLOORING OVER AN ANNULAR RING
by Russell Houchen   50

PLATFORM LEGGING
by Karl T. Pope   51

IMPROVED LEGGING FOR WOODEN
PLATFORMS
by John Chenault   53

HYBRID PARALLEL PLATFORMS
by Michael Glenn Ward   54

PLATFORMING FOR THE LIBERAL
ARTS SHOP
John T. Howard, Jr.   56

SELF ADJUSTING RAKE LEG
by Michael Ludwick   58

MOTORIZED TURNTABLE
by Stancil Campbell   59

STEEL TUBING REVOLVE
by Peter Bendevski   62

Scenic Construction: Tricks and Techniques

TWO SOLUTIONS FROM THE VASSAR
SHOP
by Bryan Ackler   64

BUILDING A PRACTICAL DOOR UNIT
by Leon Pike   65

MULTI-PURPOSE PYLONS
by Bryan H. Ackler   67

FOOLPROOF CORNER BLOCK
by Michael Glenn Ward   68

A BOARD STRETCHER
by Leon Pike   69

A MODULAR SCENIC SYSTEM
by Wayne Kramer   71

PLATFORM CLAMPS
by John T. Howard, Jr.   73

HEXEL HONEYCOMB PANELS
by John Priest and Pierre Cayard   73

ACTOR-PROOFING FURNITURE
by Patrick Reed   74

CREATING LAMINATED CURVES
by Allan Fanjoy   76

LAMINATING CURVES FOR SCENIC
CONSTRUCTION
by Thomas J. Corbett   78

FLAME TEXTURING WOOD
by Keith Arnett   80

CONTOURED HILLS
by Stancil Campbell   81

TAPERED FLUTED COLUMNS
by Mark Freij   82

Rigging and Roll Drops

ENDLESS LINE RIGGING
by Thomas J. Corbett   84

THE TRADITIONAL ROLL DROP
by Allan Fanjoy   86

A VARIATION ON THE ROLL DROP
by James Fay   88

THE VERSATILE CUT DROP STAGES A
COMEBACK
by Barry L. Bailey   90

CHECK YOUR RIGGING
by William Lord   94

Uncle Dunc and Scenic Artists' Techniques

UNCLE DUNC'S TIPSHEET
by R. Duncan Mackenzie   98

FLAT JOINT IDEAS   98
BUBBLE FILM   98
UNCLE DUNC'S
CHEAPO AIR CYLINDER   99
HAND-HELD FEET/INCHES/SIXTEENTHS
CALCULATOR   99
UNCLE DUNC'S PUSHMI-PULLYU
ACTUATOR   100

CABLE-TENSIONING DEVICE   100
CATALOGUE PICK   100
AIR-POWERED CURTAIN TRACKS   101

SCREENWIRE PANELS
by David Glenn   102

TEXTURAL FIBER HANGINGS
by Karen Huffman   104

STAINED GLASS
by Leo Gambacorta   107

SOLUTIONS FOR PAINTING AND
PLUMBING
by Phillip Grayson   108

SCENIC SOLUTIONS WITH FIBERS
by Carey Wong   110

OUT OF THE HOSPITAL AND ONTO
THE STAGE
by Gregg Olsson   115

SUPERGRAPHING SETS AND COS-
TUMES FOR THE LIFE OF ORESTES
by Carey Wong   117

A WOOD GRAINING TOOL
by Richard Slabaugh   122

**Shop Built Hardware and More
Pneumatics**

LIFT JACKS
by John T. Howard, Jr.   125

SHOP-BUILT HANGING IRONS
by John T. Howard, Jr.   125

HYDRAULIC WALL JACKS FOR THE
THEATRE
by Everett Littlefield   126

HIGH SPEED ELECTRIC SCREW
SHOOTER
by Mike Stair   128

MULTI-PURPOSE CLAMPS
by R.J. Loyd   129

AIR CYLINDERS AT THE GUTHRIE
by Terry Sateren   130

UPSIDE DOWN AIR-BEARINGS
by Pete Davis   131

THE AIR-BEARING CASTER
by Robert Scales   132

HYDRAULIC CASTERS
by Terry Sateren   133

AIR-STAPLER AND SCENIC
CONSTRUCTION
by William Miller   134

**Robert Scales' Lab Theatre:
Hydraulics and Pneumatics**

PNEUMATICS, PART 1
by Robert Scales   136

PNEUMATIC FLUID POWER SYSTEM
BASICS
Part 1: generator, circuitry, working
device
by Robert Scales   138

PNEUMATIC FLUID POWER SYSTEM
BASICS
Part 2: valves, regulation, protection
devices
by Robert Scales   140

HYDRO-PNEUMATICS
by Robert Scales   143

THE REMOTE SWIVEL BRAKE CASTER
by Robert Scales   146

PNEUMATICS: SINGLE MOVEMENT
EFFECTS
by Robert Scales   148

EARTHQUAKES
by Robert Scales   151

CABLE CYLINDERS
by Robert Scales   155

FLUID POWER
by Robert Scales   159

BIOGRAPHICAL INDEX   164

SIDEBARS

HOT GLUE DETAILING   4

PLASTICS AND SAFETY   9

POLYURETHANE FOAM   11

PLASTIC FOAMS AND SAFETY   13

STYROFOAM SAFETY   24

FOAM CASTING IN SAND   31

DISSENTING ON THE UNIVERSAL
CORNER-BLOCK   69

SHOESTRING SLIDING DOORS   78

CONSTRUCTION TIPS   104

VARIATIONS ON FOAM CORE
CONSTRUCTION   105

ELEGANT ETCHED GLASS   107

FLAT BLACK SOLUTION   108

STYROFOAM AND CANVAS   108

50 CENT BEAMS   108

SPATTER TECHNIQUES   109

KINETIC LEAVES   120

ACRYLITE LOGO   121

Basics: Adhesives, Plastics, Wood, and Steel

Glue and You

by Daniel Koetting

As the process of constructing scenery and costumes progresses with the times, the theatre technician can benefit from what I call "split vision"—one eye toward the good products and solutions of the past that are sometimes overlooked and one eye toward the future, with its new products and solutions to common problems. This article will focus on old and new adhesives and their uses in wood construction, plastics construction, painting and texturing, and costume construction for the theatre. Note: This overview of available products is not all-inclusive. Mention of a particular product by trade name, unless specifically noted otherwise, does not constitute a recommendation; names are used as examples of various kinds of adhesives.

Wood construction

Several varieties of glues are used in wood construction. *Hide glue* (made from animals' hoofs, hides, and bones) is one of the oldest glues used in woodworking. It is available in a syrup-like liquid form. Similar to hide glue is *carpenter's glue,* which is available in small flake or large grain form. Before use, carpenter's glue must be soaked in water and then cooked in a double boiler or glue pot—resulting in a distinctive odor. Hide glue and carpenter's glue must be clamped until dry (18-24 hours). Both are good gap fillers and relatively cheap; neither is waterproof.

Various synthetic adhesives are replacing the above-mentioned glues in many areas of woodworking. The most popular synthetic glue used in scenery construction, commonly referred to as white glue, is *polyvinyl resin glue.* Available brands include: Elmer's Glue-all, Wilhold White Glue, and Swift's.

Another popular synthetic adhesive is a yellow- or cream-colored glue made specifically for wood joints— *aliphatic resin glue.* When applied according to directions, it creates a bond that is stronger than wood. Air-exposure causes this glue to dry to the touch in 10 minutes and to dry completely in 45 minutes. The quick set-up time may cause problems when gluing large objects or surfaces. Aliphatic resin glue has a low water resistance and is more expensive than white glue, but has a higher heat resistance than white glue. Available brands include Elmer's Professional Carpenter's Glue and The Bond Glue from Franklin Industries. Note: Aliphatic resin glue is sometimes called carpenter's glue.

Casein glue is another adhesive often used in scenery construction. Made from milk curd, it is available in powder form and must be mixed with water for each use. Casein glue is a good gap filler, dries in two to three hours, and is

water resistant (but not waterproof for outdoor use). Possible disadvantages include wear and tear on tool edges and staining of certain woods.

When a very strong, waterproof joint is needed—such as for properties construction—*resorcinol resin glue* is the adhesive to use. The heat caused by the chemical reaction produced by mixing the liquid (resin) with the powder (catalyst) sets this two-part glue. After mixing, the glue must be used within one to two hours. Resorcinol resin glue takes a long time to dry, leaves a dark stain where it soaks into the wood, and is quite expensive. However, it is very strong and holds well when exposed to extreme heat or extreme cold.

The glues I have discussed so far are the "work horses" of theatrical scene shops. Most wood lamination—the gluing of layers of wood—is done with one of these glues. There are, however, many new synthetic adhesives available that are good for special jobs. *Plastic resin glue* is a strong, water resistant glue useful for close-fitting joints (it is not a good gap filler). This adhesive is available in powder form and must be mixed with water and used within four hours. Plastic resin glue dries in approximately 16 hours and does not stain.

Another adhesive used primarily for very close-fitting joints is *urea resin glue.* It is used mostly in furniture assembly shops or other high-output wood shops. Application is by electric or high-frequency glue machines.

A third special application glue is *Scotch Grip Brand Wood Adhesive,* used to glue plywood floors to joists. It can be used for other wood joints too. This adhesive is available in tube form and is applied with a caulking gun.

Several other glues, also available in tube form, are used to hold paneling in place or to glue wood to other surfaces such as concrete and brick. Available *panel glues* include: Wilhold Glu On Panel Adhesive, Wilhold Builders Construction Adhesive, Wilhold Panel Adhesive 29, and #4314 Scotch Grip Construction Mastic.

Hot melt glue is similar to panel adhesive, but has a faster drying time. This general purpose glue is available in pellet form and must be heated in an electric glue gun until it becomes a viscous liquid. It is useful primarily for small applications, since it dries in 10 to 60 seconds. Hot melt glue does remain somewhat flexible, however, and can be resoftened by heat once applied.

Many types of *contact cement* are available for theatrical application. Some types are better for joining certain materials than others, but woods, metals, plastics, wood laminates, and hardboards can all be glued with contact cement. To use, both surfaces of the material to be joined are coated with the adhesive. When the cement becomes tacky, the pieces are joined in an instant bond. Proper alignment is very important, because some contact cements cannot be moved once the surfaces touch. Available brands include: Wilhold Professional Contact Cement (neoprene rubber base), Wilhold Smooth Spreading Contact Cement (neoprene rubber base but not as thick as Professional), and Scotch Grip Contact Cement #4488 (polychloroprene base). Available non-flammable contact cements include: Wilhold Contact Cement 21 (neoprene base), Wilhold Contact Cement 40 (latex/water base), Scotch Grip #5034 Contact Cement (water base), Scotch Grip #4729 Contact Cement (water base), and Scotch Grip #2226 Contact Cement (water base). A special contact adhesive for plastics and theatrical use is RoscoBond (see Plastic construction). Note: Almost all contact cements emit some form of toxic vapor. Read and follow all directions carefully.

Epoxy glue is especially valuable for small gluing jobs such as properties. This two-part adhesive consists of resin and a catalyst adhesive. Epoxy glue, although expensive, can be used on a wide range of materials and dries quickly (30 seconds to five minutes). It forms a waterproof, high-strength bond and is a good gap filler.

Plastic construction

Different types of plastics are being used increasingly in scenic construction. Many adhesives are already available for plastic applications and new materials and new techniques are being introduced rapidly. Some of the more common adhesives and their applications to plastics are discussed below. Rigid foams such as Styrofoam, polystyrene, urethane, and Ethafoam are used for textured walls, carved moldings, and applied details. Several types of adhesives for foam have recently been developed to replace polyvinyl glue. (White glue needs air to dry, and drying time for rigid foam glued with polyvinyl adhesive takes several days, if it dries at all). Special adhesives for rigid foam should be applied to both surfaces to be joined, allowed to dry for several minutes, then clamped together if possible. Available brands include: B.F. Goodrich PL 200, Dow Mastic No. 11, Wilhold Panel & Foam Adhesive, Scotch Grip Plastic Adhesive #1099 (spray on), Scotch Grip Contact Cement #1390, Scotch Grip Insulation Adhesive #35 (non-flammable solvent, spray on), and Sobo's Quik.

Sheet plastics, such as Plexiglas and sheet acrylic, require special glues. These adhesives are actually *solvents* that cause the plastic to dissolve and weld together as the solvent dries. Consult your plastic supplier for the best adhesive for your particular plastic.

Vacuum-formed plastics can be joined together by two types of adhesives—the *solvents* used for sheet plastics and *bodied adhesive*. Bodied adhesive contains a filler material made of the same material as the plastic and is particularly useful with very thin plastics. For more information on vacuum-formed plastics and their adhesives, see *Thermoplastic Scenery for the Theatre, Volume I* by Nicholas L. Bryson (currently out-of-print; try your library).

Two glues work well with plastic films such as Mylar, foil,

and vinyl. *Sobo's Quik* glues plastic film to porous surfaces, such as cloth and wood, and is flexible when dry. *Rosco-Bond* glues plastic film to porous and non-porous surfaces. Both adhesives must be thinned with water prior to this kind of use and do not give off any harmful vapors.

Scene painting

Adhesives are used often in scene painting, but they are best understood in the context of painting rather than adhesives. *Gelatine glue,* also known as *ground carpenter's glue,* is available in flaked or granular form. It must be soaked in water and then heated in a double boiler before use as size water. The size water is then mixed with dry pigment and acts as a binder. (Although this method is no longer widely used, some scene painters still prefer it to other methods.)

Polyvinyl glue can be thinned with water and used as a binder for priming and painting. It can also be used to glue canvas to flat frames and to glue other fabrics to various surfaces. Some of the polyvinyls, such as *Sobo* and *Sobo's Quik,* dry flexible. In addition, Sobo can be dry cleaned after it has dried. Polyvinyl adhesives are particularly useful on fabrics that must move, such as curtains and drops. For more information on adhesives and their uses in scene painting, see *Scenery for the Theatre* by Edward Cole and Burris Meyer (available from Little, Brown Publishers) and *Design and Painting for the Theatre* by Lynn Pecktal (available from Holt, Rinehart, and Winston).

Several other adhesives work well for specific applications. Rubber-based *clear latex* can be used as a binder for paints to be used on drops and scrims. *Wheat paste* and various kinds of wallpaper pastes are useful for attaching wallpaper and photo enlargements to other surfaces. *Spray adhesives* are good for prop work and for attaching certain kinds of paper to various surfaces. These adhesives, such as Scotch Spra-Ment and 3M Spray Adhesive #77, are available in aerosol form.

Costume construction

Adhesives are used basically two ways in the costume shop: to attach decoration to a portion of a costume and to create designs out of the glue itself. *Sobo,* a polyvinyl, is the most widely used adhesive for costume work. Its advantages, as previously noted, are clear drying, flexibility after drying, and a capacity for dry cleaning. These attributes are especially important in costume construction.

Hot melt glue is a popular adhesive for costume work. It can be used in the same way as the polyvinyls and, in addition, dries very quickly. One drawback—sometimes costumes decorated using hot melt glue cannot be dry cleaned or laundered because the heat employed causes the glue to remelt.

New adhesive products and new applications of adhesives for theatrical use become available almost daily. If you are interested in new glues and how to use them, write to the manufacturers and ask to be placed on their new products mailing list.

Originally published in April 1981

Hot Glue Detailing

Inspired by Mattel's Creepy Crawler Thing-maker, we have developed a method of copying decorative detail by using God's gift to the theatre: the hot glue gun.

First, make a negative mold by imbedding the detail piece in the plaster. After the piece is pulled from the mold, clean up the impression by filling in holes with plaster or spackling compound.

Coat the mold generously with petroleum jelly, though not enough to cover up the textures in the mold. Squeeze the hot glue into the mold, using the tip of the gun to push the glue into crevices and corners. When the mold is filled, use the tip of the gun to smooth out the top surface. When the glue is sufficiently cooled, begin to pry out all the edges until the entire piece can be pulled out.

Occasionally, we have made copies of larger molds that made use of the glue gun impractical. For these, we melted glue sticks in a double boiler and simply poured the glue into the mold, again using the gun's tip as a trowel to smooth and fill in areas. In this method, dry pigment can be added to the glue to color it. The dry pigment retains its darker wet value and dries to its lighter color.

Painting the glue details is easy, as it readily accepts spray paints. Other flexible base paints can be used if the detail is first sprayed with a workable fixative. As mentioned before, dry pigments can also be used to color the glue in a double boiler.

RONALD NAVERSEN
Northern Kentucky University
Highland Heights, Kentucky

Adhesive Formulation

by Thomas J. Corbett

Most scenic designers and technicians have a good idea of how paint is formulated; but adhesives are a similar supply item for the theatre that few of us know much about.

Paul Shattuck, president of Adhesive Products, Inc, of Albany, California, recently outlined information about formulating adhesives.

Adhesives have several basic ingredients, which can be adjusted to alter the properties of the finished product. These basic ingredients determine the product's application and suitability. According to Shattuck there are six basic categories of adhesives. Not all of these adhesives are genuinely useful for theatrical application. They do have differing properties, however, and therefore differing utilities for theatre.

Vegetable bases
The simplest form of adhesive is vegetable-based. Starch is one. Flour and water paste or wheat paste, once used in hanging wallpaper, is an immediate binder with low tack. Sugar, by contrast, has a high tack and will make your fingers very sticky. Tack indicates contact adhesion—to what degree a glue tends to grab two surfaces and resist their being separated.

Many natural materials exhibit adhesive properties, among them wood resin, natural rubber, salt, and clay. All of these are used alone or in combination to make an adhesive with its own characteristic properties. A typical natural-based adhesive might be mixed by using cooked starch (as a base), salt (added for flexibility), and sugar (added for stickiness). Clay provides body and stiffness, as does superfine sawdust. Cornstarch and/or flour can be used as thickener also. The amount of water added will affect both pene-

tration and speed of set for the compound. Clay is an interesting adhesive base and one we have all dealt with on repeated occasions. Walking through mud becomes hard work as the mud sticks to your shoes. When walking through clay the problem increases, for the fine particles cling to each other and to boots, and are heavy besides. The fine particles of clay hold water and do not let air beneath their fine contours. This results in a mechanical bond created by suction.

These mechanical bonds are weaker bonds than chemical bonds, but are useful. When building flats, for example, we use a heavier bond adhesive to hold the canvas onto the frame. If the same adhesive held the dutchman to the flat's joint, when the dutchman is removed the canvas would rip from the flat frame. We therefore choose a lighter bond adhesive, such as wheat paste, so that the canvas remains on the frame when the dutchman is struck.

Animal by-product bases
Carpenter's glue, a second type of adhesive, is compounded from animal by-products made by cooking fish heads or animal hides and bones in vats until residue comes to the surface. This residue is gelatin and is skimmed off the top. These glues include fish glue and animal cake glue. Interestingly, there is now a much better world market for gelatin than there is for carpenter's glue, while costs for these raw materials have escalated disproportionately. Animal glues have therefore fallen out of favor in the last few years, although they remain a versatile water-based adhesive system.

Synthetic glues
Water-based synthetics are the next order of adhesive. White glue is the

most popular. It is also the most basic, because it can be compounded to make other kinds of adhesives for differing utilities. The most common use is wood-to-wood bonding, or paper-to-paper binding. As wood and paper are both cellulose, either wood or paper have interchangeable adhesive utility.

White glue is standard in the scene shop and has largely filled the void left by carpenter's glue. (It is difficult to say if indeed there was a void as there seemed to be a shift away from the bother of double boilers and toward the simpler and more convenient white glue even before the gelatin became more desirable in other financial markets.) Because white glue can be cut with water, it can be mixed to different strengths just like carpenter's glue; it is therefore useful for the range of sizing through paint base and to gesso, just as animal glue has been.

Carpenter's glue mixed 15:1 with water and with a little dutch whiting makes good sizing for sealing and filling the pores of new canvas prior to painting. Mixed 5:1 with powdered paint pigments added, and maybe some whiting for either pastel tones or for filler, it makes a fine scenic paint. Mixed 1:1 with considerable whiting and maybe some color it makes a gesso which can be trowled, squeezed from a cake-decorating bag, or otherwise worked for texturing scenic elements. This kind of gesso mixture lacks mechanical flexibility, however, and tends to crack and break off the set without a protective coating of gauze.

White glue base is an oil derivitive manufactured by chemical distillation. This process yields a large family of resin adhesive bases that are stable and mix well with water. Because white glue can be cut with water it frequently is diluted by the supplier. Some white

glues have much less adhesive base than others. At this point, there is no required labeling for adhesives that will tell the customer how much adhesive base he is buying and, therefore, how much the glue can be cut usefully. (Shattuck points out that some of his products are as high as 95% adhesive base and, therefore, have excellent adhesive properties, and are more useful to the customer if cutting is desired.)

When other chemicals are added, flexible padding glue results. Padding glue is used in bookbinding and for binding tear-off pads. San Francisco Opera Company buys this padding cement in bulk as flex-glue for ground cloths, texturing, and other shiftable applications.

Interestingly, not all of the many forms of white glue surface into the retail mainstream. Less expensive white glue bonds wood to wood, or paper to wood for example, but more expensive derivitives bond vinyl to cloth, vinyl to vinyl, and plastics to wood, and are generally much more useful. From Adhesive Products, the 183AL-1 binds vinyl to wood, cloth, and other surfaces, as well as cloth to plastic and dissimilar materials with nonporous surfaces.

Rubber bases

The fourth adhesive type uses a water vehicle and a rubber base. Rubber has a natural self-adhesion although it does not adhere to many other surfaces. This makes a pressure-sensitive self-sealing envelope that does not need moistening to seal. It also makes contact cements that have a very high tack.

Rubber bases using solvent

Close to these are the fifth kind of adhesive, the rubber-based using a

solvent (in whole or in part). Adding solvent gives speed to the adhesive. Whereas water must ventilate and leave the bonding surfaces, some situations cannot vent to free air, demand faster adhesion time, or otherwise require speed. Because the petrochemically-based solvents are constantly increasing in price these adhesives are more costly. Generally, they will form bonds with a wider range of surfaces and are desirable for broad usage. Solvents can also cut through many surfaces and are a valuable ingredient for penetration. Many of these adhesives and/or solvents need chemical clean-up, however, and some are hazardous because of the chemicals involved in either their manufacture or their basic composition. Flammability and flash point are several concerns.

One example of the hazards associated with solvent adhesives involves a worker who used a chlorinated solvent adhesive and drank an alcoholic beverage at the same time. The solvents were absorbed into the blood stream through topical exposure and respiration and entered into chemical combination with the alcohol, resulting in severe illness. (Avoid using spray adhesives. They may contain hazardous solvents with an aerosol propellant that readily invades the lungs and subsequently the bloodstream.) This, coupled with other hazards associated with solvents, leaves many of us willing to reexamine water vehicle adhesives.

Hot melt glues

The last basic adhesive category discussed is thermoplastic or, as they are called, hot melts. Sold in solid form, these adhesives must be dispensed with a hot glue gun or a melting pot, which puts the adhesive into semi-liquid state. When the adhesive cools, a rugged and durable bond forms.

Hot melt adhesives are used commercially for box making and in other production applications, as well as in the domestic and retail consumer market. Thermoplastic adhesives have been used in iron-on patches (thermoset adhesive impregnated into cloth), laminating tapes, and specialty items extending beyond the domestic and industrial realms.

Thermoplastic adhesives are made from wax and wood resin (for stickiness), and contain other ingredients, such as polyethylene for film forming. Ingredients are cooked and then injected into cooling systems to make continuous bands that are cut into wafers or slugs for stick guns. The stick guns accept small sticks (about 1/2" diameter) or large diameter sticks (about 1"). The sticks are available in short stock as well as longer stocks of about 12". Manufacturers of commercial and domestic thermoplastic systems sell heating guns at low cost in order to open the market for their glue sticks. The stick diameters are not standardized in an effort to maintain individual markets. Although convenient, these glue sticks are expensive, costing as much as three times the wafer-form thermoset. You can buy commercial thermoplastic guns that will accept the wafers, but they have an industrial tool price. It pays to invest in the tool, however, if you use thermoplastic adhesives to any extent.

Use in the theatre

For theatrical use Shattuck recommends a limited number of adhesives. Five forms will fill most gluing needs. Most theatres can use hot melt, woodworking white glue, white glue designed for adhesion to plastics, flexible film glue for backdrops or ground cloths, and water-based pressure sensitive adhesive for foam-to-foam adhesion. Shattuck recommends that most theatres stay away from solvent systems. Technology and consumer demands are replacing most of the solvent systems with water-based pressure sensitive adhesives. Fire regulations, health hazards, consumer activism, and government regulations have accelerated the move away from solvent adhesives.

A publication called *Adhesives Red Book* lists all manufacturers and suppliers, along with their specialties and other information. The manufacturers listed represent a considerable geographic spread. The same publisher, Palmerton Publishing of Atlanta, Georgia, also prints a magazine for the industry called *Adhesives Age*. The articles tend to be very technical and of little value unless you're a chemist. The advertisements, however, are very useful to both manufacturers and users, including those in the theatrical trades.

What should the theatrical user look for in an application adhesive, other than its ability to make two (or more) things stick together? The following terminology may help you speak with clarity with your local adhesives supplier.

Wicking is the penetration of the adhesive or the rate at which water or another carrying agent is absorbed by the surfaces being bonded. As the water is being absorbed, it is carrying the bonding agent into the surface and giving the glue holding power. An adhesive with more water wicks faster and deeper but thinner.

Some surfaces demand penetration power. A printed label, for example, tends to repel the water carrier. Some decorative boxes are coated with plastic or lacquer that gives them a shiny gloss but inhibits wicking. Solvents are sometimes mixed into water carrier adhesives to give the surface penetration necessary to glue a gloss-coated box together. The penetrating agent allows the carrier to wick into the substrate.

Initial tack is desired for holding objects in place while the adhesive sets up. Without high initial tack clamping may be necessary while the adhesive dries.

Flexibility is sometimes desired. With vegetable and animal-based adhesives, sugars and salts work as plasticizers as they retain moisture. More sophisticated plasticizers involve adjusting the hardening time and the final cure. Moisture retention is the plasticizer for water vehicle systems.

Resistance to environmental conditions is sometimes necessary, and special additives can be used to help the adhesive maintain tack, form a skin while it cures, or otherwise prevent adhesive failure before it has had time to cure.

How fast the adhesive forms a *film surface* is adjustable as well. This film may retard curing, assist environmental resistance, or otherwise provide desirable results. The nature of the final film is frequently important to theatrical users, as direct painting is usually desirable.

Viscosity is not only important when the product is new but also as the glue ages. Fillers and extenders are sometimes used in adhesives, and they must remain stable and in even homogenous distribution as well as resist oxidation, for viscosity is adversely affected by these changes.

Drooling and skinning are what these terms imply. Drooling is when a low-viscosity adhesive runs out from under the surfaces being glued. Skinning is a premature reaction with the air where the surface of the adhesive forms a barrier.

Open time is the amount of time that the user has to work with the adhesive and its surfaces after the glue is applied and before the two surfaces are put together.

Simpler adhesives form mechanical bonds, the more compounded adhesives form chemical bonds. The simple mechanical bond between a paper label and a glass bottle is formed not because of surface penetration of the adhesive into the bottle but because the glue makes a suction bond to the glass. This simple suction bond may have to form 700 times a minute, as it does on the Michelob bottling line in Los Angeles.

When penetration is involved more factors enter in and the user needs to be more concerned with each application. Sometimes the obvious eludes us in our efforts to be complete. For fear of omitting the most important part of gluing, some process reminders are in order. Cleanliness is foremost. Dirty surfaces prevent full surface contact between those faces being pressed together. The glue must then act structurally, which places a new burden on the bond. If the bond is a mechanical one, such as a suction bond, the gluing will necessarily be very weak. Clean and dry are the by-words in the shop.

Adhesives have been replacing fasteners for many years. Speed, convenience, and the range of new adhesives have contributed to this shift away from old techniques. It is not just new homes where subfloor adhesive helps prevent squeaks and panel adhesive hangs furring strips onto concrete walls. It is the whole industrial climate. Theatre is as responsive to change as any other industry, if not more so, for our fiscal balance has always been tenuous and always demanded a component of inexperienced help. Our production time frames are as rigorous as any industry's and our artistic dimensions more demanding. Knowledge of adhesives is therefore necessary, and time spent studying the opportunities presented by new products pays itself back readily. Stick with it, and you will be bound to use more adhesives.

Materials

Adhesives manufactured by Adhesive Products, Inc, 520 Cleveland Avenue, Albany, California 94706, and of use to the theatrical community. Including tapes, hot melt adhesives, animal cake glues, and a wide variety of starch and white (synthetic) glues. They are responsive to user queries and are willing to supply special adhesives for unusual application problems. That may be one of the reasons they supply the San Francisco Opera with carpenter's glue, flexible adhesive, and foam glue.

140CG-1 All-purpose woodworking glue (natural fibers only). Polyvinyl acetate emulsion (white glue), thicker than many retail brands. For building flats, and similar applications.

183AL-1 Broader range of materials, such as wood/wood, paper/paper, plastics/paper, cloth/plastics. Will glue foam to foam.

183BW-3 White glue with a dash of solvent to speed drying and increase penetration. This is a stronger white glue and will stick to plastic.

134W-1 Padding cement. High viscosity, natural cellulose penetration. Flexible film adhesive for backdrops, groundcloths, and similar uses. Commercially used for bookbinding and padding.

4ZA-1 Water-base contact cement, pressure sensitive adhesive. Only one surface needs coating. Adheres to a variety of plastic surfaces.

74DZX Hot Melt, plastic to cork, and so forth. Hot melt thermo-plastic glue is sold by the pound in wafer form.

Originally published in August/September 1982

Garbage to Grandeur

Found object transformation and textural solutions with flexible urethane foam

by James R. Bakkom

Flexible urethane foam opens up a Pandora's box of possible solutions for the scene, prop, or costume shop. Flex foam is light. It's strong. It will withstand the abuse of a long run. It is fast and easy to work with. It can transform found-object garbage into viable props. Flex foam can create a variety of surface textures where before there was only corrugated cardboard illustration board. It can be used to cast body parts or to cast prop food. By mixing flexible urethane foam and found-object garbage—anything from plastic packing chips, rope, shot gun wads, and salvaged pine cones to crumpled newspaper, corn flakes and macaroni—a whole range of complicated textures can be quickly and easily fabricated. The possibilities are almost endless. Flexible urethane foam can be a boon to any theatre with limited time and a limited budget.

There is a *but*. You have to know how to use it. You have to buy some and experiment with it. You have to find out how to create the textures. Learn how long it takes to cure. Discover what happens when you add pigment to the mix. You have to develop a creative flexibility. In addition, you need to develop an eye for found-object potential. A cruise through Kresge's. A visit to a garage sale. A stop by the local surplus store. A perusal of your local alleys and loading docks. And you're on your way from garbage to grandeur.

What is it?

What I call flex foam is more properly known as flexible urethane foam. It was originally formulated for insulation. It is a two part, A and B component foam. Part A is essentially inert. Part B is the catalyst. When equal parts of A and B are mixed together and stirred they catalyze. Once mixed, it takes approximately three to five minutes before the resulting foam has set up—or is no longer liquid. Once set up, you can no longer work with the foam, except for carving. Internal curing can take anywhere from 30 minutes to several hours.

Sources and packaging

In doing workshops around the country, I have encountered several different kinds of flexible urethane foam. They vary in density and color. I have found that urethane foam is usually available through companies who are concerned with insulation, fiber glass, ship or boat building, or sometimes from paint companies. Unfortunately, these are the kinds of concerns who are not usually interested in dealing in the small amounts we, in the theatre, would be buying.

Because the difficulty of obtaining small amounts I am now packaging component foam under the name Theatre Flex in one and five gallon containers. These are sizes that most

Originally published in September 1978

1   2

Flexible urethane foam is a two part, component foam. Part A is the inert matter and part B is the catalyst. Basic necessities to begin experimenting with the foam are: sufficient containers, mixing sticks (1), and a well-ventilated place in which to work. The first and simplest experiment is the straight mix and pour technique. Measure equal amounts of A and B components in separate containers (2). Add the B catalyst to A component. Stir. The foam will begin to get warm and change from a dark chocolate to a milk chocolate color as the mixture catalyzes. Pour out. Let rise. Result is a pancake (3) shape. Or, with successive pourings, an irregular cobblestone pattern (4). After the mixture has set up (hard, but not completely cured), it can be painted. Bakkom estimates that for theatre use, painting can begin about 30 minutes after the pour. Depending on the colors and the number of glazes, the end result could be rain-slicked cobblestones (5), ground cloth surface, a vertical wall texture, or simple pancakes.

3

4

5

theatres can use easily. Two one-gallon containers (one each of A and B) of Theatre Flex brand urethane foam sells for $49.60. In the five gallon size, the cost of the two components totals $192. To give you an idea of how far one gallon of each component will stretch, approximately 2 ounces of each, when mixed, will cover an area about 1½' square to a depth of ½". The Theatre Flex brand is available from The Studio, Box 7008, Minneapolis, MN 54407.

Raw materials, releases, solvents and safety

To begin experimenting and working with flex foam you need containers to pour the components into, stirring sticks, and a work surface. If you are running on a budget, saving discarded food cans will help cut costs in this area. Food and soup cans usually have rings embossed on the inside of the can that can be used as easy measuring devices. If you do not have cans, 16 ounce wax-coated, Dixie cups (that you can usually buy in bulk from a Dixie distributor) are a good size and easy to work with. I recommend wax cups because you can usually peel the fired foam residue out of the cup and reuse it. You will also need sticks to stir the mixture.

For your first textural experiments, I recommend using something like shirt cardboards or discarded illustration board. Remember, flex foam will adhere to any surface except polyethylene plastic ones. So be sure to cover your work table and or surrounding floor with plastic sheeting. The mold release agent is Vaseline or mineral oil. Acetone is the solvent for urethane foam—but only while in liquid form. Once it has fired, acetone will have no effect on it.

Of course, you need a well-ventilated place in which to work. Respirators are recommended. In its liquid state, the foam is very messy and sticky. If you get it on your skin, wash it off before it catalyzes. People who are sensitive to it might want to work with rubber-based, disposable surgical gloves. They are inexpensive and thin enough not to loose the tactile control of working with the foam. You might also consider using safety goggles. Do not smoke while using the foam.

Mixing procedure

When you are opening new containers of component, I recommend venting the

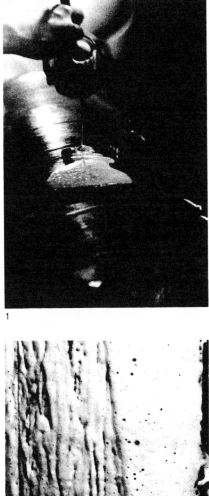

1

2

3

4

Using a curved, concrete forming tube as a base, Bakkom can turn out a tree trunk in approximately 30-35 minutes—a time span which includes 20-25 minutes of setting up and curing time before the finishing. Using a technique which he has dubbed mis-mixing, Bakkom mixes two parts of B catalyst to one part of A inert. This produces a smoother, lower textured foam when poured and textured (1, 2). To add textural variation and detail, standard mix 1:1 foam is also added to the surface (3, mis-mixed foam left, and 1:1 foam right). The set-up and partially cured tree can be painted with commercial wood stains, aniline dyes, latex-based house paints, or scene paints (4).

Plastics and Safety

As a plastics engineer in the field of special effects, I would like to comment on the article entitled "Garbage to Grandeur" in the September 1978 issue of Theatre Crafts.

Flexible urethane foam can be an easy, exciting medium to use, but your readers should know well in advance of using the foam that it is highly toxic, a proven carcinogenic, and has caused serious health problems for individuals that experiment with it without benefit of professional safety conditions:

(1) Respirators—one that is approved by OSHA and the Bureau of Mines for organic vapors—should always be used. If the wearer starts to smell the chemical through the mask, filters should be changed. Masks should be stored in an airtight container when not in use so they do not continue to absorb vapors and filters will have a longer life.

(2) Preferable working area would be outdoors. If that is not possible, one should install an exhaust system to rid area of all lingering vapors.

(3) Immediately after working with the materials, dispose of all mixing containers, rags, brushes, etc. If not, they will continue to emit dangerous vapors into the working atmosphere.

(4) We also recommend working with disposable clothes, gloves and headgear. After initial use, these articles should also be discarded.

Plastics are the most creative medium in the world, but if they continue to be used improperly all we can expect is that they will eventually be unavailable to the general public.

JOYCE SPECTER
The Plastics Factory, New York

1

2

Once familiar with the simple mix and pour procedure, the next step is to experiment with creating textures that might suggest solutions in set, prop, or costume work. Using a piece of masonite (1) as a testing ground, Bakkom mixes equal parts of A and B component, stirs and pours out. Then with a stick, moves the catalyzing foam around (2). Depending on how long you wait before you start working the foam, how the foam is manipulated, how many times the air is knocked out of the rising foam, a variety of textures can be achieved, including a stringy rope-like or cobwebby texture (still tacky 3, and cured 4) and a surface that suggests pock-marked, broken and peeling plaster walls (5). By pouring the foam mixture out, waiting a minute until the foam begins to form a skin and then hitting the foam to release the build-up of gasses under the skin, you can create a textural solution for twisted metal (6). By adding powdered graphite to the still-wet foam surface (7) and then polishing after the foam has cured, the twisted foam acquires the proper metallic patina.

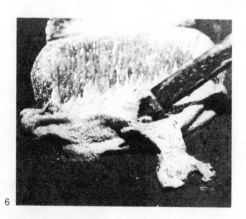

6

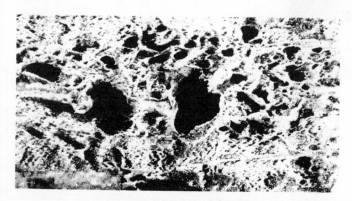

7

1

2

To create a brick wall texture inexpensively and quickly, Bakkom uses discarded illustration board as the base, and spreads it with the urethane foam mixture. Then, using the foam as an adhesive, he lays in old pieces of Dorvon bead foam salvaged from furniture packing (1). The Dorvon foam pieces become the bricks and the urethane foam both the adhesive and the mortar (2). Once dry, the illustration board retains its flexibility and could be easily applied to another surface. Bakkom recommends utilizing a found object like discarded illustration board rather than plywood because it cuts the cost and does not inhibit the flexibility. Once the urethane foam has cured, the bricks can be spattered with acetone (3, 4) to achieve a worn and pock-marked look. The acetone that will dissolve Dorvon has no chemical effect on the urethane mortar so the line of the brick will always be retained. To finish the brick wall, apply a light coat of flexible glue or polymer before painting with a vinyl-based paint. Or, if using a paint with a strong body like one of the Rosco line, the glue can be omitted.

3

4

Polyurethane Foam

Recently, while visiting some of my former students and colleagues, I picked up a copy of the May/June 1979 issue of *Theatre Crafts*. My shock and surprise must have been very noticeable, for I was asked, "What's wrong?" I pointed to the cover and replied, "I'm astonished to find that anyone is still using polyurethane foam for theatre scenery, knowing what is known about the combustibility of this material." I am flabbergasted that anyone would be willing to accept the risk of having polyurethane foam on stage, exposed and jeopardizing the lives of hundreds of patrons.

When I was TD at the University of Wisconsin, Stevens Point, we discontinued the use of foam in 1975, after it was discovered that polyurethane was very definitely *not* flame retardant or self-extinguishing as the manufacturers had led us to believe. It will support combustion extremely well, expecially if other combustible materials such as wood, cloth, paint, etc. are present to help the foam reach its ignition temperature.

I am now working as an insurance agent where my primary market is Wisconsin dairy farmers. My company, and many others, will refuse to insure any structure, such as a dairy barn, where exposed polyurethane is used as insulation. The Reinsurance Association of Minnesota has produced a film showing how a garage-sized building, lined on four walls and the ceiling with 2″ of rigid polyurethane board, was completely engulfed in flames less than two minutes after a standard plastic trash bag stuffed with crumpled newspapers was set afire in one corner. Such an occurrence in an occupied theatre would surely result in multiple fatalities, especially among the staff who remain to evacuate the patrons. Your life expectancy in such a situation may be less than two minutes, due to the toxicity of the gases produced by burning polyurethane: phosgene (a type of "nerve gas," which paralyzes the respiratory system) and hydrogen cyanide, hydrogen chloride, and ammonia.

K. CLARKE CRANDELL
National Farmers Union Insurance Companies
Stevens Point, Wisconsin

container to release the trapped gases before you open the spout. Thoroughly mix each component, using a stick. It is usually easier to work with if you pour some of each component into a manageable-sized container such as a coffee can. Then pour equal parts of A and B into separate, smaller cups or cans. If you are using a Dixie cup with a design on it, holding it up to the light will make measuring easier.

A manageable amount of component is two to three ounces of each. The directions call for equal parts of each, but I have found that it is not imperative to be absolutely exact. Remember, the containers you pour one component into have to be large enough to accommodate an equal amount of the remaining component and allow sufficient space for easy stirring and for the foam to rise in the cup as the catalyzation begins.

Once you have measured out equal amounts of the two components, the general procedure is to pour the B component—which is lighter and more liquid—into the container of A. As you start to mix, you will feel the cup begin to get warm. It will not get so hot that you have to drop the cup. As it begins to catalyze, the foam will start to rise in the cup. There is a certain Vesuvian quality about it. Do not panic. Keep on stirring. There is a tendency, when mixing, to just swirl the upper half of the mixture. Be sure to stir all the way down to the bottom. When the mixture has changed color it is then ready to be poured out.

The time elapsed between combining the two components until the mixture is ready to be poured out is not exact. You learn by trial and error—but it is not more than a minute or two. Once poured out, the foam will continue to rise until it hardens and sets up—also not long.

If simply poured out, the foam will form a pancake shape. Take a stick and begin to move the foam around; spread it and begin to play with creating textures. Each time you hit the foam with the stick, you knock the gases out of it; the foam will collapse and then begin to rise back up. By continuing to knock the gases out, you slow the hardening of the foam and can vary the depth and design of the texture. I find that continued working of the foam suggest different scenic and textural solutions.

Once you have mastered this step you can begin to experiment with the three other ways to create texture with flex

2

3

1

Bakkom points out that one of the great advantages to working with flexible urethane foam is that it allows creative transformation of found objects into viable scenic solutions. Assume that the theatre company has changed production plans at the last minute. There is virtually no budget and the shop is called upon to produce a group of shields, inexpensively and quickly.

The first problem would be to find an item that might serve as the armature for the shield. In Bakkom's case, he turns to the collection of bushel basket lids he has been saving. Using the found object's intrinsic shape, Bakkom mixes foam, pours (1) and spreads it over the lid (2). Before the foam begins to set up, he sprinkles some graphite and gold bronzing powder on the surface (3). Once cured, the shield is polished with neutral shoe polish or Johnson's wax—whatever is handy—to set the graphite and bronzing powder, and then buffed to a deep luster with a soft cloth or newspaper.

4

5

Another approach is to add coloring to the B component before mixing with the A. For the second shield, graphite and gold bronzing powder were added and then the mixture spread (4) on the bushel basket lid. Instead of the natural urethane foam, bread-crust color of the first shield, the result is a deep metallic gray through which the gold color shines. This shield is completed with a simple buffing (5).

6

7

Further variations on the theme use the bushel basket lid and add other found objects. By adding Liquitex acrylic paint to the B component before mixing and pouring, the shield acquires a pigment color which is enhanced with the surface dusting of gold bronzing powder. The addition of a dime store, paper doily and a piece of sheepskin create one more distinctive, yet related, shield for this army (6). In the finishing, acrylic paints the same color as the pigmented foam to make the source of the lacy doily design less obvious.

Another simple solution is the addition of a sheepskin (7) or any other appropriately rustic fabric to the urethane foam. Some graphite is also added to the setting up surface.

Bakkom points out that handles could be added at the beginning. He recommends screen door handles, jute twine or leather throngs as easy solutions. The total time from start to finished object of each shield is approximately 30-35 minutes. Of that, about 25 minutes is setting up time during which other shields can be worked on.

Plastic Foams and Safety

In response to some commentary on plastic foam flammability in (the Letters Column of the January/February 1980 issue) of your magazine, I would like to offer some moderation. The main points to be made are:

1. Flame retardant plastic foams do exist, and are used in special areas, such as aircraft interiors, which are required by law or regulation to meet flammability standards.
2. Treatment of plastics to make them non-flammable is best done in formulation before foaming, but it can be done as a coating after construction.
3. Testing flammability can be subject to a lot of variation, but the National Fire Protection Association match test is sufficient for a set designer to use *prior to purchase* of plastic foams as a ranking test.

Hence, there are plastic foams which may be used in theatre set design without fear, if one takes the time and trouble to search out and test to be sure. The unreasoned fear of all plastic foams is almost as senseless as the unreasoning usage of any plastic foam without a thought to safety.

R. D. ATHEY, JR.
Manager
Polymer & Coating Project Research

foam. One method is what I call mis-mixing. If you double the amount of the B catalyst component, you will get a smoother textured foam with a lower rise. Other textures can be achieved, once the foam has been poured out, by embedding textural items in the surface—things as widely disparate as dime store doilies and corn flakes. Or you can mix textural items like shot gun wads, jute, newspaper, into the B components before you mix the foam for still a different textural effect.

Coloring the flex foam

The type of flex foam that I use is, when cured, a light tan, bread crust color Fine, if you're making croissants and brioche. But if not, there are a whole range of ways to color flex foam depending on the desired final effect, what you happen to have available in the shop, or what you can afford. Color can be added before the foam is mixed, sprinkled on the setting-up foam, or painted over the cured foam.

Painting a cured foam form is usually possible once the initial curing is complete (or until it is no longer tacky) about 30 minutes. I have found that all paints work on it: casein bases, Luminols, vinyl acrylics like Liquitex, latex housepaints, and the Rosco paints. For costume work and small prop painting, I find the range of iridescent, metallic opaque and transparent colors from acrylic Liquitex and Hyplar invaluable. They are somewhat expensive for any extensive use, however. The type of wear that the foam will be subjected to usually determines the paint I use on it. Rosco is the strongest and I will use it if I know that the piece will be in use for a long time. But if it is a short—say three weekend—run, the cheapest paint you have handy will probably suffice.

Aniline dyes and French enamel varnish are very effective glazing mediums. But, if you cannot afford them, using standard hardware store wood stains is one of the easiest and best ways to achieve similar effects.

If you want a light dusting of metallic sheen, graphite or decorator bronzing powders can be sprinkled on the still-wet surface of the foam before it has set.

If you want a solid, opaque color, you can add coloring media to the B catalyst before mixing the foam. Number 1 and number 2 graphite, aluminum powder, and decorator bronzing powders will create effective metallic looks. You can

1

2

3

Many textural refinements are possible. If the problem is to create a stucco wall that has been inscribed mix equal parts of A and B component. Stir. Pour out and spread much in the manner of icing a cake. While the foam is still wet and soft "VIVA" (1) is inscribed in the surface. As the foam sets up and cures, the letters fill in somewhat, but the indentation is still visible (2). Once the foam has cured Bakkom applies successive coats of light and dark colored water-based acrylic paints, wiping dry between applications to achieve the impression of aged graffiti (3). The technique could be used for other things like carving "Dan'l kilt him a baar here" in a tree trunk.

also add dry scenic pigment or wet, pre-mixed pigments, vinyl acrylics, Liquitex acrylics, wet Gothic casein or Rosco paints. Two things to remember: the dry scenic pigments do not always come out the pure color you selected; and, the addition of elements to the foam will make it softer and springier.

What flex foam will not do

I have found flex foam the answer to so many scenic and prop projects that it might be helpful to know the few things I have discovered flex foam is not good for. I have cast body parts out of it, but it has a stiffness that makes it unnatural for prosthetic pieces. It cannot pick up the muscle movement the way foam latex does. Flex foam is very difficult to

apply, in a controlled way, to an already vertical surface. So, apply the texture while the scenery is horizontal or apply texture to something that can be attached to the vertical surface. Also it will not successfully reproduce minute details.

Experiment

The key to using flex foam is to experiment. Your only handicap is lack of adventure and imagination. You don't need the famous MFA from Yale to mix A with B, stir, and pour. Once you've learned to master the foam and done some imaginative garbage collecting, you've got a wealth of show biz techniques at your fingertips.

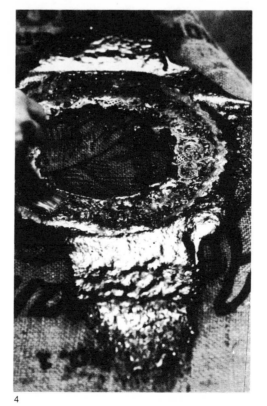

Using another found object—a burlap potato sack (1)—Bakkom creates a simple tabard costume for a mythical production of *Caucasian Chalk Circle*. After slitting the sides and cutting a neck hole, mix a 1:1 batch of flex foam with graphite added. Using the sack's printed design as a base, pour the foam (2) in a circle and imbed a paper doily (3) in the foam. Sprinkle the still-wet foam with powdered graphite and let the tabard cure. Finish with Liquitex metallic acrylics. Let dry (4). The finished tabard is flexible (5) and can be stretched slightly by rolling the foam to loosen it further. Several things to remember when working with fabrics and foam: don't do it over your favorite cutting table unless you have first put down a layer of polyethylene plastic; and foam should be applied to only one layer of fabric at a time.

1

2

3

4

5

Sand Dunes That Travel

by William Daniel File

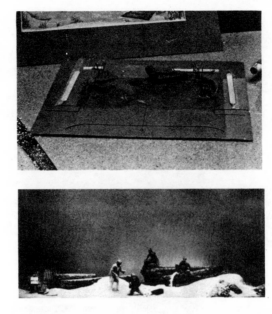

A recent production of Edward Albee's *Seascape* (left) at Northern Michigan University was designed for touring. The unit set, both dunes and rocks (above), had to replicate their natural counterparts. They also had to be light enough to travel and sturdy enough to withstand numerous performances. Contouring of the plastic foam closely followed designer William Daniel File's original scale model (top left).

The second production of the 1979–80 season at Northern Michigan University's Forest Roberts Theatre was to be Edward Albee's *Seascape*. It was also scheduled to be the university's ACTF entry. As the designer, what that meant to me was that *Seascape* had to be ready to tour. Not wishing to tour with a two-ton dump truck of sand and wishing to solve as many of the common tour problems as possible, I began experimenting with various methods of creating a "desolate, sandy beach area with rocky outcroppings".

Two qualities became most important in the construction of the dunes. First, the dunes had to look as if they were sand. Second, the dunes had to react like sand—"give" under the feet of the actors, retaining slight footprint impressions, but make no appreciable noise. Experiments brought me to two distinct solutions, each emphasizing one of the qualities at the expense of the other.

The solution that emphasized the reaction quality was to shape the stage space with modules similar in concept to bean-bag chairs. While this was the closest we could come in the time we had to experiment, the solution had several serious drawbacks. No matter what we filled the bags with, they made considerable noise as the actors climbed, jumped, and rolled on the material. Another problem was how to hide the seams where one module met another. The thought of a custom-made ground cloth was offered, but time and expense were problems, and, anyway, the cloth covering would

simply muddle the very effect that made the bean-bags so enticing— sand reaction. The final major problem was that, no matter how we tried, we could not mask the fact that each successive footprint forced each prior footprint to bulge back up. All things considered, the solution created more problems than this particular effect was worth.

The second solution, and the one we opted for, was to use sculpted bead-board or plastic foam.

Process

After making a watercolor sketch, I sculpted a 1/2" scale model of the dunes in children's modeling clay. The model proved to be indispensable because with it we could take measurements, calculate square and cubic footages, and generally be more precise in duplicating the design.

I had worked with plastic foam before, at the Guthrie Theatre, in Minneapolis, with Jim Bakkom, and knew that it would be relatively easy to shape and texture. I also knew that it had a great tendency to "chip/chunk" at surface joints, it could squeak loudly if pieces moved against each other, and that it obviously would not react like sand at all.

It became apparent that we would have to build the dunes as a solid unit, to keep the inherently dead, solid sound plastic foam possesses. We purchased the plastic foam in 4' by 8'

sheets of varying thicknesses (6", 10", and 12").

We divided the design into three sections and used rigid pour foam to laminate the various thicknesses of plastic foam in order to create the mounds. The pour foam comes to us as two liquids (Chempol #32-1730 and #32-1601, available from Freeman Chemical Corporation, of Port Washington, Wisconsin) that, when mixed, form a third material which expands greatly in volume and cures to a solid state in about 90–120 seconds. (Pour foams have been the subject of a number of previous articles in *Theatre Crafts*.)

Note: after pouring the mixed liquid components and placing one sheet of plastic foam on the other, it is important to have enough weight to force the foam to expand out along the seam, rather than up. We had four to six students sit on the top plastic foam piece immediately after positioning it, and we found that satisfactory.

The Chempol pour foam we chose has about the same density as the plastic foam. Therefore, when it came time to cut, sand, and shape the dunes, there was practically no visible seam.

Contouring

We began the contouring process by cutting the squared edges off the plastic foam blocks and, paying close attention to the clay model, shaping the major mounds and slopes. We used hand cross-cut saws to do the first, roughest cutting. The saw that was the most useful, however, was a Sawzall, which is an electric reciprocating saw. We attached a 14″ tapered blade to it and found that it would do most of our more detailed cutting.

The final contouring and shaping was done with an electric belt sander, using coarse sandpaper. One note on the sanding process: an immense number of small plastic foam particles are generated. These particles pose two real problems. The first is that they have a static electrical charge, which helps them cling to plastic goggles, glasses, tools, and clothing. This necessitates time-consuming clean up breaks during work sessions. The second problem is that the particles can be inhaled easily, which makes the use of inexpensive paper-type respirators mandatory. We found that having an assistant keep the nozzle of a vacuum close to the sander gave us considerably less dust and fewer particles, but by no means solved the problem.

Once we got the major shapes roughed in, I could mark the levels on the mounds with charcoal, much like a contour relief map, and the students could follow the marks when cutting or sanding. This had to be done with the rocky outcroppings in place, so that we could relate the dunes.

Finally the sculpture was ready to be treated in order to:
1 fireproof or retard the plastic foam and pour foam;
2 seal the surface for further textural treatment;
3 strengthen the surface to prevent the chip/chunking, especially at thin spots (1″ or less), such as where the plastic foam mound met the stage; and
4 allow some "give" to the surface, which is a natural effect of the plastic foam that we wished to keep if possible.

After experimentation, the following materials were layered onto the surface over a period of three days, allowing complete drying between each application unless otherwise indicated.
1 The entire dune area was painted with leftover Supersaturated Roscopaint, in a neutral gray. Because it was a mixture of paint remnants from previ-

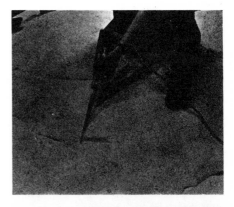

The *Seascape* dunes were made of varying thicknesses of sheet plastic foam (right) laminated together with rigid pour foam (top and above). After roughly shaping the mounds and slopes with a hand cross-cut saw, a Sawzall reciprocating saw with a 14″ tapered blade was used for more detailed cutting (right top). The final contouring was achieved with a sander (right center).

ous productions, its exact ratio of water to paint is not known, but I would estimate it to be between five and eight parts water to one part paint. We rolled and brushed the paint on to cover the surface completely. Caution: if the paint is applied too heavily it will seep into the plastic foam and take two or three days to dry completely.

2 Next, with our Hudson tanks, we sprayed a mixture of one part flexible glue and one part water over the whole dune structure.

3 We then brushed household texture paint—diluted 1:1 with warm water—over the surface. The texture paint is the same material used to commercially texture walls and ceilings. Because its base is latex we reasoned that it would "give" or flex somewhat under the actors' weight, while holding to the sealed plastic foam.

4 We mixed some Supersaturated Roscopaint to match the sand color we were going to use and sprayed that over the dried texture paint.

5 We next mixed a rather heavy animal glue size. While the size was still hot, we sprayed it over the dunes in small sections (about 4' x 4') and immediately spread real sand over the wet size. We left the set undisturbed overnight.

6 Finally, we took the same mixture as in 4, brushed off the excess sand from 5, and repeated 5 but spraying the mixture from 4.

We found the surface surprisingly resiliant, tough, and very quiet. Although it did not react like real sand, our sand dunes looked identical to natural sand dunes, even when scrutinized closely. We did have to do minor touchups after each performance—primarily sweeping the loose sand back up over the dunes prior to the next performance. As some of the new sand fell when the actors initially traversed the set, it appeared to the audience that footprints were actually being made. Our director also blocked a rather frantic fight scene, with a great deal of jumping, falling, and throwing, and we had to patch an occasional piece of the layered crust back on, but little, if any, plastic foam actually chip/chunked.

Initially, I was concerned that the entire set might shift during the more frantic scenes, since the plastic foam is so lightweight. We had glued a strip of canvas (about 15" wide) to the front edge of the dunes, reasoning that we could anchor at least part of the set by putting quantities of sand on the canvas. As it turned out, the plastic foam provided enough friction with the stage deck that the extra sand was not needed, technically. The sand and the canvas lip did help our strike and cleanup, however, and it probably helped keep the thin leading edge of the plastic foam in one piece, as the sand absorbed much of the abuse that the plastic foam would have to take if unprotected. It also provided an aesthetic way to hide the meeting of the plastic foam dunes with the stage deck.

Touring

The set was cut into three pieces, essentially a stage left, a center, and a stage right section. By a little planning, luck, and coincidence, two of the pieces fit together piggy-back style, as one was flipped over and on top of the second piece. The bottom piece cradled the top one and, since the top piece's flat bottom was facing up, the third set piece simply sat on top of the first two. The loose sand, which was carried in doubled plastic garbage bags, was then wedged around the three set pieces to provide added stability and prevent as much shifting as possible.

The rocky outcroppings were essentially platforms with removable legs and textural fronts, and could be broken down rather easily. The rest of the materials (wrap-around cyc, sand fence, plants, grasses, weeds, and props) fit into five small to medium-sized trunks. All fit neatly in the box of a 12' x 20' truck.

The setup was a reversal of the strike process, with one difference: the three set pieces needed to be glued together. The glue was the same rigid pour foam which we used to laminate the plastic foam. After the pour foam had cured (about three minutes after mixing) it was ready to be sanded and touched up (steps 4 and 6). In less than one hour, the dunes were ready.

An added note about the rocky outcroppings: the textural fronts were made by attaching turkey wire fencing to the shaped platform lids and then weaving whatever flexible material we could find into the holes. We used burlap, paper towels, scrap nylon, newsprint, and more. When the turkey wire was filled, we placed the platform on its back (so that the filled wire was facing up) and poured alternating rows of flexible and rigid foam over the material. (Flexible foam is Chempol #30-1947 and #30-2013). The two foams have slightly different textures, and we heightened the differences by dragging a spatula over the partially cured and sticky foams. These techniques helped us create the striations we were looking for. We also made sure to begin the top striation (the one closest to the platform lid edge) with the flexible foam, since the actors were going to be climbing and sitting on the platforms. We reasoned that the flexible qualities would be less harsh on the actors and costumes, and probably would not chip, as the rigid foam might.

Finally, we painted the rocks with Supersaturated Roscopaint. We occasionally mixed aluminum powder with the paint to help some of the striations read better or, at least, differently.

While Northern Michigan did not advance to the regional ACTF competition, we did perform a benefit after the close of our regular run, which gave us the opportunity to test our tour capabilities. We struck and set up within the ACTF's requirements of personnel, time, and space, and found that the planning and process were successful. And although this was not necessarily a low budget set, it came in under our allotted $1,200.

Originally published in May 1982

Poor Man's Vacuum-form Machine

by Michael Hottois

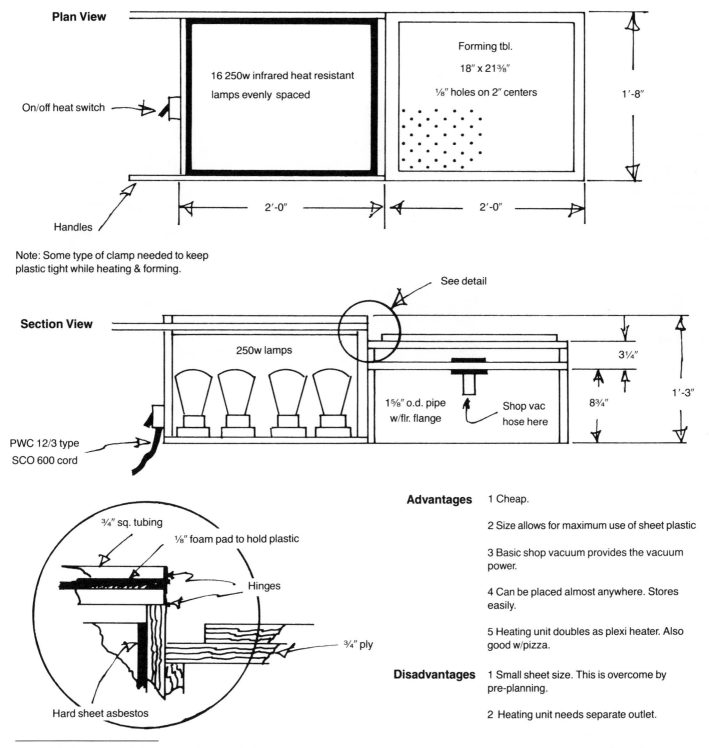

Plan View

16 250w infrared heat resistant lamps evenly spaced

On/off heat switch

Forming tbl.

18" x 21⅜"

⅛" holes on 2" centers

1'-8"

Handles

2'-0"

2'-0"

Note: Some type of clamp needed to keep plastic tight while heating & forming.

Section View

250w lamps

See detail

3¼"

8¾"

1'-3"

1⅝" o.d. pipe w/flr. flange

Shop vac hose here

PWC 12/3 type SCO 600 cord

¾" sq. tubing

⅛" foam pad to hold plastic

Hinges

¾" ply

Hard sheet asbestos

Advantages

1 Cheap.

2 Size allows for maximum use of sheet plastic

3 Basic shop vacuum provides the vacuum power.

4 Can be placed almost anywhere. Stores easily.

5 Heating unit doubles as plexi heater. Also good w/pizza.

Disadvantages

1 Small sheet size. This is overcome by pre-planning.

2 Heating unit needs separate outlet.

Original design: Joe Ragi, Actors' Theatre of Louisville. Revised: Michael F. Hottois, University of Louisville

Originally published in October 1983

Lathing Foam Spindles

by Thomas J. Corbett

The ability to turn decorative spindles for a setting can sometimes be the factor that makes or breaks scenic design. Two possible methods of carving decorative spindles involve modified lathes that allow the technician to trim Styrofoam quickly and easily.

The first method involves a new way of using a floor model drill press—the drill press is used as a vertical lathe. To do this:

- The table of the drill press is lowered to accomodate the length of the desired spindle.
- A length of threaded rod is used as the axle on which the Styrofoam turns. It is driven by the drill press chuck and rotates in a wooden block clamped to the drilling table. The threaded rod is either pushed through one long block of Styrofoam or through sections of built-up Styrofoam block.
- If the rod axle is sharpened before insertion into the foam, it will insert faster, and follow a truer course through the foam. Resting the point on the drilling table makes an improved bearing for the turning.

One way to insert the rod through a long single piece of foam is to use a hand-held power drill and "thread" the rod through the plastic foam, turning it at a very slow speed and carefully ensuring that it is inserted on a center line both vertically and horizontally. When turning Styrofoam spindles, the San Francisco Opera shop builds the raw turning stock by stacking 6" rounds of Styrofoam. These rounds are band saw pre-cut and pre-glued so that they easily skewer onto the spindle. Pre-cutting round form disks saves having to "round" off the square

1

2

(1) After mounting the block of Styrofoam on the drill press, the block is slowly turned to remove the edges. The stock is rounded out with a surform to prepare it to be cut into a decorative shape. (2) A small round file is used to cut the deeper grooves. Bracing the file heel against the template and turning the rasp slowly into the work yields a very good cut. (3) The Masonite template is clamped onto the drill press stand with an appropriate amount of material left for a center thickness. Notice the gridding produced by laying out the positive shape on the Masonite. Also note the 1x3 used as a bottom pivot clamped to the drill press table.

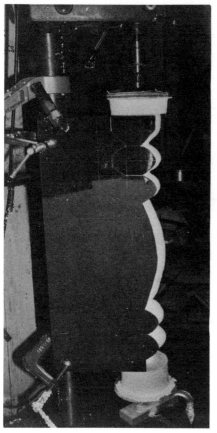

3

corners from fragile foam stock. The rounds can also be sized and stacked according to the final profile outline—the turning is left to a final shaping operation.

■ With the rod inserted into the foam, a plywood disk is threaded onto each end of the assembly, and retaining nuts are turned onto the rod to hold the Styrofoam in place. Nails can be driven through the plywood disk into the foam to assure non-slip rotation. Use longer double-headed nails for easy removal.

■ Place the bottom end of the completed assembly into a block of plywood clamped to the bottom table of the drill press. The rod can turn in a hole drilled in the plywood while resting on the drill press metal table. It acts rather like a metal-to-metal bearing with minimal drag.

■ After placing the bottom of the threaded rod holding the Styrofoam stock into the bottom centering and pivoting disk, the rod's top end is tipped into position under the drill press chuck and inserted into the chuck. If the rod is inserted into the chuck first, the bottom centering plywood is put on the lower end of the rod and pulled into position over the trueing table. It is then clamped. Either procedure is possible.

■ Set the drill press for the slowest possible speed, clamp the template for the spindle to the column of the drill press, and you are ready to turn the shape. The carving tools are passed along the edge of the template and the shape is eased out of the Styrofoam. Do not rush the Styrofoam. It is soft and easily carved, and you might feel that deep cuts could speed up the work. However, deep cuts can easily break the foam or pull it off in deep rips.

TOOLS

Carving tools that can be used are a Stanley surform, files, and wood chisels. Standard wood turning tools are also very helpful. Even sandpaper is adequate as the spindle's rate of speed is variable. Faster rotation of the work can allow a smoother cutting tool and a finer surface.

The carving tools can be handled in one of two ways. The template can be used as a positive of the desired spindle shape. Clamp the template to the drill press post and pass the tools along the template with the cutting tool protruding perpendicular to the template. As the Styrofoam turns beside the template, the chisel removes excess material. Make sure that the template is mounted to allow enough Styrofoam center in the finished spindle. The deepest cuts should not sever the spindle.

The template can also be cut as a negative of the final desired spindle shape, and the tools can be handled differently. Place the tools along the template's surface with the template mounted straight off the axis of the rotating foam. Using a finger as a guide, move the tools along the template maintaining even spacing off the template edge. Holding the end of the tool equidistant from the template's edge will yield a finished form that matches the template. When the form is close to completion and needs to be checked, move the template in and against the turned foam to look for irregularities in the turning.

Using a negative template is sometimes the more desirable method for making a foam spindle, as cutting and tool manipulation is easier and the operator can accurately check the turning. A positive template allows the operator to see the final spindle shape and make a visual comparison of the turning as it progresses.

If the spindle needs to carry weight,

4

and therefore be reinforced with pipe, the threaded rod can be turned through the Styrofoam with a portable drill, and worked back and forth to enlarge the opening. After the reinforcing pipe is inserted, the exterior surface of the spindle needs to be gauzed to prepare it for painting.

The San Francisco Opera shop built a Styrofoam lathe specifically to turn multiple spindles. A motor is used to turn a rod axis and an enlarged platform over a Styrofoam chips collecting bin. This lathe design turns the work horizontally and makes the entire process more convenient for the operator.

A ¼ or ⅓ horsepower motor is mounted with a small v-belt pulley that drives a larger v-belt pulley bolted to a plywood disk. The plywood disk rotates around a center shaft mounted with thrust bearing and three rigid castors close to the edge of the plywood disk. The disk is then centered while the rigid castors prevent the disk's edge from shimmying. Near the center of the disk are three or four

nails protruding through the plywood to catch the Styrofoam and prevent it from turning independently of the drive disk.

A ⅜" smooth steel rod is run through the center of the Styrofoam stock and meets the rotating disk at the center shaft. The opposite end of the steel rod is supported by a plywood cut out that acts as legs. A small block of Teflon is mounted on the plywood frame where the steel rod penetrates. This Teflon block acts as a bearing. Two steel rings encircle the shaft and are locked against the foam with a set screw. Like the threaded rod with its lock nuts, these rings tighten the foam stock against the driving disk. The plywood end fits onto the base frame of the lathe over a dust collection bin. By sliding the end member along the frame, the lathe can be adjusted for smaller- or larger-sized work.

Attached to one side rail is a ruler that allows the operator to conveniently turn the spindle and even work from scaled drawings. The ruler, however, is not accurate enough for finished turnings. Large

¼" plywood outside calipers were fashioned for this purpose.

A handmade enlarged cutter shaped from mild steel flat strap was attached to a closet pole handle. The tool was sharpened on the end opposite the handle, and rested along the guide rail. The frontal, downward rotation keeps the cutting tool resting on the guide rail. A plywood profile is cut to guide the operator and to check the formation. A negative profile cut from ¼" tempered masonite or plywood can do the final shaping if the operator slowly pushes it into the rotating Styrofoam.

Both methods described here are variations on a simple lathe. Small lathes, however, are designed to grip rigid stock. Either of these tool descriptions provide a more positive grip on the porous Styrofoam than any woodworking lathe, can be easily fabricated, and will allow your shop to "turn out" shaped spindles in quantity.

Originally published in August 1984

5

(4) The plywood disc is mounted around a thrust bearing and shaft. A driven wheel is bolted to its motor side. Rigid castors help align the disc and minimize wobble. The smaller rod that centers the foam fits into the shaft centering the disc. (5) Jay Kotcher, charge man for the San Francisco Opera shop, holds a plywood sweep to judge the shape of a spindle under construction. (6) A hand tool reminiscent of the one Captain Ahab used on Moby Dick was fashioned for a large-scale Opera turning. Here, it is held against the guide rail. Notice the dust collection bin used as the base of the lathe.

6

Styrofoam Safety

For the Intiman Theatre Company production of *Shadow of a Gunman* our scenic artist was asked to melt Styrofoam with a torch to produce a crumbly brick texture. Because of the cyanide gas produced, good ventilation was essential. However, the technique required fine control of the flame so that it was not possible to work in a drafty area. Standard cannister type respirators only trap particulate dust and are inadequate protection against cyanide gas. Masks that plug into an air supply cost $85 to $140 and require auxiliary equipment, which could bring the total cost for one operating mask up to $300.

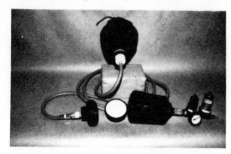

It was time to do a little scrounging. A trip to a local Army-Navy surplus store produced a serviceable military-type gas mask. To the intake valve on the mask I attached an old air hose, which I plugged into a low pressure regulator. The regulator was then plugged into the shop air system. Between the regulator and the mask I attached a cannister from a Protex series 7500 respirator, using ABS fittings, which traps any oil vapor, water, or dust contamination in the compressor-fed air. Care must be taken to keep the intake of the compressor away from the source of the fumes.

The advantages of this system are as follows:

1 The user is fed a steady stream of clean air.

2 The flow can be adjusted from a quiet trickle to a pleasing gale, making it unnecessary to suck air through a cannister.

3 Stray vapors cannot be inhaled through a loose-fitting mask, as there is positive pressure within the mask.

4 Air flow keeps the lenses from fogging up and the mask stays cool.

5 With some scrounging the whole system can be made for $25, excluding regulator.

This system may not be OSHA approved, but with most theatres unable or disinclined to invest in adequate respiration systems, the simplicity and low cost of this system makes on-the-job health protection practical.

RICHARD KLYCE
Technical Director
Department of Speech & Drama
University of Alaska
Fairbanks, Alaska

What— More Wire Cutters?

by Thomas J. Corbett

Every scene shop has its own way to cut plastic foam for cornice and molding pieces. Two of the best methods I know are the hot wire cutter used in the San Francisco Opera shop and the hot band cutter developed at Musson Theatrical in San Jose.

The hot wire cutter

The most straightforward hot wire cutter is that found at the San Francisco Opera. It is the most inexpensive device to construct. Essentially, a length of nichrome wire is stretched between two short lengths of dowel. The dowels act as handles. Two operators, one at each handle, pull the heated wire taut and draw it through the plastic foam to be cut or shaped.

To cut a complex piece of architectural ornamentation, such as a column or a cornice, a cross section of the desired shape is drawn on ¼″ masonite. Then, two layers of masonite are simultaneously cut for use as templates. These templates are pinned to nails to each end of the foam billet. Power is fed to the nichrome wire by clipping two lengths of stranded flexible copper lead wire with two battery clips to the cutting wire. These two leads are attached to the cutting wire near the dowel handle. The operators start at one end of the cornice template to make their first cut. It is important that they reach the cutting plane corner at the same time. If one end of the hot wire cutter rounds the corner before the other, the edge being cut will be rounded and irregular.

The cutting nichrome wire must be connected to a series register. The register acts as a current limiter and prevents the line fuse from blowing. In order to stay under 20 amp draw at line voltage, total load resistance needs to be at least six ohms. Apply Ohm's Law for the specific resistance requirements at local voltage levels. For a variety of reasons, autotransformers are more reliable than registers.

The useful size autotransformer is determined by the supply outlet. The transformer should have its own circuit breaker protection rated specifically to the dimmer being used. A 2,000w autotransformer is sufficient for a 20 amp wall outlet supply. A smaller variac—such as a 1,500w with a 15 amp breaker mounted on its container—is fine for most cuts. The fuse on the unit protects the variac and the supply outlet if the voltage is set too high or the cutting wire is drawing too much current.

Adjusting the variac will change the heat of the wire and the speed of the cut. In cutting through plastic foam, heat is drawn off the wire and the cutting slows down. For long cuts, therefore, the operators need to increase the voltage. A handle, similar to the knee-activated levers on some sewing machines, might be rigged so that an operator could advance the voltage while cutting.

Safety

Because foam cut with hot wire gives off toxic gases, the operators should work next to a large exhaust fan and wear respirators. The SFO shop uses active carbon combination cartridges screwed onto a Mine Safety Appliance mask (Mine Safety Appliance Company, Pittsburgh, PA 15208. Cartridge number GMC-H). Although the foams suitable for hot wire cutting include expanded bead styrene, Styrofoam, ethafoam, and urethane foam, these respirators do not filter the toxic gases given off by the urethane foam. Specific respirators' defined chemical

Originally published in January 1984

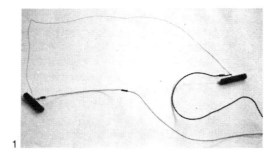

1

A hot wire cutter can be constructed from nichrome wire with a dowel handle at each end (1). The variac supply is clipped to the other end and the wire is pulled through the foam (2). An improved circuit offers a warning light, dead man's switches for the operators, and a GFI for shock protection (3). A short length of wire built into a single handle can be used by one person (4).

2

activity should be checked before the cutting begins.

The San Francisco Opera's electrical shop added a number of safety features to its hot wire cutter. The variac was mounted in a steel cover box with a power switch, fuse, circuit breaker, line cord, and pilot light. The light reminds the operators that, in addition to disconnecting the power clips from the cutting wire when the cut is completed, the system power must also be shut off.

Two dead man's switches, rigged on foot pads and placed under each operator's foot, are also recommended. These normally open, spring-return switches should be attached in series with the primary of the transformer. If a wire operator should get a shock, his/her startled response would probably remove his/her foot from the switches, and the circuit would open. Foot switches can be run by a low-voltage relay which, in turn, controls the load circuit. This isolates from the switch shock hazard.

Installing a GFI (ground fault interrupter) rather than a simple circuit breaker on the variac primary is another necessary precaution. A GFI will sense whether there is any leakage to the ground or an imbalance between the hot and the neutral wires. This is the best protection for the operators, especially if they have ignored such standard safety measures as insulated gloves, rubber-soled safety shoes, and rubber foot mats. If even trickle voltage occurs, the GFI will cut the circuit.

Supplies

Nichrome wire can be purchased in a variety of gauges, each with a different resistance and tensile strength. The wire used in the San Francisco Opera shop is Nic-chrome straight, which is a solid, single strand wire. Nic-chrome is avail-

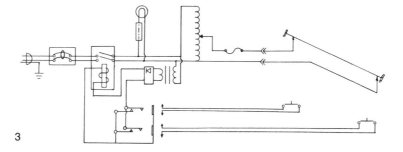

3

4

127,224

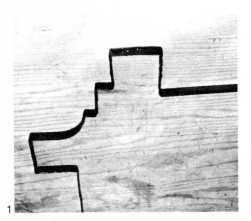

A mild steel strap used for a hot cutter can be pre-shaped using hand tools (1). A bench provides a surface along which to slide the plastic foam as it passes through the cutter (2). To prevent the drag of the cutter from pulling the foam away, holding blocks may be attached (3). Luan plywood is glued to the top side of the compound curve (4).

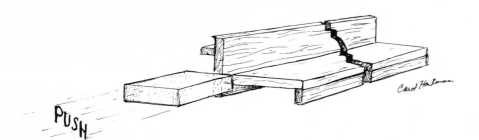

2

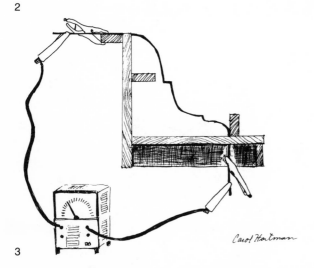

3

4

able from Waage Mfg. (Chicago, IL 60612). SFO stocks four gauges: 26 gauge (2.67 ohms per foot resistance), 22 gauge (1.05 ohms per foot), 19 gauge (.53 ohms per foot), and 18 gauge (.42 ohms per foot).

The flexible hot wire cutter has been used successfully many times in the San Francisco Opera's shop for cutting cornices, molding, and columns. Size limitations are defined by the foam stock. The wire can be any length, remembering that longer cutting operations may demand lower resistance nichrome wire. Using this method the Opera has cut columns over 20′ long in a single pass.

The hot band cutter

Unlike the flexible hot wire cutter, the hot band cutter is a rigid metal form fashioned from mild steel strap. Whereas the wire cutter is drawn through the plastic foam, the band cutter employs the opposite process: the foam is pressed through the band.

The band cutter was first made with a steel strap ¹⁄₁₆″ thick, ½″ wide, and 18″ long. The steel band was formed in the shape of a cornice, including convex and concave curves and right-angled corners. Almost any steel strap will work. Thinner straps cut less of a kerf in the plastic stock, while wider bands hold heat better as the material is passed through.

An arc welder provides ideal voltage and current for power. The AC stick welder, fundamentally a step-down transformer, provides a selection of operating voltages while maintaining enough current to heat the low resistance steel strap. The ground clamp is attached to one end of the strap and the stick clamp attached to the other. No special lugs are required, and the welder need only be unclamped to convert it back to welding. The welder's line supply fuses will indicate if the steel's resistance is too low and thus overdrawing the secondary of the welder transformer. If desired, a clamp-on ammeter can be placed around the welder cable to monitor the draw amperage. The power leads are clamped onto the steel strap outside the strap's attachment to the cutting bench.

The cutting bench used to hold the steel band can be little more than a plywood table with a backstop fence attached at right angles along one side and a slot in the middle for holding the steel strap. If the foam block being fed through the cutter turns away from the table or the fence, guiding blocks can be clamped or nailed in place.

To attach the strap to the bench, use two Vice Grip pliers and clamp the strap to a block of wood on the underside of the table. Since the block is mounted along the slot in the table, the pliers grip the steel strap on its edge. The only problem this attachment creates is that the internal heating from the current passing through the strap tends to char the wooden clamping blocks. Mill-board can be used here as a heat barrier to protect the wood blocks.

One of the great attractions of the band cutter is that long and complex forms can be pulled through in one pass, making them easier to attach to flats than smaller sections that must be glued together. To attach foam pieces to the flats, glue lengths of ⅛" luan plywood to the top edge of the cornice. Use panel

adhesive. Make sure the luan extends away from the shaped face to overlap the top edge of the flat. Use small nails to tack the cornice to the flat's top edge.

A good foam for use with the hot band cutter is Dow Blue Board foam insulation. It comes in 2' x 8' billet-sized stock as well as thinner sheets. (See Dow's technical bulletin for specific product information.)

When passing the foam through the cutter, maintain a constant rate of speed. Fluctuation will produce a wavy form. During the cutting, small beads of hot plastic will collect along the length of the cut molding or cornice. These beads will not be visible to the audience. Plastic will also cake around the cutter as it cools, but is easily cleaned off by flexing the steel band prior to reuse.

Safety
As with the flexible wire cutter, the steel

band cutter requires close attention to safety precautions. Cutter operators should work in a well-ventilated area and wear masks. The gases given off by band cutting foam plastics are extremely toxic and are the greatest hazard of working with plastics.

Power connections to the cutting strap should be shielded from workers. If someone touched both power leads at the same time, a severe electrical shock would result. To prevent sparks, always connect the welder leads with the power off.

With the abundance of hot wire cutters on the market, another one may seem unnecessary. This cutter, however, is easy to assemble, works well, cuts complex shapes in one pass, and, if a welder is already owned, is inexpensive to construct. It should become a permanent tool in every shop.

Template-Spun Polystyrene Foam for Stage Furniture

by Richard H. Chapman

Polystyrene foam, turned on a lathe and using a template, is a practical and inexpensive way to create detailed stage furniture. The basic forms can be made simply of plywood and pipe, then filled out with the foam details you design and build. Post-production, the foam can be stripped off and the forms reused by adding different foam details.

The advantage of turning the foam on a lathe and using a template to reproduce the sections is uniformity (over hand carving). Also, the lathe and template method of foam carving is simple to learn and can be executed quickly. A step-by-step guide to making foam table legs follows:

Make a template. ⅛" plywood (doorskin) works very well; so do masonite and ¼" plywood. Cardboads won't

hold up; tinplate and other metals are rather difficult to work with. (1) Cut

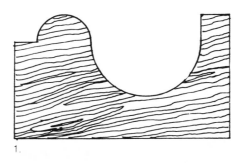
1.

and glue polystrene foam. Be sure all blocks are square and accurately cut to proper size. Important: all glued joints should be roughly perpendicular

to the turning axis. Glued joints parallel to the turning axis will cause problems.
Locate the centers (2)

2.

3.

4.

5.

6.

7.

8.

9.

10.

Attach center plates. The method used here was to make two 2″ x 1/4″ masonite disks drilled to accept center pins and anchored with two 6d nails each (3). Using a gouge, rough the block to round. If a 6″ round is needed, start with a 6″ square and turn until flat faces just disappear (4). The next step will go much faster if you rough in any deep gouges in the finished form at this time (5). Remove the tool rest and anything else that might cause fingers to get caught. Using the template as the cutting tool, turn the workpiece to its final shape. If a 6″ finished diameter at the highest point is desired, use a 6″ round workpiece to start with and stop the moment you can no longer see daylight between the template and the workpiece (6). Using a hot wire cutter, cut a hole in the foam to allow for the pipe leg and assemble the parts of the finished leg (8). Finish as desired. In this case, tissue paper and paint with some glue added were used for the base coat (9). The round side table, the bed, and the dining table were all constructed from plywood, pipe, and polystyrene foam (7, 10).

Originally published in November/December 1977

A PVC Gazebo

by Raynette Halvorsen Smith

The use of PVC (polyvinyl chloride) in the theatre is not news. Extensive use of the product in an unusual manner, however, led to the development of new forming and joining techniques in a recent production at Loyola University, Chicago, where I was guest designer.

Director Dennis Zacek decided to abandon the traditional staging style for George Bernard Shaw's *Misalliance*. He wanted the set to provide ample movement possibilities to counterbalance the lack of action in Shaw's rather wordy play. My design solution was to move the setting from the traditional conservatory to a gazebo in a terraced garden, thus creating more acting areas.

The problem

The dome of the gazebo, and the archway leading to it, was designed to reflect the graceful sweeping lines of the art noveau style. It provided our most difficult technical problem. The gazebo needed to be lightweight, built

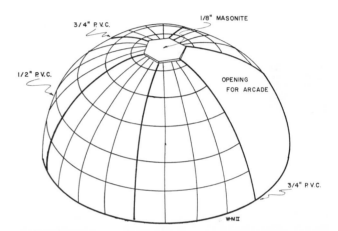

A recent production of *Misalliance*, at Loyola University, departed from the traditional staging of the play by substituting a gazebo (top) for the usual conservatory setting. Set designer Raynette Halvorsen Smith chose PVC plumbing pipe as the principle material for the gazebo's construction (diagram, center). Two 12″ hexagons cut from ½″ masonite formed the gazebo's top (left bottom). Pipe ends were force-fit over small dowels (above, detail cross joint construction) to strengthen joints. To secure the base of the gazebo to the floor, nails were driven into the floor and bent over the pipe (left top, detail vertical joint construction).

quickly, inexpensively, and with mostly student labor.

While working on the design I had envisioned the structure in metal conduit pipe. Unfortunately, the scene shop lacked metal forming equipment and, as a basement scene shop, did not provide adequate ventilation for welding.

After abandoning metal I investigated plastic pipe. For structural reasons I needed to permanently form the pipe in the desired shape, rather than merely bending it. To force the pipe into curved shapes meant that I would have to use stronger joining techniques, detracting from the delicate look desired. Three-quarter inch and 1/2" PVC plumbing pipe was the right size for the desired look. Schedule 125 pipe was cheap, but too thin-walled and hence not strong enough. Schedule 80 was expensive and also tempered, making it very difficult to form. I selected Schedule 40, which was strong enough, formable, and readily available.

A technique that could form the pipe into long sweeping curves was needed. A heat gun provided unsatisfactory results. It could heat only 6" to 12" of the pipe at once. The product was a very uneven curve and the high heat of the process produced noxious fumes. Some attempts were made at using steam to heat the pipe, but equipment and safety problems led us to consider another technique— dipping the pipe in boiling water. The water heated the pipe thoroughly and evenly so that when pressed against the form we achieved a smooth, even curve without distorting the diameter of the pipe.

The procedure

To hold the boiling water we made a trough from a 10' length of rain gutter. The ends were plugged with a piece of 2' x 6' cut to profile the gutter and caulked in place to prevent leaks. A hole was drilled in the lower part of one of the end pieces and a plug inserted to allow water to drain out of the trough.

The actual forming procedure for the long structural members was as follows:

1 Enough water was boiled in galvanized pails to cover several pieces of pipe in the trough.
2 The number and lengths of pipe to be formed were selected and placed in the trough.
3 The form against which the pipe was to be formed was placed as near as possible to the trough.
4 Boiling water was carefully poured over the pipe in the trough. We allowed the pipe to heat in the water until it began to bend (approximately five seconds).
5 The pipe was lifted out of the trough with wire hooks, one end higher than the other, to drain the water from the pipe.
6 The hot pipe was pressed against the form for about ten seconds.

When the water temperature dropped below about 190°F the pipe became harder to bend. Consequently only a few pipes could be heated at one time. Also, the pipe cooled quickly once out of the water, so we had only seconds to actually form the pipe. We made L-shaped hooks out of heavy gauge wire to lift the pipe out of the trough quickly and safely. Thick gloves were a necessity when directly handling the pipe. The form we used was the edge of a turntable that had the same 6' radius as the gazebo dome. After a few reheatings the pipe became tempered and increasingly difficult to bend.

The shorter cross-members were made with a much simpler technique. Since these were only 6" to 18" long, we simply boiled a large kettle of water and heated many of them at once. Our forms were 3/4" plywood sweeps of varying radii. The radii of these pieces were determined by their position on the dome. The longer pieces, with larger radii, formed the rings near the bottom of the dome. The shorter, more tightly bent pieces formed the rings nearer the top.

A large plywood jig was cut to form the attached arcade canopy, which formed an ellipse instead of a semicircle in section. The pipes for the arcade were then formed in the same manner as the pipes on the dome.

Assembly

After all the members were formed, construction of the gazebo began. Starting with the two longest pieces of formed pipe, a circle was laid out on the floor to create the base of the dome. The ends of the pipe were force-fit over a small section of dowel to create the joint. Hot melt glue was used to seal and strengthen the joint. The pipe was secured to the floor with nails driven into the floor and then bent over the pipe.

The very top of the gazebo was fabricated from two 12" hexagons shaped from 1/4" masonite. A wooden spacer, as thick as the outside diameter of the 3/4" pipe, was placed in the center between the two hexagons. The formed vertical pipes were then threaded between the pieces of masonite and secured with a screw from the top.

The other end of the formed pieces was attached to the ring on the floor with plumbers tape. When the main dome supports were in place, installation of the 1/2" vertical pipes was done in the same manner. After this, only the 1/2" cross-members remained to be installed. Because the pipe was preformed into curved shapes, there was very little stress on the joints. This allowed us to use a weaker but tidier-looking technique invented by John Yeck, the technical director.

These joints were secured with a double-pointed nail and a piece of dowel. A 6-penny nail was driven into one end of the dowel. Then the head of the nail was removed on the grinder. The dowel was forced into the short horizontal member and the other end of the nail was pushed into a predrilled hole in the vertical pipe. Loose joints were caulked with hot melt glue.

Finishing

The entire structure was sprayed with flat black enamel. To render a glass-like effect, synthetic chiffon in pie-shaped wedges was glued to the inside of the dome with hot melt glue. Magic markers were used to paint stained glass on the chiffon.

Rigging

The supporting columns of the gazebo were bundles consisting of a 1″ iron pipe flanked by ³/₄″ PVC pipes on either side. Each was attached to the bottom ring of the dome with plumbers tape. The bundle went through a hole in a 6″ platform and into a flange on the stage floor. For aesthetic reasons, there could be no cross bracing to hold the columns rigid. This problem was solved by tying a guy wire from the top of the dome to a pipe batten. The batten was carefully flown out until it created a tension throughout the structure which helped to prevent movement and swaying. Wires were strung across the inside of the dome to prevent possible distortion of its shape. When the arcade unit was joined, it further braced the dome. The arcade was tied to a thoroughly braced flat wall.

Conclusion

The solution to this design problem proved to be lightweight and inexpensive. The fact that very little special equipment was needed saved much time and money. But most important of all, the unit was visually very effective.

Budget (dome and supports only)

³/₄″ PVC pipe, Schedule 40	
180′ at .30 a foot	$ 54.00
¹/₂″ PVC pipe, Schedule 40	
210′ at .20 a foot	42.00
Plumbers tape—1 roll	.59
¹/₄ sheet of ¹/₄″ masonite	1.15
⁵/₈″ dowel	
3′ at .50 a foot	1.50
25 sticks of hot melt glue	(stock)
Flat black spray paint	
3 cans at 2.50	7.50
10 yds. of chiffon at	
2.00 per yard	20.00
40′ of 1″ iron pipe	(stock)
10′ of rain gutter	(stock)
Total	**$126.74**

Warning: *polyvinyl chloride releases toxic fumes (carbon monoxide and hydrogen chloride) when burned. Extreme care must be taken when heating this material.*

Originally published in August/September 1982

Foam Casting in Sand

We have been able to duplicate decorative detail and create original forms by using dampened sand to form negative molds with the following method.

First, make a small sandbox big enough to fit the object. Pour in the sand and dampen with a spray mister. Press item into the sand and remove. Imperfections can be touched up and new features sculpted or pressed into the sand at this point.

Next, mix two-part A-B foam (we have used both polystyrene and polyurethane) and pour into the mold. When the foam has cured, it can be pulled easily from the box. Brush away excess sand and trim any excess foam.

For smaller forms requiring greater strength, use automotive body putty thinned down with fiberglass resin so it can be poured into the sand mold.

The only problem we have encountered is improper curing of the foam, due to the acidic nature of most commercial sand. To neutralize the acidity, add baking soda to the sand.

RONALD NAVERSEN
Northern Kentucky University
Highland Heights, Kentucky

Welding Basics for Strength and Design Flexibility

by David Sealy

One law of any scene shop is that no two shows are alike. Even if a show is revived, the demands on the scene shop may be different. This means that flexibility and versatility are essential for the successful shop operation. An area that can add to a shop's versatility is metals. Even though a structure might traditionally be made out of wood—a better and less expensive product might result from using metals. For example, a circular stair was required for the University of Iowa's production of *A Midsummer Night's Dream;* the diameter of the circle was 40″ with a rise of 6½″ for each tread. The design called for as open a construction as possible. We constructed it in metals. If this same structure had been made from wood it would have cost more than the steel, and the open construction would have been impaired.

Metals are not difficult to deal with. They do, however, require some specialized tools and skills. One of these skills is welding. While not difficult to learn it does require practice to become proficient.

Gas welding

Welding methods can be divided into two basic types: gas welding and electric welding. Gas welding combines a combustible gas with oxygen. (The technique is frequently referred to as oxyacetylene welding.) The flame characteristically is extremely concentrated and localized. As a result it is necessary to move along the weldment at a slow speed. This can cause problems with metal deformation and loss of temper—especially with thick metals or over a large area. However if the area

Safety precautions are important in welding—basic equipment includes safety helmet, gloves, and a body covering, in this case (top), a leather jacket. The University of Iowa production of *Tooth of Crime*, designed by Hunt Squibb with technical direction by Kathy Moore, featured a throne (bottom) created out of automobile parts that had been welded together. Photos: Peni Hall.

you are working on is small, the concentrated flame is useful. As in the University of Iowa's production of *'Tis A Pity She's A Whore* when a set of human masks was needed. The masks were two dimensional and made from #10 steel wire. They ranged in size from 8″ to 10″ high and from 6″ to 8″ wide. A full scale designer's elevation was made and wire was cut and bent into proper shape. The pieces of the mask were then welded together with a gas welding torch. The concentrated flame allowed for good control of the weld over a small area. Oxyacetylene welding has many other applications in fabricating props or small set pieces.

Another application of a gas system is metal cutting. Many times metal can be more efficiently cut with a cutting torch than with a hacksaw or a bandsaw. For example, if a piece of ¼″ plate steel needs to be cut it might be quicker to cut the pieces with a cutting torch. A good "weld ready" cut can be achieved with practice by an oxyacetylene torch.

Other processes available with a gas system are soft soldering, hard or silver soldering, and brazing. These processes are not welding processes, as such, in that they do not heat the base metal to a melting point. They also need a complimentary metal to "glue" the base metals together.

Electric welding

In electric welding (frequently referred to as arc welding) an electric current is passed from one side of a transformer through an electrode. The other side of the transformer is connected by a "ground cable" to the work. When the electrode is touched to the work the electric circuit is completed and a current flows. When the electrode is drawn away from the work the air is heated and is ionized. The ionized air carries the current and an arc is struck. The heat of the arc is used to melt the base metal to make the weld.

In choosing an electric welding machine, there are two ratings to consider: amperage and duty cycle. The amperage is an indication as to the capacity. The duty cycle is an indication of how long the machine can operate at rated capacity before it must be allowed to cool.

The duty cycle is listed as a percentage of a ten minute period. For example, a machine might have a duty cycle of 60% at 125 amperes. This means that the machine can be operated at 125 amperes for six minutes. The machine must then idle and be allowed to cool for four minutes before using it again at rated capacity. If the machine is used at a lesser amperage it can be used for a longer period of time before cooling. Conversely, if it is used at a high amperage the duty cycle shortens.

In a theatre scene shop a machine rated from 125 to 200 amperes at a 60% duty cycle is quite satisfactory. Higher duty cycles and amperages are needed for production welding in industry.

By using solid state circuitry, electric machines can achieve a 100% duty cycle at full rated capacity. The solid state circuitry also allows the user to strike an arc more easily and maintain a better arc while welding. A welder that uses solid state (i.e. transistors, SCR's etc.) in the weld and/or the control circuits is far more flexible than a traditional machine.

Some machines use an alternating current or ac for welding. One advantage of an ac machine is that it has fewer electrical parts that a comparable direct current or dc welder. Thus, it has a lower operating and maintenance cost. Another advantage is that an ac machine can be used as a base for other welding processes, such as TIG (Tungsten-Inert-Gas) for welding aluminum.

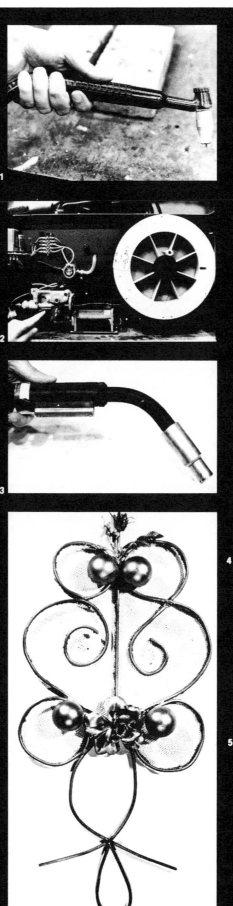

ASPECTS OF ELECTRIC AND GAS WELDING

The electric TIG (Tungsten-Inert-Gas) system uses a special torch (1) and strikes an arc between a non-consumable tungsten electrode and the work. Also electric is another inert gas shielded welding process, MIG (Metallic-Inert-Gas). It uses a continuously fed consumable wire electrode that is stored on a reel in the machine and pushed into the weld area by a friction drive motor (2). The MIG gun has a switch on the handle that controls the process of feeding the wire to the weld area (3). Other MIG machines carry a smaller reel of wire electrode in the gun itself (4, interior, 5, exterior). The gas welding process combines combustible gas with oxygen to provide a concentrated flame to a small area. This oxyacetylene process was used for masks fabricated from # 10 steel wire for a recent University of Iowa production of 'Tis a Pity She's a Whore (6, front view).

TIG systems

A TIG system uses a special torch. The arc is struck between a tungsten electrode and the work. The tungsten rod is considered to be non-consumable in that it does not become part of the weldment. A filler rod of the same material as the base metal is sometimes used. The arc is surrounded by a shield of inert gas, usually argon, that excludes the surrounding air and helps prevent oxidation. A high frequency component is added to the welding current to help stabilize the arc. TIG can be used for welding other metals, such as mild steel. It is more expensive than stick welding but the quality of weld is much higher. An accessory package containing an electronic box that adds the high frequency component, a TIG torch, and a gas regulator can be purchased and added to an existing ac welder.

MIG systems

Another type of inert gas shielded welding is MIG (Metallic-Inert-Gas). This is sometimes referred to as "wire welding." MIG uses a continuously fed wire as a consumable electrode. The arc is surrounded by an inert gas. In MIG welding carbon dioxide can be used as it is cheaper than argon. If carbon dioxide is used then the wire must contain a deoxidizer. If MIG and TIG are both used then it might be cheaper to use argon as a single shield gas.

There are several advantages to MIG welding:

1. The process is much faster than stick welding. There is no need to break the arc to change electrodes. Many welding flaws occur where the weld is broken and restarted.
2. MIG is a simple process to learn. Anyone who is a proficient welder can pick it up in a short time.
3. There is no flux or slag to remove. Also, spatter is kept to a minimum.
4. It produces a small heat-affected area.
5. With its short circuiting transfer technique, thin stock is easily welded.

The wire electrode is stored on a reel in the machine and is pushed into the weld area by a friction drive motor. The distance between the machine and the gun is limited to about 15 feet. Some machines carry a smaller reel in the gun. This can be awkward to use, but it does allow for a greater distance from the machine to the welding location because the wire does not have to be pushed the full distance.

The wire contacts the work creating a short circuit between the electrically "live" wire and the work. As the wire heats it melts breaking the contact and creating an arc. The wire continues to melt depositing the metal from the wire onto the weld area. Finally, the arc is broken. As the wire is being continuously fed by the machine, the wire contacts the work again and the cycle repeats itself.

When the operator uses a MIG gun, a microswitch on the handle controls the process. When the switch is closed the process begins. This allows a great deal of control in placing the weld exactly. It is difficult to place a weld when trying to strike an arc in stick welding.

This control of placement can be very useful when welding irregular shapes. For example, for the University of Iowa's production of *Cabaret* it was necessary to weld some irregular shapes made from 5/8" reinforcing rod. The individual pieces were cut with square ends rather than resetting the saw each time at a different angle to mitre the ends. The pieces were then laid out and MIG welded at their proper angle. The wire electrode was used to fill in the gaps. There was no slag so the pieces could be immediately painted without a lot of time needed for grinding. The job was completed in about a tenth the time it would have taken without MIG.

The big disadvantage of MIG is the initial cost. An ordinary dc welder costs about 1/5 as much as a comparable MIG welder. MIG packages can be purchased for existing arc welders. The machine should be a dc welder. If both

TIG and MIG are needed, there are machines available that supply both ac and dc. Once a MIG system is purchased the cost is comparable to coated electrode welding. The cost of wire, gas, etc., is about the same as a comparable weight of coated electrodes.

Resistance welding

The last process is resistance welding. The pieces of metal to be welded are placed between two electrodes. A low voltage high current is passed between the electrodes. The materials own resistance causes the metals to heat to weld temperature. The current is then stopped either manually by a switch or automatically by a built in timer. The electrodes are left in place to apply pressure while the weld cools. The most common use of resistance welding is spot welding. Spot welding is useful for joining pieces of sheet metal.

Machines and magazines

A simple single process welding machine might be purchased at a savings. However, the trade-off is a decrease in flexibility and versatility. There are machine packages on the market that include several of the processes that were discussed. One would do well to investigate these package systems.

Guidelines set out here should help you evaluate the individual systems. Also I do recommend the magazine *Welding Design and Fabrication*. It is available free to qualified receivers (shop foremen, department heads, etc) from the Industrial Publishing Company, 614 Superior Avenue W. Cleveland, Ohio 44113. While this magazine deals mainly with industrial welding it does keep you abreast of new equipment and techniques.

Originally published in September 1976

Steel Tubing

by Richard W. Durst

As inflation continues to drive scenic construction costs higher and since the availability of good quality traditional materials is becoming scarce, we are all searching for low-cost, lightweight, readily available materials that can be quickly assembled. In our scene shops at the University of Minnesota (Duluth), we have turned to square steel tubing as one solution to the problem. The relatively easy and inexpensive setup process coupled with simple operator training makes scenic construction with steel tubing an attractive option for school and small shops.

Equipment

The initial cost of equipping our shop to work steel tubing was nominal, considering the time saved and the potential long-range use both of the equipment and scenery built. We equipped an old table saw with a Rockwell Abrasive Cutting Wheel (cat #12174) to cut tubing lengths. Each wheel, under normal usage, will last two to three shows and is much more satisfactory than those purchased at a hardware store. The price, $7.40, is well worth the investment. An oxyacetylene torch is the least expensive type of equipment you can use to weld the tubing. Use an "O" tip with pressure settings at 1-2 on both tanks for welding. Set the torch to a neutral flame and weld with 1/16" steel rod. Total cost for the torch, gauges, and hose is about $125. Tank rental varies with locales, but the average seems to be $4.50 per month. If you have the cutting torch attachment, you can also make odd-angle cuts and notches in the tubing. If you can afford it, a wire feed, CO_2 MIG welder is invaluable. Any student can learn to weld with it in five minutes and it produces no warpage at the welded joint. We purchased a used Linde MIG welder with .030 wire for $475 from a welding manufacturer and it has cut steel fabrication time by 25% to 30%. Hand-held welding shields for eye protection are available from any welding supply outlet for about

$2.50 each. They are excellent for use in fabricating and in demonstrations where the cost of helmets for all would be prohibitive. An abrasive-wheel grinder (air or electric) is handy for smoothing welds, but is not an absolute necessity. Our Rockwell Angle Grinder (cat #96296) cost $74 and we are still using the original abrasive wheel. To attach wood, plywood, and masonite to the tubing we use a Milwaukee magnum screw shooter (see *Theatre Crafts*, Nov/Dec '78, p. 85) with ¾" to 1½" TEK screws. These screws are self-drilling and save untold amounts of time. Our screw shooter cost $94 on bid and the screws are $18/thousand. The screws can be used only once in the tubing, but we save the TEK screws after strike of any scrapped construction and use them for wood screws.

We have constructed flying door and window units, revolves, circular step units, Cinderella's pumpkin coach . . .

What you can actually construct with the tubing by itself, or combined with other types of steel, is limited only by your imagination. We have constructed flying door and window units, revolves, circular step units, Cinderella's pumpkin coach, and other non-standard scenery, as well as stock units, from tubing, flat iron, sheet stock, and rod. Non-standard steel units are cut up with a cutting torch and reused for other construction. When pieces get too small to use, they are sold to a local scrap metal dealer for about *15% of the original cost* of the steel.

Process

Stock platform and wagon units are not only easily constructed but also lightweight, easily stored, inexpensive, and last the life of the sheet stock top. (No more broken rails!) Construct the rails

Originally published in November/December 1979

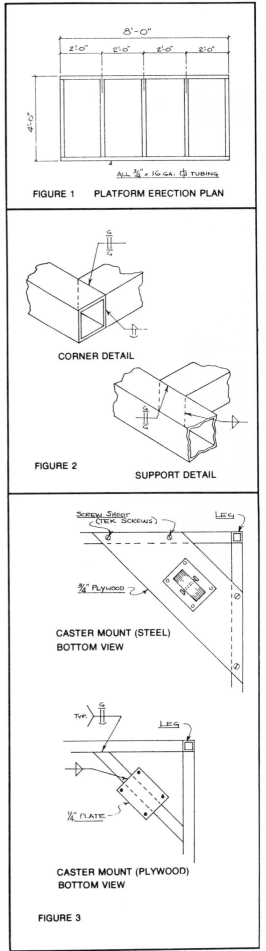

FIGURE 1   PLATFORM ERECTION PLAN

CORNER DETAIL

FIGURE 2   SUPPORT DETAIL

CASTER MOUNT (STEEL) BOTTOM VIEW

CASTER MOUNT (PLYWOOD) BOTTOM VIEW

FIGURE 3

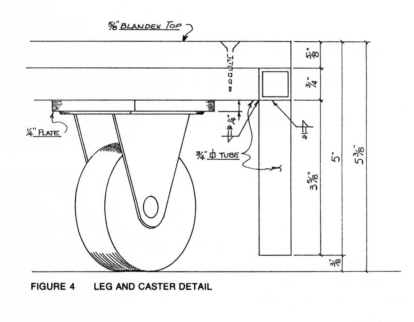

FIGURE 4   LEG AND CASTER DETAIL

FIGURE 5   LEG DETAIL

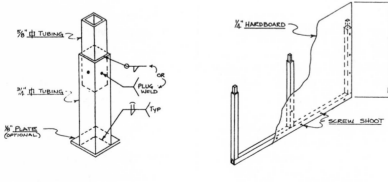

FIGURE 6   LEG UNIT DETAIL

and internal supports of 1″ × 16 gauge square tubing welded on four sides; grind the top surface so the platform top sits flat, and grind the bottom surface so the legs fit squarely. Internal supports should be on 2′ centers (see figures 1 and 2). Caution: Tubing thicker than 16 gauge is considerably more expensive, heavy, and difficult to cut except with a cutting torch. Sixteen or 18 gauge has more than adequate strength for most theatrical use.

If you anticipate using the platform as a wagon, we have found two methods that work well. Weld a 45° beveled tube in each corner and in the center of the long sides; weld a ¼″ plate, drilled to match the caster plate, to the bottom surface of each tube. Or bolt casters to 45° beveled piece of ¾″ plywood and screw-shoot the whole assembly to the platform rails (figure 3). For either method, caster spacing should be at 4′ intervals. Insure that caster movement is not impeded by the legs that will be attached. Attach legs of 1″ tubing at 4′ intervals around the perimeter of the platform. The legs are 3⅜″ to allow a ⅜″ floor clearance when used as a wagon with our 3¾″ casters (figure 4). Screw-shoot the platform top (⅝″ Blandex) to the tubing with 1½″ TEK screws. The overall platform height including the top is 5 ¼″ Blandex, a relatively new wood product, has some obvious advantages for platform tops: it is nearly as strong as ¾″ plywood and weighs virtually the same; it is 40% cheaper than ¾″ plywood; and it is much lighter than particle board and doesn't break or chip.

To leg up the stock platforms we use two methods. Up to 1′ in height we use 1″ tubing legs with a ¹³⁄₁₆″ tubing-splice (an exact inside match to 1″ tubing. ⅛″ flat iron can be welded to the bottom to prevent floor damage (figure 5). If you keep the legs in stock, platform heights can be altered in seconds. For platforms above 1', a frame is welded of 1" tubing (again with the $^{13}/_{16}$" tubing splices) and, if facing is required, covered with ¼" hardboard that is the height of the total

The added feature of selling the scrap metal further reduces construction costs

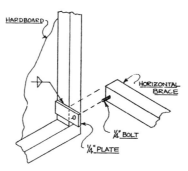

FIGURE 7   HORIZONTAL BRACING

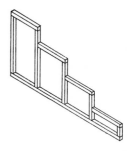

FIGURE 8   STEP UNIT CARRIAGE DETAIL

platform (figure 6). Care must be taken to insure that placement of the legs on the platforms is exact so these leg units can be interchangeable from platform to platform.

If horizontal bracing is required, weld drilled flat iron to the inside of the legs or leg units at a standard height. Weld ¼" × ¾" bolts on the proper length tubing brace and bolt it in place (figure 7). You can, if you wish, eliminate the bolts and screw-shoot the brace through the drilled plate. Several platforms can be hooked together with casket latches, bolts, C-clamps, or loose pin hinges.

Stock step units can also be constructed from steel tubing. The carriages can be welded (figure 8) and the width of the unit changed by changing tread lengths.

These platforms and step units are lighter, more economical, and take up less storage space than those made of wood. They can be reused and recycled indefinitely. The added feature of selling the scrap metal further reduces construction costs.

Cost and weight analysis for a 4' × 8' stock platform		
Steel: 5" high	Cost	Weight
Approximately 38' of square tubing	$ 6.75	14 lbs.
One 4' × 8' sheet of ⅝" Blandex	$11.65	64 lbs.
	$18.40	78 lbs.
Wood: 4¼" high		
Approximately 36' of 2 × 4	$ 8.01	33 lbs.*
One 4' × 8' sheet of ¾" plywood	$21.25	60 lbs.
	$29.26	93 lbs.
Approximately 36' of 2 × 4	$ 8.01	33 lbs.*
One 4' × 8' sheet of ⅝" Blandex	$11.65	64 lbs.
	$19.66	97 lbs.

*Approximate—depends upon water and sap content.
Due to variable life of wood, we cannot adequately compare length of usage.   □

Wood Words

by Daniel Koetting

Although little formal statistical data has been gathered, anyone involved in the construction of scenery can tell you that wood is the basic element. Lumber is our only renewable natural resource and has been used in the theatre since the Greeks. Approximately 40-60% of the materials' budget at the college where I teach goes for lumber. Two other noticeable factors about wood are that the price is going up rapidly and the quality is going down. I have put together some information on two kinds of wood products: boards and dimensional lumber (wood that comes directly from the tree) and plywood and related materials (wood that has undergone a manufacturing process). Hopefully, the following will help increase your consumer awareness and ease as a threatre lumber buyer.

Boards and dimensional lumber

For most scenery construction, the lumber used is softwood, from the species Pine, Fir, Spruce, or Hemlock. Lumber nearer the center of the tree is called heartwood and the lumber nearer to the edge of the tree is called sapwood. Heartwood is usually stronger and harder and resists warping more than sapwood. The board lumber is usually pine and the dimension lumber is fir, spruce, or hemlock.

1   edge grain cut

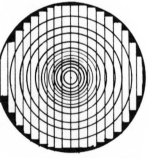

2   flat grain cut

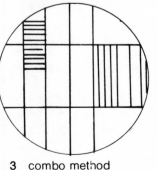

3   combo method

There are two major log-sawing methods for softwoods: edge grain cutting (1) and flat grain cutting (2). Modern sawing usually combines both methods (3). The proper terminology will facilitate purchasing:

A *strip* is less than 2″ thick and less than 8″ wide (nominal size).

A *board* is less than 2″ thick and more than 8″ wide (nominal size).

A dimensional piece of lumber is 2″ (or more) thick and 5″ (or less) thick; more than 4″ and less than 12″ wide (nominal size).

A *timber* is a piece of lumber with the small dimension 6″ or more.

The common references to dimensions of wood are not always exact. 1″ x 3″s are actually ¾″ x 2½″ and 1″ x 12″s are only 11¼″ wide. Always know what your real dimensions are so your figures won't be thrown off. In addition, the decrease in size means a proportionate decrease in strength.

Wood costs

The price of lumber is determined by the grade and the amount. But in the theatre, you often have to order in a hurry (due to changes or failure of the designs to arrive in the shop on time) and you often order specialty items not always stocked by every lumberyard. At the same time you always must try to get the best lumber for the dollar.

Given these factors, it is important to do business with one or two lumber yards that will appreciate your business and will help you out in a jam. Of course, that does not mean that you should take terrible wood or pay extremely high prices, but remember that not every single board has to be perfect. For example, some dimensional lumber like 2″ x 4″s are bought by the box car and are graded #1 construction. But grading allows for 60/40; that is 60% #1 and 40% #2. If you order ten pieces only 6 have to be #1 grade and the others may be #2. If you need ten #1 then you have to pay more. Another example is that you may need one or two sheets of Upson board and even though the lumber yard does not stock it, in lieu of past business and hope of future business they may get it for you. So try to develop a good working relationship with a couple of yards.

If your theatre can store a large amount of lumber it may prove useful to issue bids to several companies. This may help get a better price but it does take more time. When writing a bid be extremely clear about amounts (size in width and lengths), the grade, and the species. By specifying that the lumber should be grade stamped (done at the mill or railroad siding) it might cost a slight bit more but you will be sure of what you are getting. Also, specify your delivery date since that might also affect the price.

Grading wood

Grading is the process of defining the quality of lumber. Generally speaking, the production budget and how long the scenery is expected to be used are the two factors that determine choice of grade. The two most often used grades are "c" select (sometimes humorously referred to as "c" or better, but don't wait for the better because somehow it never makes it). The other grade is #2 common. I use "c" grade for stock platforms, door units, reusable flats, and certain pieces where extra-heavy wear is expected. Most colleges and smaller groups use #2 for everything.

Any grade lower than #2 will contain more and larger knots

than useful wood and therefore should be avoided. Grade #2 should have no warp or splits.

In grading dimensional lumber your yard may use one of two systems. One system is, in descending order of quality: construction, standard, utility, economy. The other system runs, in descending order: select structural, #1, #2, #3 economy. Stud grade usually refers to pieces under 10′ long and fits in somewhere between #2 and #3. There is also a stud economy grade that is not recommended for most theatre applications.

Dimensional lumber can be bought either air-dried or kiln-dried. Kiln-dried lumber has been dried to a specific moisture content (about 12% for general usage), and care must be exercised to keep kiln-dried wood from exposure to moisture so it will not warp.

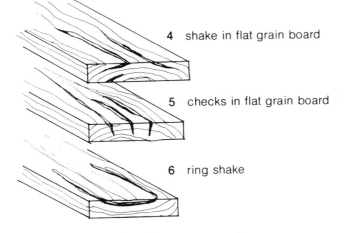

4 shake in flat grain board

5 checks in flat grain board

6 ring shake

Knots and other defects

In addition to grading, defects must be considered to insure that you receive good lumber. A shake is a separation along the grain between the annual growth rings (4). A through shake is a crack running completely through a board from face to face. Checks in a flat grain (sawing method) board are separations across the annual rings (5). Checks along the medullary rays can be caused by too-rapid drying. A ring shake (6); boards having this kind of shake may also be warped. A knot, either intergrown or encased (7). Knots are formed where limbs of a tree meet the trunk. If the limb is

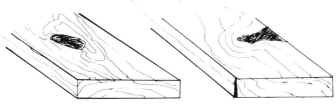

7 knot—encased or ingrown

alive, the knot formed is called intergrown. If the limb dies and the sapwood covers the knot, the knot is called encased (the fibers of the trunk are not continuous with the knot and encase the knot, ergo the name). Encased knots are usually accompanied by less cross grain and therefore are usually less serious. Knots which are firmly in place are called tight knots.

Knots reduce the strength of wood for several reasons. Clear wood is displaced by the knot or the fibers around the knot are distorted, causing cross grain. Or there is a lack of continuity in the fibers which causes stress concentrations. Also, checking occurs around the knot during the drying due to a different rate of drying for the knot. The wood in a knot is usually much harder and has a higher pitch content than other parts of the wood, therefore it is harder to machine and often warps. The size of the knot in relation to the total width of the board affects the board's strength. A large knot in a 1″ x 3″ can make the board useless except for short lengths.

Wood warpage

Wood warpage can be a major problem in lumber. As wood dries after it has been cut it tends to bend several ways (8, 9).

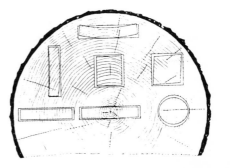

8 shrinkage shown in log

New wood can contain up to 200% more moisture than it should have to be used properly. For construction use, wood should contain 9-12% moisture. Do not accept water-logged lumber from the yard. (You can usually feel the difference in the weight of the wet lumber.)

Tell the yard to cover your delivery on rainy days—especially important with kiln-dried lumber—and, if possible, let the wood dry for a few days in the shop before using it.

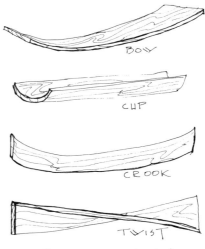

BOW

CUP

CROOK

TWIST

9 warpages, extracted

Warpage can be discouraged by proper storage. Always store lumber in a cool, dry place that is well-ventilated. Support it adequately and keep it flat.

Plywood

The second major grouping of wood products used in scenic construction is plywood and related items such as particle board. Plywood is thin layers of wood called veneers which are laminated together. The grain of each layer alternates direction. This gives the ply more strength both with the grain and across the grain. Although there are many types of plywoods available to the scenic builder, plywood made of softwoods is usually sufficient for theatrical use. Hardwood ply is much more expensive. There are two methods of grading ply: appearance grades and engineered grades. Each front and back layer of veneer is graded with one of five letters ranging from A-A to C-D (appearance). The engineering grades cover the structural properties of the plywood and range from C-C to C-D. These plys are usually unsanded. Almost all American plywood is grade stamped on the back face. Most American plywood consists of three or five layers. Imported plywood has no grade stamp and sometimes is seven layers thick. The type of glue used in construction also differentiates categories of plywood. Exterior glue is water-proof and interior glue is moisture-resistant, but not necessarily waterproof. There is a third type, intermediate glue, that is more moisture resistant than interior but not made for permanent exposure to water.

Due to its composition, plywood is handled differently than wood. Useful joints for plywood are a bevel joint (10) that should be 5 to 12 times as long as the ply is thick, a rabbet joint (11), often used at corners, and a shiplap joint (12).

As a general rule, do not nail into plywood parallel to the front or back faces. Also, use nailing blocks (13) and glue. When drilling through plywood, either clamp a block on the back or drill halfway through from the back, turn the piece over, and finish drilling from the front. Use a wood bit for best results.

Sometimes a type of ply called "plugged and touched sanded" is available (one face has been plugged and the sanding is coarse). This variety is usually adequate for theatre work and it costs a good deal less than regular ply. Imported ply also may be cheaper but check the quality with the lumberyard. Plywood made for underflooring also may be cheaper than regular ply, but it often has a soft core. This type should not be used where strength is vital.

Shop panels are similar to clothing store seconds. These panels have failed to pass grading and often are out of square. However, you may be able to cut them up for smaller pieces. Again, if strength is not your primary consideration, you may want to substitute a 3/16" soft mahogany ply panel for 1/4" ply. This will decrease your cost per panel by more than 50%.

Plywood-related products

In the area of plywood-related products, perhaps the closest to ply is a product called particle board, sometimes referred to as Nova ply. Particle board is made of sawdust mixed with resin-type adhesive, formed and heated and pressed into a dense, smooth panel. On the plus side, particle board is cheaper (anywhere from 33% to 50% less) than plywood. It has no grain, so it is equally strong in both directions, and a smooth surface that finishes smoothly.

On the minus side, particle board is very heavy. Since it is made up of various wood chips and glue it is difficult to nail or screw into without pre-drilling and is hard on saw blades and other machine tools. If not supported properly or if dropped the edges can chip or break off. A small amount of paraffin is used to make particle board and it can cause problems with the paint or the finish you apply. Try a small sample first. Also, the density of the particular brand may vary and that too will affect how the paint adheres.

There are several kinds of hardboard that can be used for theatre construction. Hardboard, such as Masonite, comes in three types; standard, tempered (standard that is treated with chemicals and heated to give one face a very hard surface), and service (less dense and weaker than the others). It is available with one or both sides smooth, or the rough side comes with a screen pattern on the back (helpful if you are gluing the panel to some other surface).

Several types of plywood indoor siding, though expensive, can be used to good advantage in the theatre. These range from 1/4" to 5/8" thick and have various textures and patterns in them, such as reversed board and batten, rough sawn, channel grooved, and brushed textured. Even though the initial cost of these sidings may be more expensive, you may be able to save on the labor costs and end up even in price.

When it comes to purchasing the best woods or wood products for your uses—find a good lumberyard and don't hesitate to ask questions.

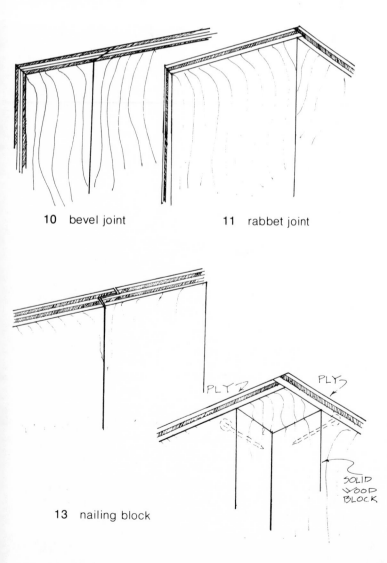

10 bevel joint   11 rabbet joint

PLY PLY

13 nailing block

SOLID WOOD BLOCK

Platforms, Flooring, Escapes, and Revolves

Spiral Stair Design and Construction

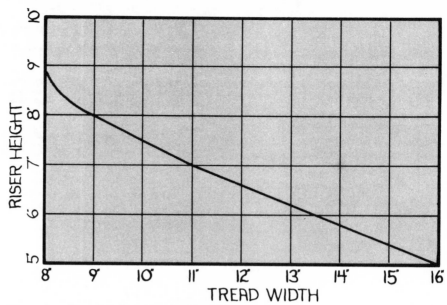

Figure 1. Riser height versus tread width

by Jeffrey Sultan

Spiral staircases are virtual necessities for many operatic and musical productions. Yet their construction presents complex problems for stage designers and technicians because it is extremely difficult to produce sufficiently accurate working drawings of a spiral staircase unit by conventional design graphics.

Typically, a spiral staircase is drawn in plan view and elevation with an inner and outer radius, height, and, perhaps, an angular measurement for the treads. The technician must then make construction drawings having only those four measurements actually given by the designer. The method described here will allow the technician to calculate all of the additional dimensions he needs without any scale rule measurements.

A designer should avoid making the technicians determine dimensions with a scale rule whenever possible. The reason is precision: a scale rule measurement is only accurate within ± ½ inch on a typical ½ inch = 1 foot scaled drawing. For a stair unit with ten steps, the final construction could be off 5 inches or more if the tread width is determined solely by a scale rule measurement. That much error could conceivably affect the overall composition of the design. The precision could be improved either by using a larger scale or by adjusting and fitting in the shop.

The biggest problem in the usual method is laying out the treads of the staircase; that is, calculating the proper plan view and transferring it to the working drawings. Once that is done, the final framing can be accomplished by any of the traditional methods, such as gates, carriages, pipe legs, etc. The particular construction method must be suited to the production needs of shifting, storage, touring, loading, and the designer's concept will determine the ultimate structure.

The geometrical method presented here is a simple, no-cost way of producing accurate design drawings. While the dimensional errors introduced by other methods can be eliminated in later phases of construction, it is not easy. Carelessness and unprofessionalism are factors only when the errors are overlooked or intentionally ignored.

For a production of the opera *Albert Herring* at Stanford University, a simple method was devised to design and construct the treads of spiral staircase units. Spiral stairs are different from any staircase unit in that the tread width decreases towards the center. Each tread must be wide enough to accommodate all of the actors who might be on it at the same time. This method devised at Stanford imposes a minimum of constraints on the designer and does not involve elaborate geometrical or mathematical computation. It is based on the

geometry of circular segments, but only multiplication is required for a solution, and the process can be further simplified by the use of a table of decimals of a foot or by metric measurements. The geometry involved imposes but one limitation, which does not seem too severe: that the whole staircase must describe an angle of 90 or 120 degrees. No other limitation as to shape or size is imposed by this scheme.

For any staircase, spiral or otherwise, the relationship between tread width and riser height is very important. When a person climbs steep steps, weight is transferred to the balls of the feet and a narrow tread width is needed. Conversely, less steep stairs require wider treads. Figure 1 gives the tread widths which are appropriate for riser heights likely to be used in stage settings. Major variations from this chart should be carefully considered to avoid hazards and uncomfortable situations for actors. Stair units with too-narrow treads on which actors appear to be in danger of tumbling headlong are all too common in stage settings.

For a circular staircase, which has wedge-shaped treads, the riser-tread relationship applies to the portion of the tread which is used by actors. If two or more actors must use the stairs abreast, care must be taken to assure that the width is correct for each person. An-

Two feet from the outer edge is the part upon which an actor would walk, and Figure 1 shows that a width of 1'-2-1/8" would be consistent with a rise of just under 6". Eight six-inch steps reach an overall height of 4'-6"; there is an additional rise from the top step to the landing. It is up to the designer to adjust, by trial and error, the number of steps, the inner and outer radii, and the overall height to insure that the rise-to-run relationships of Figure 1 are maintained.

Once the designer has made his decisions, the carpenter need only be given the measurements for the outer radius (R_O), the inner radius (R_I), and the length of the chord which is the outer width of the tread (W_O). $R_I = 0$ if the tread converges on the center. He can then proceed in the following manner:

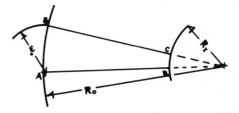

1. Swing arc with radius R_O and mark center.
2. From the same center swing arc R_I, if R_I is not zero.
3. Draw a line from center to any point on outer radius (A).
4. From A mark chord of length W_O on outer radius (B).
5. Draw a line from center to B.
6. ABCD is the template for the stair treads. If $R_I = 0$, the template is the whole wedge from AB to the center.

The method described above can be as accurate as one wishes. Most architectural and engineering handbooks have tables of decimals of a foot in 1/16" increments, the closest tolerance to which a scene shop is likely to work.

For *Albert Herring* this method greatly speeded the construction of the grand staircase. It should be even more useful for smaller or more intricate spiral staircase units where lack of precision would be objectionable.

Originally published in November/December 1974

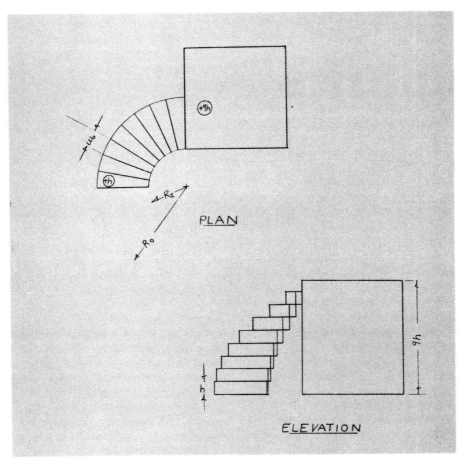

Figure 2. Elevation: basic spiral staircase unit, no scale.

other important factor in the design of stair units is the use of equal riser heights throughout the whole unit. A person tends to subconsciously "measure" the first few steps and is likely to stumble if a subsequent step is misaligned. Many building codes restrict the variation in riser heights to a maximum of 3/16" for a given run.

Figure 2 is a plan and elevation of a basic spiral staircase. To determine the width of the tread (length of the chord of the arc) at any radius, multiply the given radius by the value of C from Figure 3 for the appropriate number of steps and the correct angle. For example, on a circular staircase with an outer radius of 8 feet, an inner radius of 4 feet, and eight steps:

the outer tread width =
8.0 x .196 = 1.568' = 1'-6-13/16"
the inner tread width =
4.0 x .196 = .784' = 9-7/16"
the tread width at 2'-0" in from the outer edge =
6.0 x .196 = 1.176' = 1'-2-1/8"

Number of Steps	C 90°	C 120°
3	.518	.684
4	.390	.518
5	.313	.416
6	.261	.347
7	.223	.298
8	.196	.261
9	.174	.232
10	.157	.209
11	.143	.190
12	.131	.174
13	.121	.161
14	.112	.149
15	.105	.140
16	.098	.131
17	.092	.123
18	.087	.116
19	.083	.110
20	.079	.105
21	.075	.100
22	.071	.095
23	.068	.091
24	.065	.087
25	.063	.084
26	.060	.081
27	.058	.078
28	.056	.075
29	.054	.072
30	.052	.070

Figure 3.

Rota-Lock Stairs

by William Anderson

A solution to a design problem for a production of *West Side Story,* at the University of Iowa, led to the development of a totally flexible staircase system. The set design, by G. Eric Ulfers, called for a pipe structure, with various levels depicting different locations. These levels were connected with staircases, which had to be built, in keeping with the design, out of pipe. As technical director for the produc-

tion, I had to come up with a way to build these staircases. With the help of master carpenter Greg Hambleton, a solution was devised.

The pipe structure for the set was built out of 1¼″ schedule 40 standard steel pipe. The pipes were held together by Rota-Locks. These devices are used to connect two pieces of pipe at right angles to each other. They consist of an endless loop, which

fits around the two pipes, and a separate adjustable saddle, which fits in between the pipes and the loop. This saddle is tightened down on the pipe and acts as a wedge holding the two pipes together. With this as the basis, we worked out a way to build the staircases using the same materials as the rest of the set.

The staircases were made of 1¼″ pipe, ¾″ x ¾″ x ³/₁₆″ angle iron, and ¾″ plywood. The angle iron was cut to length and drilled to receive a ¼″ x 1¼″ flathead machine screw. The 1¼″ pipe was cut and had the ends reamed to remove any burrs. Next, a jig was made to hold the pipe and two pieces of angle in place while welding. The angle was welded to the pipe from underneath to keep a smooth surface on top for the tread. After the welding was completed, the plywood treads were bolted onto the unit, completing the tread part of the staircase.

The stringers were also made from 1¼″ pipe. The staircase was assembled by attaching the treads to the stringers one side at a time. This proved to be the hardest part of building the staircase. After all treads were attached to the stringer pipes, the complete unit was attached to the levels requiring the staircase. Since the treads can revolve to any angle around the stringer pipes and are adjustable as to the rise according to the needs of the staircase, it was very easy to adjust these staircases to fit the specific needs of the design. It should be noted that adjustments to the treads should be made after the staircase is put into position. This method is much faster than trying to make adjustments while the unit is on

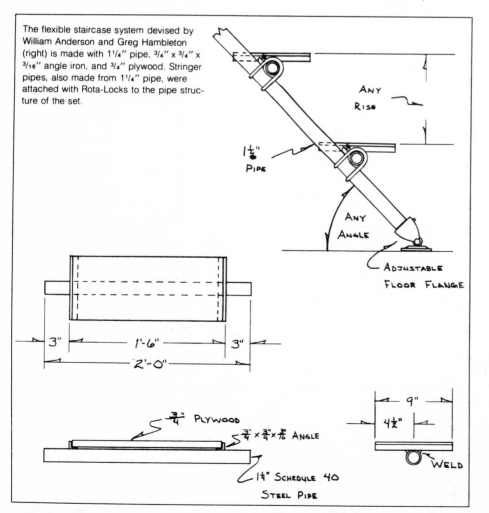

The flexible staircase system devised by William Anderson and Greg Hambleton (right) is made with 1¼″ pipe, ¾″ x ¾″ x ³/₁₆″ angle iron, and ¾″ plywood. Stringer pipes, also made from 1¼″ pipe, were attached with Rota-Locks to the pipe structure of the set.

Improved Step Units

by A. Evan Haag

the floor. We used some adjustable Speed Rail floor flanges to attach the ends of the stringer pipes to the floor. The tops of the stringer pipes were attached with Rota-Locks to the pipe structure of the set.

These staircases spanned a distance of about 9′ at approximately a 45° angle. For greater spans, support legs should be added. Although no hand rails were called for in the design, they may be attached to the staircase, along with supporting legs, with Rota-Locks or any other available pipe clamps.

Although these staircases were not used as escape stairs for *West Side Story,* they have since been used to build escape staircases of varying configurations for many different productions at the University of Iowa. They have proven to be a fast and economical method of providing adjustable and reuseable staircases.

SOURCES
Rota-Locks
UP-RIGHT SCAFFOLDS
1013 Pardee Street
Berkeley, CA 94710
(415) 843-0770

Speed Rail pipe fittings
HOLLAENDER MANUFACTURING
10285 Wayne Avenue
Cincinnati, OH 45215
(513) 772-8800

Originally published in April 1981

In the design and construction of step units for the theatre, there are several problems that frequently arise:

1 Flimsy facing often gets kicked in or comes loose before the end of the run. Facing needs attention when the unit is pulled from stock and reused.
2 Nailing through the facing into the back edge of the tread often causes the tread to split along the back.
3 The span distance limitation (from left-to-right) usually is limited to the allowable span of the tread material.
4 The difficulty of fastening facing to the thin edge of a stair through the front of the tread.

In construction, facing material is frequently ¼″ plywood. This material has properties which, when used correctly, will allow it to span much greater distances (left-to-right) than most tread materials. If you use ¼″ plywood efficiently and effectively you can construct units that will solve many

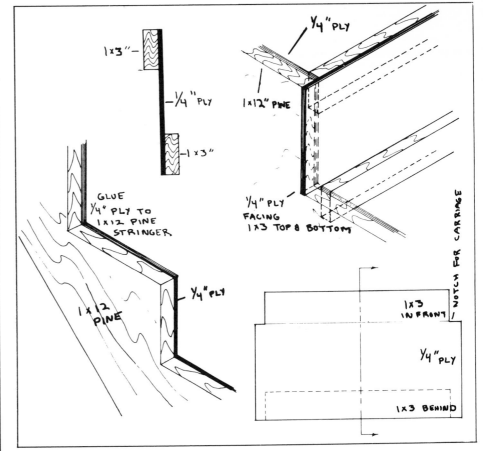

A. Evan Haag's step unit uses ¼″ plywood facing as the structural left-to-right member and has it support the treads (isometric view of step unit and construction diagrams, top).

of the common problems. In addition, it will create a strong, durable, and lightweight unit.

The system is one I developed to build long-lasting stock for audience step units for the Studio Theatre of the University of California at Santa Barbara. The units had to support the combined weight of audience members who congregate on them during intermissions or at the end of the show. They had to be as lightweight and maintenance free as possible— the ideal for any kind of unit that will be reused. The span, left-to-right, had to be 3' in order to conform with fire laws for aisle widths. An additional consideration was silence—audience members feel safer on stairs that do not squeak. And, late audience members should be able to get to their seats silently.

To understand our solution it is important to remember the strength of plywood when it is used on-edge. Simply, the solution is to use the 1/4" plywood facing as the structural left-to-right member and make it support the treads. Quarter inch plywood, on-edge, will support a great amount of weight, providing that it can be securely fastened not to flex or buckle. When it moves out of a perfectly vertical position it loses strength very rapidly. To keep the facing in place and to assure that the top and bottom edges of the facing remain immovable I added two elements to the step unit design (parts C and D in the figure).

Part C is glued and screwed to the facing. The facing is fastened to the tread above by screwing (after gluing) through the tread and into the top of part C. Glue on all joints will engage a large surface areas and assure strength as well as assuring that the joint will be noiseless. Most noise in units is caused by the various parts rubbing against each other.

Part D (at the bottom of the facing) is designed to hold the lower edge of the facing rigidly in place. It is glued and screwed to the facing. The tread below actually sits on part D. The facing is fastened to the tread below by screwing (after gluing) through the tread and into the top of part D. The fasterners used to secure part D to the tread must be positioned so that any force tending to move the facing away from the back of the tread causes the fasteners to resist withdrawal laterally instead of axially, as would be the case if it were nailed through the fac-

ing and into the back edge of the tread. Fasteners generally are more resistant to withdrawal laterally than to a force tending to remove them along their axis. Parts C and D keep the 1/4" plywood facing in place, allowing its strength in a vertical position to be used to support the tread from left to right. The 1/4" plywood facing piece is also notched at its ends so that it sits on the carriage or stringer. This does away with a left-to-right support that is end-nailed through the side of the carriage. This joint, when glued and screwed, is extremely noiseless. It makes the facing (rigidly stiffened by parts C and D as well as the fastening through the facing and into the carriage) act as a beam, sitting on a support at each end.

This system has worked extremely well in the step units for which it was originally designed, and the system has been successfully used in a show where the staircase had to be 6' wide. The use of the facing as the support member left-to-right allowed for an otherwise unsupported 6' span using only 12" x 2" fir for parts C and D with 1/4" plywood as the facing. This system would be useful wherever a long, unsupported span is needed, and it would be lighter and more maintenance-free than many other systems.

The carriage shown in the figure also uses 1/4" plywood in a vertical position. The 1" x 12" pine (clear) combines with the 1/4" plywood to give the carriage considerable strength and the 1/4" plywood keeps it from splitting. The 1" x 12" also facilitates fastening into the carriage.

Using this method creates a lighter unit than that created by using 2" x 12" carriages and a 2" x 4" under the tread as the structural member, and it is just as strong. Additionally, splitting out of the carriage is almost non-existant with this method. Obviously, the strength and integrity of this unit depends on fine tolerances and accurate, square cuts. However, even without those, this system will be better than most because of the surface areas involved and because of the way fasteners are used. Finally, this system creates a truly lightweight unit relative to the weight it will bear. It would work well in a touring situation where strength and lightweight are of great importance.

Originally published in April 1981

A Portable Dance Sub-Floor

by Charles Purchase

If all dancers were to voice their most common fear when touring, it would be of cold theatres with hard stages. Turning up the thermostat can lessen the chill, but little can be done with a hard stage.

The ideal stage floor has resiliency. Dancing on a hard, non-yielding floor overtaxes tendons, joints, and muscles. Muscles and joints become the shock absorber, instead of the floor. In jumps, a dancer adjusts by changing the way his feet leave and return to the floor, thereby altering the body's natural kinesthetic tendencies. This unconscious attempt to protect the

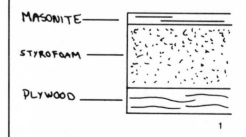

body causes undue strain on compensating muscles; this can lead to shin splints. Shin splints and injuries to the knee are perhaps the most common but by no means the only problems related to hard floors.

In the past, one of the more popular ways a touring dance company could deal with hard floors was to carry enough battleship linoleum to cover the performing area. Although this may be fine for a huge company with huge trucks and huge stagehands to cart it around, it is impractical for most of us.

The portable sub-floor used by the American Festival Ballet is a sandwich of masonite, Styrofoam, and plywood (schematic 1, facing page). In construction, after the decks are glued together muslin is dutch-manned around the edges (2 and 3). The muslin protects the soft edges of the decks and draws the pieces together to make an even surface. When three sides of the deck are finished, the decks are stacked on the uncovered edge (4).

Many touring companies travel with a lighter weight floor made by Marley, Tarkett, Stagestep, or Roscofloor, but these alone do not compensate for an unyielding floor.

The American Festival Ballet, of Moscow, Idaho, plays in all kinds of facilities, from grade schools to high school auditoriums to major theatres to gymnasiums. In most of these places the floors are hard, primarily because they were not designed specifically for dance. Even some of the gym floors are too hard: we once found a gym with outdoor carpet laid directly over concrete. (Pity the poor basketball players.)

Here is one solution. The idea is not new, but the way I have developed it makes it work well for us. It is a portable sub-floor made of a sandwich of plywood, Styrofoam, and masonite. The Styrofoam provides the resiliency and the plywood and masonite protect it. Constructed in 4′ x 8′ sheets, the deck is lightweight and, with proper handling by stagehands, should give many seasons of service. Following is a step by step description of the building process.

Step 1 The plywood was laid on a working surface or floor, with the rough side down. Tite-Bond glue was then applied in six large spots, in a nail pattern, and spread with a stick. Care was taken to spread the glue all the way to the edges of the wood.

Step 2 The Styrofoam was placed on top of the glued wood. Glue was then applied to the top side of the Styro-foam. Again, care was taken to get the glue all the way to the edge. We did not spread the glue all over either surface, to lessen the chance of warping.

Step 3 Using an abrasive disk, the tempered side of the masonite was scored in the places it would contact the glue. This gave the glue something to stick to.

Step 4 The masonite was placed on the glued Styrofoam, with the rough side up, and sandbags or other weighty objects were placed on it as a clamp till the glue dried.

We made a stack of decks as the glue was drying, simply moving the sandbags to the top piece as each deck was completed and added to the stack.

Step 5 When the glue had dried, muslin was dutchmanned around the edges, using white glue in a half and half mix with water. The muslin should extend in at least 6″ from the edge. It was stapled to hold it in place until the glue dried.

Care must be taken with the muslin. Its purpose is to protect the soft edges of the decks and to draw the pieces of the sandwich together to make a completely even surface. Unless the plywood and masonite are free of warps and bumps—rather unlikely—a slight bulge may appear along the edge here and there. Stretching the muslin tight in these spots should take care of that problem.

Three sides of the deck were done with dutchman and the decks were stacked on the undone side. When dried they were turned over and the remaining side done.

Step 6 The assembled pieces were painted with latex paint. This is to protect them from the rain and snow storms they are sure to go through. The plywood sides were painted in two separate actions, again to lessen the chance of warping.

The completed sub-floor was then ready to be used under a portable dance surface, such as a Marley floor. The weight of the Marley keeps the sub-floor from shifting. The decks should be laid with the masonite side up. The masonite spreads out the weight of the dancers and keeps the Styrofoam from being compressed. Care should be taken in transporting the decks, in that they should not be run into walls or protruding objects, nor stacked in the truck so that heavy objects can fall on them. Keeping this

in mind, it is easier if each piece is handled by two stagehands—although the temptation is for one person to do it alone. The decks are awkward for one person to handle and could be damaged too easily, destroying their integral resiliency.

Materials list:

The materials listed here are for 32 pieces of deck, enough to cover an area 32′ x 32′.

Plywood, 1/2″, shop grade (CDX might do)	$370
Masonite, 1/4″	$230
Styrofoam, 2″	$370
Muslin, approximately 4 sq. yards per deck	$250
Tite-Bond glue, four gallons	$52
White glue, three gallons	$32
Latex paint, five gallons	$35

Brushes, rollers, staples, and other supplies of that sort all came from regular shop stock and are not counted in the budget. Our costs were lower than budget because we used a lot of scrap muslin, and a nearby lumber mill sold us reject plywood for under $2 a sheet. There were no obvious defects in the plywood and it has worked well for us. Moreover, we found paint on sale for $5 a gallon.

For further reading I recommend: *Dance Injuries: Their Prevention and Care* by Daniel D. Arnheim (The C.V. Mosby Company); *Teaching Young Dancers* by Joan Lawson (Theatre Arts Books); *Dance is a Contact Sport* by Joseph H. Mazo (Da Capo Press). This project was funded by a grant from the George Frederick Jewett Foundation of San Francisco.

Originally published in April 1981

Solve the Flooring

by Charles L. Riccillo

We've all seen the problem before—you aren't allowed to paint the stage floor. Either the theatre is running the first show of the season, and technicians won't have access to the area until set-in, and then only all-too-briefly. Or, the shows "roll" in rep, perhaps even tour to different locations where they play a week or more at a time.

The list goes on. Even in resident university theatre, where you've tried both fabric and wood, the results could be termed only modestly successful. Somehow all the glue and staples, the stretching and sizing, the filling and sanding just didn't qualify as your ideal way to spend an already hectic weekend. And the net effect seldom stood up to close scrutiny.

The floor problem, in sum, is durability, shift-ability, the demands of stock application, dance-ability, and acceptability as a canvas for the scenic artist. You tell your spouse, the costume designer, about the problem and the budget limitations. You sit at home, bleary-eyed from tech of the last show, consciousness dissolving in front of the mind-mush machine. Typical late-night television: a commercial, then another, and another, and . . . wait a moment! What is it they're doing to that vinyl jacket? Why, mending it! Sealing it with a hot iron. Why not the same principle applied to a floor—a big, touring or stock floor of vinyl? It is available 12′ wide in huge rolls. What's to keep you from "mending" seams, to create surfaces 24 or more feet wide?

Vinyl flooring, commonly called linoleum, is the answer. You can use the flip-side, which is an absorbent composite of vinyl and flexible fibrous substances or even retain the option of flopping it over to the finished side for use as the real interior flooring it is. How boring.

What advantages does vinyl flooring have over duck-canvas or other similar fabrics? Obviously, it is both thicker and more resilient. It also accepts pads and seams beneath—while hiding more of the cracks and unevenness—and does not require stretching or sizing, laying flat nicely. In addition, vinyl floors need a minimum of taping or adhesive, and even then, usually only around the periphery. Storage depends upon the individual circumstance, but the long, compact rolls may be practical enough for most theatres.

Wooden decking in luan or ply may be laid under it as a base. These need not be filled or sanded and will be re-usable —with undamaged edges and a clean, unpainted surface—when it's taken up. But obviously, in laying a "seamless" vinyl floor, the smoother and flatter the surface beneath, the neater the result.

The bottom line is always of great concern. Armstrong vinyl flooring was available—on sale—for about $4.00 a running yard in 12' wide rolls. This compares very favorably with $10.00 a running yard for 104" wide duck-canvas or 142 count muslin. The salesman, without doubt, will eye you as a lunatic when he learns your purpose for the flooring, but then, in our bastard profession, I've learned to accept the same from carpenters, plumbers, hardware salesmen, welders and roofers.

This type of floor was used for two productions at Duke University in a recent summer season. The first was for a set I designed for Michael Weller's *Loose Ends*, wherein the linoleum was painted in a partly abstract, partly earthen, partly marble effect with a style reminiscent of Jackson Pollack on a bad day. With the proper template lighting, these intentionally ambiguous textures were capable of evoking a variety of different locales and settings: a shady park, the dirt yard of a New Hampshire cabin, a New York apartment's terrace, and a 1950's linoleum floor in an old Boston apartment.

In the second setting, designed by Duke scenographer/technical director Steve Judd for Tom Stoppard's *Night and Day*, a 16' x 20' vinyl floor was painted as polished slate in a modern African millionaire's home. In retrospect, we might even have applied heat and pressure to achieve the further realistic effect of grouting. In both cases, after production, the floors were rolled up and saved in their entirety or in large pieces.

The Process
The tools you will need are the usual for measuring and squaring, like a tape measure and carpenter's square. A long, metal straight edge will be invaluable. A watercolor marker is also useful. Be careful. Indelible Magic Marker would bleed up through most paints later.

For cutting—depending on the shapes and your preference—you need a pair

of electric rotary shears, a utility or linoleum knife, and a putty knife. You will also need a caulking gun. (Good quality vinyl caulk works well. However, I suspect that acrylic and silicone caulks might bond even better, and maintain plasticity when dry.) Next, be sure to have a highly adhesive strong duct or gaffer's tape. And finally, a roll of heavy-duty aluminum foil.

An electric iron is the only other tool you will require. It has been suggested that an iron with a Teflon-coated face—or, alternatively, a Teflon coating sprayed on the usual stainless steel might eliminate the need for the foil. You'll probably remain more popular if you refrain from borrowing a trusted friend's from the costume shop.

Avoid tearing or creasing the vinyl flooring. Handle it gently when moving it. When it is rolled, you will find it best to keep it intact and straight.

Now begin to work. Lay the flooring seam to seam with its finished commercial side up, then tape the seams. Make sure the surfaces are flat and the edges are aligned with a thin but consistent gap. The tape should be pressed down smoothly and firmly. Here you will realize the advantage of flooring with very little or no embossing.

Now carefully re-roll the partially-joined flooring in preparation for turning it over without damaging it. I found it useful to roll it under and away from myself as I go. This allows you to quickly unroll the piece with the commercial bottom-side up.

Take your choice of caulk, and, using the appropriate gun, lay a thin, even bead on the seam. Smooth this with the putty knife. For the cleanest, most presentable results, do not spread the caulk out from the seam. Instead pick up the excess by cleaning the surface with a firm drag of the knife.

After a few minutes of dry-time, smoothly lay the aluminum foil, shiny side down, on the flooring seam. Set your iron on its highest non-steam temperature. Then carefully, somewhat slowly, iron the seam. Allow it to cool for a least five minutes before peeling the aluminum foil slowly back—not up.

Finishing
You now not only have a floor, but a canvas you can proceed to prepare for painting. Do so by preparing a latex, vinyl, or acrylic undercoat of approximately the same color as the flooring. With this you may either coat the entire floor or soft-spray the repeating Armstrong or other manufacturers' signatures. If you choose to undercoat—or in your base coat—you may find it useful to add a small amount of Rosco-Bond or other strong acrylic adhesive. Add no more than one part adhesive to ten parts paint. This will aid in bonding and generally strengthen the surface.

Whenever possible, use a fairly thick consistency of paint, and more paint rather than more layers. This will cause less buckling of the surface. The flooring responds a great deal like some watercolor papers when it is too saturated with water—it absorbs extraordinarily well, and becomes smooth again only as the water evaporates.

When you've painted the effect you desire, you may wish to seal the surface. Depending on the finished look you prefer and the availability of products, I recommend one of three mediums, all chosen for their combination of strength and flexibility when dry: Rosco Gloss Medium, Rosco Matte Medium, or Johnson's Future acrylic floor wax. Though more expensive, you may find the Future less disconcerting since, in my experience, it not only dries clear, but also is clear in application. All three mediums, however, have a tendency to bubble and froth if worked too vigorously by brush, and care should be taken to apply the substance evenly. Because of this step, your floor will withstand damp-mopping when necessary during the show's run. A new application of your chosen sealant will also revitalize its finish.

Now you need only lay and secure the floor. Start with a bead of vinyl wallpaper adhesive around the periphery of the area. This, or a similar type of "gummy" cement, will hold down the flooring, and later on, can be removed from the building's floor with a simple rubbing. However, tape, wooden, metal, rubber, or other kinds of strips also work for this purpose. The more you protect the surface from staples and tears, the longer it will function.

Originally published in May 1984

Flooring Over an Annular Ring

by Russell Houchen

The stage floor of the proscenium theatre at Wake Forest University's Scales Fine Arts Center is equipped with a 7' wide permanent revolving annular ring turntable. The ring's overall diameter is 32', with a stationary, trapped center section measuring 18' in diameter. The first production on the stage posed a unique technical problem concerning the revolving ring. As designed, the scenery dictated back-to-back settings that covered most of the revolving ring and the entire center section. The scenery floor had to be 18" above the stage floor, support two full sets and 17 actors, and move quietly and safely as a single unit. The specific problem, then, was how to span the stationary center of the revolving ring with a quiet, moving unit that could support almost two tons of weight.

After examination of several alternatives, a giant but simple "lazy Susan" device was decided on. The perimeter of the raised scenic floor or platform would set on legs attached to the turntable, with the center of the platform resting on a pivot mechanism positioned in the center of the 18' diameter trapped area inside the annular ring. A single, weight-supporting pivot mechanism would solve both the major engineering problems inherent in the design: the set floor would have a solid mechanical support over the stationary stage floor inside the annular ring, yet still be able to rotate uninhibited with the turntable.

The weight-bearing pivot mechanism had only two requirements: it had to support slightly less than two tons of actors, scenery, and lighting equipment, and it had to rotate slowly but freely as the whole set floor turned on it. Investigation into industrial power transmission showed our particular problem seemed to be best solved by fabricating a unit using two self-aligning, open-ended, pillow block bearing assemblies separated by a shaft of solid bar stock. The bearings were slipped onto collar insets machined into the ends of the bar stock, with the bearing mounting plates facing away from the bar stock shaft. The bottom bearing mounting plate simply was lag screwed to the stage floor, and the top bearing mounting plate attached to the underside of the platform's gridwork via angle iron guides. The bar stock shaft provided both the required 18" overall height as well as the necessary solid mechanical support for that portion of scenic platform located over the stationary stage floor, in center of the annular ring.

The raised scenery platform consisted of two large, wooden gridwork frames with a $3/4''$ plywood deck. Standard 2" x 6" stringers on 24" centers and 2" x 4" cross braces on 48" centers composed the gridwork frames. The 2" x 6" stringers covered the 9' span from the annular ring to the pivot bearing. Short pieces of 2" x 6" served as compression legs, at the gridwork perimeter, to raise the whole scenic platform to the required 18" height. Once the stringers and cross braces had been cut, the gridworks were laid out, air-nailed together, and set in place. The framed gridworks rested on the compression legs, on the turntable, and on the pivot bearing, in the center of the annular ring. The $3/4''$ plywood deck was applied and air-nailed down. In three hours we had a set floor 32' in diameter 18" high. This unit rotated via the power of the turntable yet covered the dead, trapped area inside the ring. Padding, canvas, and the vertical scenic elements for the two back-to-back sets were put in place easily and quickly to finish the design.

In practical application the bearing assembly proved to be most effective. The unit easily handled the production demands, supporting all the actors and scenery while allowing the whole design to rotate silently. Since the bearings were self-aligning, any error in placement of the assembly and/or any slight incongruity in the revolve itself was compensated for. The assembly is reusable and needs only a change in the length of the bar stock shaft to render different height applications. In short, the unit resulted in a quick, quiet, solid, and compact solution to the problem.

Originally published in April 1981

Platform Legging

by Karl T. Pope

Platform legging is one element of set construction that continually threatens to be a problem. Economy requires that legs and platform frames must be able to withstand continual attaching to one another and removal over a prolonged period of time. Safety requires that the joint between the leg and frame be as strong as possible, in order to withstand performer weight and movement. Time pressures require that the legs be capable of being attached quickly and removed easily. And storage availability usually requires that legs and platforms not need much storage room.

These requirements appear to work against one another. If the legs and platforms are to be re-used, joining needs to be quickly made and easily parted. Conversely, however, if the platform is to be secure the leg joint must be tight, strong, and able to withstand the pressures of action, all of which seem to rule out easy dismantling and re-use.

The following discussion considers two traditional methods of platform legging, and then suggests two methods of improved construction and joining. The procedures include mid-platform legging as well, but for convenience the examples only cover the more difficult corner joints.

Perhaps the most familiar method of securing a leg to a platform frame is to use common nails to affix the leg to the inside corner of the platform (figure 1). For added strength, nails are usually driven from two directions—through the platform frame into the leg (into the flat side of the 2″ x 4″ leg) and into the edge.

Although this method of attaching

Originally published in April 1981

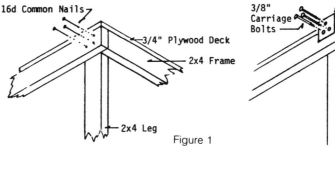

Figure 1

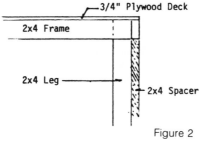

Figure 2

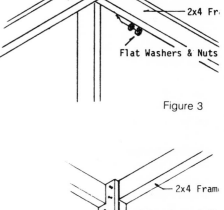

Figure 3

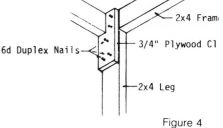

Figure 4

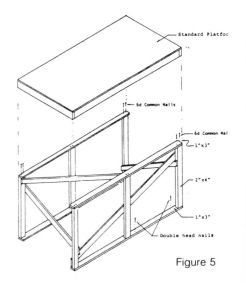

Figure 5

the legs is simple, fast, and inexpensive, it immediately creates three problems which negate its primary advantage. First, the joint is weak, since all of the weight of the platform is resting on the nails. The weight and movement of the performers may cause the nails to bend (allowing the frame to sink) or the legs to split, causing the whole structure to become unstable. Second, as new nails are continually driven through the frame and into the legs during the setup, and withdrawn during the strike, the wooden frames are torn and splintered, and soon must be replaced. Third, since the leg must be placed on the inside corner of the platform frame, it is the width of the frame away from the platform facing. Therefore, a spacer (figure 2) must always be added before the face of the platform can be covered.

The second of the traditional joints solves the problem of instability. It uses the same positioning of the legs—in the inside corner of the platform frame—but instead of nails, carriage bolts, nuts, and washers are used to attach the legs to the platform (figure 3). The spacer problem, however, still remains, and new problems are added. First, in removing the bolts during the strike, the threads often are damaged, requiring either time to "chase" the damaged threads or the purchase of new bolts. Therefore, if bolt legging is the usual method of joining it can be quite expensive unless time and care are exercised during the dismantling process (both of which also drive costs up). Further, a platform frame is soon rendered worthless by continually drilling new holes for legs—unless a template is used to ensure uniform holes in both the platforms and the legs. And finally, the bolted leg supports only part of the frame corner—one member being carried only by the nails that hold the frame together.

Improved legging

The suggestions for improved legging overcome most of the objections raised thus far.

The first method is especially effective for freestanding single platforms. The leg is placed under the platform frame and supports all the weight. On the corner it is positioned so that it supports both ends of the frame where they meet at the corner—thus prevent-

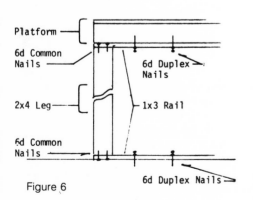

Figure 6

ing any movement from an unsupported member. The leg is attached to the platform by means of a cleat cut from a piece of ³/₄" plywood (3¹/₂" x 8") and 6d duplex nails (figure 4). If the

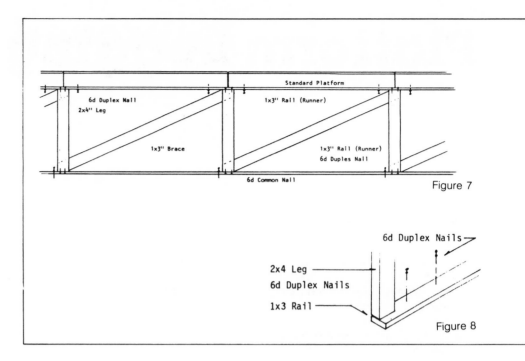

Figure 7

Figure 8

cleat is notched to accommodate the frame, the leg may be placed flush with both the end and side of the platform, thus eliminating the problem of a spacer and allowing the facing to be nailed directly to the platform legging. The 6d duplex nails are quickly driven and removed, allowing rapid setup and strike. Also, legs with cleats already attached may be stored for future use. Cross bracing is attached to the inside of the legs, also using duplex nails.

The second method of legging is useful in quickly putting up a series of platforms where large sections of a stage need be covered, and particularly where the action is rigorous and safety demands are high. (It may, of course, also be used for legging individual platforms.)

After the individual platforms are completed (using a 2" x 4" frame), legs are cut from 2" x 4"s—allowing for the thickness of the platform, plus a runner (or rail) above and one below for total length of the platform (figure 5).

Usually the runners are constructed from 1" x 3"s, although in certain instances ¹/₄" plywood might be used for the bottom rail. Legs are normally spaced on 4' centers, but may be placed closer according to weight and strength requirements. Top and bottom runners are then attached to the legs with 6d common nails. After squaring the structure, diagonal bracing is

added and the unit is ready for the platform. Legging constructed in this manner may be pre-constructed for a single platform or sufficiently long to support many. It should be noted that this procedure may be used either for a level platformed area or for raked platforming. Where open platforming is to be viewed, the edges of the runners may be beveled to make them less noticeable.

Duplex nails are then used to attach the top runners to the frame and the bottom runners to the stage floor (figure 6). When installing a series of platforms, usually it is advantageous to line up all the legging units and nail them to the floor. They will then stand (temporarily) while the platforms are moved into place and nailed to the top rail.

With the addition of cross bracing, the whole platform or platformed section then becomes a stable, tight acting area (figure 7). Yet at strike the duplex nails are easily pulled, the platforms removed, the bracing knocked off, the legs separated from the frame, and all stored and ready for re-use.

Perhaps the greatest advantages of this method of legging—stability and the elimination of toe-nailing (figure 8)—are provided by the bottom runners. Whenever legs are toe-nailed to the floor, there is always the threat of splitting a section off the bottom and losing the entire leg (figure 9). At the least, the angled nail holes weaken the

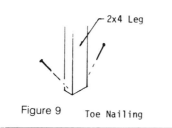

Figure 9   Toe Nailing

leg severely, and the difficulty in removing the nails increases labor costs and damage to materials. Also, until they are nailed to the floor the bottom runners allow relative ease in the movement of the platform unit.

The main requirements of platform legging are safety and economy. By using cleats or runners, as I suggest, safety is enhanced and the premature wearing-out of leg and frame pieces prevented. Cleats are inexpensive and quick to make, and all materials can be re-used. The construction and strike time are minimal. In short, this process is sturdy, inexpensive, and saves time, materials, and anxiety.

Improved Legging for Wooden Platforms

by John Chenault

For many scene shops with limited budgets, the wooden post and lintel or rigid platform with leg platform has long been a favorite method of platform construction, due to its low cost and flexibility of heights. The traditional method of constructing this type of platform is to frame a sheet of ³/₄" or ⁵/₈" plywood of the proper size with 1" x 6"s, 2" x 4"s, or 2" x 6"s, then bolt legs of 2" x 4"s to the frame with ³/₈" carriage bolts. This creates certain problems:

1 Each time you leg up with a platform, you must take the time to drill new holes in the frame and legs (or the bolt may turn in the hole).

2 This constant drilling eventually weakens the platform, causing early retirement of the unit.

3 The head of the bolt protrudes beyond the edge of the platform, making a tight fit between adjacent units virtually impossible.

4 If you drill a ³/₈" hole to reduce the possibility of the bolt turning, removal of the bolt after the show becomes quite difficult, often resulting in mashed threads if a student hits the threaded end with a hammer.

5 Invariably, on any show with several platforms at least one bolt will turn with the nut and take excessive time to get out.

The above problems can be virtually eliminated by use of a torque-washer. This is a washer, with a square hole

(to receive the square shank of a carriage bolt) and four spikes (to bite firmly into the wood), that allows you to re-use a bolt hole indefinitely and to oversize your hole slightly for easier insertion and removal of the bolt. Additionally, it is possible to set up a template for all bolt holes, allowing for the accumulation of stock legs which can be bolted in place, and to countersink the bolt head to present a smooth side.

The construction process is as follows:

1 Framing the platform. Use 2x stock to allow for countersinking the bolt head—2" x 4" is recommended.

2 After the frame is nailed together, a simple template is used to mark the locations for the bolt holes.

3 Drill, using a speed-bore type bolt, a 1¹/₈" hole ³/₈" into the 2" x 4". Be very careful to drill at a right angle to the frame.

4 Finish out the hole with a ⁷/₁₆" drill bit. Again, make sure that the hole is straight and perpendicular.

5 For additional strength, a corner bracket may be attached to the bottom of the platform.

6 Cut 2" x 4" legs, and use jig to drill ⁷/₁₆" holes in the legs. Use a drill press if available, or a hand drill if necessary.

7 Bolt legs in the normal fashion.

If you wish, you may also pre-drill the sides of the platforms to allow easy bolting together. I find that a hole exactly 1' from each corner and 2¹/₄" from the top of the platform works well. A torque-washer on the inside of the frame allows for re-use of the hole.

As of this writing, torque-washers, available from Mutual Hardware, (5–45 49th Avenue, Long Island City, NY 11101) costs approximately 16¢ each. A 4" x 5" platform will use a maximum of 20 (12 for the six legs, eight for bolting platforms together), for a total cost of $3.20. When you consider the time saved per platform and the increase in platform life, it is a wise investment.

Originally published in April 1981

Hybrid Parallel Platforms

by Michael Glenn Ward

Actors and directors seem to love the extensive use of level changes. This gives them the possibility of a variety of movements and stage picture that are not available on a flat surface. These levels are generally created by the use of rigid platforms.

Rigid platforms fall into three major types: 1) a stock platform with fixed or bolted legs; 2) the continental parallel platform; and 3) the standard parallel. Most technicians seem to prefer the rigid platform. (Such a stock platform with adjustable legs might be more economical in use over several years, but unless you buy in volume I suspect the initial investment is higher than an all wooden platform.) This is especially true if your labor force is free as in most university situations. But, because the rigid platform with fixed legs is heavier, more bulky, and, when legged for use, more space consuming than either type of parallel platform an alternative might be the answer. If your group tours or does a season in repertory, the hybrid parallel might be a solution to your problems.

There are two principal differences between the continental parallel and the standard parallel: 1) the center supports of the continental parallel are removable; and 2) each has a different hinging arrangement. These differences give the continental parallel three major advantages over the standard parallel. Because the center supporting frames are detachable, they do not interfere with the folding of the outside frames. This allows the center frames to be closer together, giving greater strength and support to the platform top. The hinging arrangement allows the support frames to be folded into a compact unit no longer than the platform. Moreover, it is possible to build a continental parallel to larger dimensions than is practical

with standard parallel, due to the possibility of additional support for the platform lid.

The length of the standard parallel is increased by its width when the frames are folded together. When more than one inner support frame is used, they will bind against each other, so that the unit cannot be stored in a compact unit. These two facts limit both the size and the strength of the standard parallel. However, it does possess several advantages: it can be shifted more quickly, because all the support frames are hinged into one unit; there are fewer parts to be misplaced in travel or storage; and, since it has fewer parts that have to be interchangeable, it will cause fewer problems and less confusion during assembly.

These statements are valid concerning these two major forms of classical scenery construction, but there is a third form that combines the good points of the continental parallel and the standard parallel. It eliminates most of the disadvantages of each and at the same time keeps the advantages. For an example of this form, I shall use a standard 4' x 8' platform. Since these dimensions are a standard construction module, its possibilities for future use are optimal and the amount of waste materials and time in construction effort is considered minimum. We will assume a finished floor height of 2' so that the elevation is above the accepted allowable unbraced length of platform legs and is in increments of a 6" stair riser.

The top should be removable and made of ³/₄" fir plywood, instead of tongue and groove white pine flooring, for three major reasons. First, it is precut in standard useable dimensions. The cost saved in labor and construction time more than offset the initial cost of material, especially when

time is at a premium. Second, the five-ply lamination helps to prevent lateral racking of the platform. Third, it is stronger than its counterpart and acts as a two-way support system, since it consists of five layers of fir laminated with its grain directions alternating.

Construction

The lid is covered with canvas over padding. The canvas is lapped and tacked (figure 1). On the under side, 1" x 2" battens are glued and screwed where indicated. Allow a ³/₄" lip around the lid and place one batten on either side of the location of the intermediate braces, for stability and continuity of the frame and lid. A ³/₄" gap should be left between battens (figure 2).

Hinge the intermediate braces as shown (figures 3 and 4). This arrangement will allow quicker and easier setup, since there are fewer parts to contend with. Also, the platform is neither increased appreciably in length when folded for storage or shipping, nor does it bind together when the additional support is added. The additional support does greatly improve the strength and rigidity of the platform and platform lid. When compared to the standard parallel, the center section still has an unbraced span of 3' 10 ¹/₂" x 4' but the two end sections' unbraced span is reduced to 3' 10 ¹/₂" x 1' 9 ³/₄". Therefore, half the platform is not as rigid as the continental parallel with the same number of braces, but the other half is stronger—it has the same number of parts as a standard parallel and requires the same storage space, yet is much stronger.

The construction of the sides, ends, and intermediate braces is very much like the classical construction technique for flat construction (figure 5).

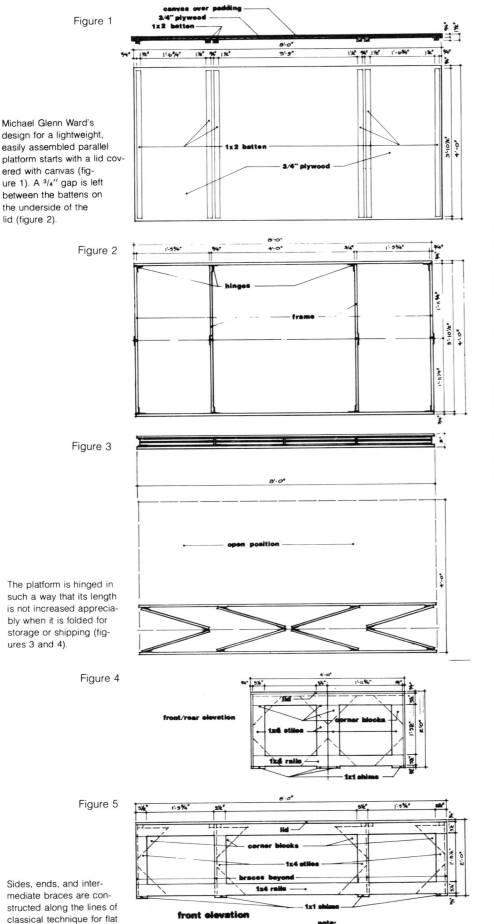

Figure 1

canvas over padding
3/4" plywood
1x2 batten

1x2 batten
3/4" plywood

8'-0"
5'-9"

Michael Glenn Ward's design for a lightweight, easily assembled parallel platform starts with a lid covered with canvas (figure 1). A 3/4'' gap is left between the battens on the underside of the lid (figure 2).

Figure 2

hinges
frame

Figure 3

open position

The platform is hinged in such a way that its length is not increased appreciably when it is folded for storage or shipping (figures 3 and 4).

Figure 4

front/rear elevation

lid
corner blocks
1x4 stiles
1x4 rails
1x1 shims

Figure 5

lid
corner blocks
1x4 stiles
braces beyond
1x4 rails
1x1 shims

front elevation

note:
cut corner block to accept hinge

Sides, ends, and intermediate braces are constructed along the lines of classical technique for flat construction (figure 5).

The only additional pieces are the 3/4'' x 3/4'' shims on the bottom rail. These act to compensate for an uneven stage and may be eliminated with no ill effects to the unit.

The quickest and simplest manner of attaching multiples of the unit together is by C-clamps. The units have flat sides that butt against each other firmly when the hinges located at midpoint on the end units are countersunk. Otherwise, a shim between units is a necessity.

The configuration of hinges and supports indicated here can be applied to any size parallel as long as the length is at least twice the width of the unit. For a platform larger than 4' x 8', however, the lid size and center unbraced span would make the unit more trouble than is justifiable. One would be better advised to use two or more smaller units that are easier to handle and of modular dimensions.

This unit is slightly more expensive than the continental parallel or standard parallel, since there are 12 more hinges to be used and slightly more work involved in the construction. However, this solution seems to answer many of the problems inherent in portable platforms. All parts of the frame are intergral, leaving only two major pieces to contend with in assembly. There are two intermediate supports, instead of one, to give additional strength and support. Therefore, larger units are more practical. The frame folds into a compact unit no longer than the platform itself.

If you have need for a lightweight, quickly assembled stock platform, this type of unit seems to solve several problems found in classical construction techniques of the parallel platform.

Originally published in April 1981

Platforming for the Liberal Arts Shop

by John T. Howard, Jr.

Most theatres have adopted some type of modular platforming. The time and money savings are obvious. The "ideal" platform is strong, modular, simple to join together, inexpensive, lightweight, and rugged. Undergraduate liberal arts shops have one more requirement: the building of the platform must teach the basic construction techniques. This requirement presupposes the belief that the shop is there primarily to teach and secondarily to produce scenery. All too frequently educational theatre shops exist in order to "grind out" scenery.

"Basic" is a very important word in this discussion, since many students are holding a hammer for the first time and are not certain that they want to do "crew" work at all. What is needed is a relatively simple technology which produces a feeling of accomplishment from seeing a project grow to completion.

For non-educational production oriented facilities, there are several construction techniques that are excellent. The oldest is the parallel, still a useful device for the road, but one which involves a large initial investment, much storage space, and the problem of inflexibility of heights. In order to be able to leg 50 platforms to eight heights, you need to build and store 400 leg units. Parallels also remove the capacity for cantilevered platforms. The platform box has all the problems of the parallel and in addition does not fold for storage.

Many of the more advanced platforming methods involve the use of steel. One can build modified scaffolding which does not rattle. There is square steel tubing for both platform structure and interchangeable legs.

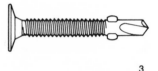

Many advanced platforming methods involve the use of steel. At the Stratford Festival of Canada, square steel tubing is used for framing and for folding legs (1). Ohio State University has experimented with fitting a pipe leg into a welded receptacle (2). TEKS screws are generally considered the state of the art solution for joining steel to wood—if the budget can afford them (3). When platforming with wood exclusively the post and lintel legging solution is a better way to engineer load support. Howard has found a doubled 1″ x 3″ leg to be the best legging method (4). Another post and lintel solution is a 4″ x 4″ leg 'with two steel pins that fit into a steel plate on the platform bottom. The jig for drilling holes in the platform (5) is made of steel layered to 1″ thickness to reduce wear and to force the drill to a 90° angle. Caster boxes (at the Stratford Festival, 6) can be homemade and are a good welding project for students.

Angle iron, Unistrut, and slotted angle for platforming have also been employed as solutions to the problem. Three years ago, Ohio State University was experimenting with a corner mounting device to accept 1¼″ steel pipe as legs for wooden platforming.

There are, however, problems with the use of steel on a large scale in platforming. The skill level is too advanced for many liberal arts shops. The students in a basic construction class need to learn how to use tools such as a hammer, a drill, and a radial arm saw. A welder is fine for 5% of the students after a semester or two.

In a world of shrinking resources for the arts, there is a cost factor. Metal work on a large scale requires a huge (for most of us) investment in equipment, fire safety precautions, and exhaust systems. The steel is more costly than wood. True, it lasts longer, but if you do not have the budget for the initial investment, it is just not possible. There is real difficulty telling a designer "I'll give you half the platforms you designed, but they will last four times as long."

A shop which does occasional metal work can get by on a minimum of expensive tools: a 10″ horizontal metal band saw—$250, an arc welder (buzz box)—$200, a gas welder—$200, and gloves, tank rental, and welding rod—$100.

A shop that shifts to all steel platforms should have two mic welders (60 Amp, 60% duty cycle)—$960, a heavy duty horizontal metal-cutting band saw—$1,150, and a welding area with exhaust system—about $2,000. (I once tried to do a big steel show with one cheap welder. It had a low-duty cycle,

so it had to rest very often. Because there was only one, only one student could weld during a crew period. It was like only having one hammer to join lumber. The result was many specially scheduled mini crews and a poor use of supervisory personnel).

There is one last problem with steel—the difficulty in attaching other materials, such as facings, to it. The TEKS screws (by Buildex) are the best answer, but they, too, are expensive.

If you decide to build wooden platforms, you have a choice between framing platforms with 1″ x 6″ (ripped to 5¼″) and 2″ x 4″. There is a school of construction, with which I agree, that believes that 2″ x 4″s, 2″ x 12″s, and 4″ x 8″s are for building houses, and that scenery should be of high quality, lightweight materials. Strength is added by glueing all joints, screwing and glueing the top on, and using T-plates and L-plates on the bottom of all the framing joints. In building one of these stock platforms (sizes up to 4′ x 8′), students get to use most of the basic tools and techniques.

There are also several methods of legging wooden platforms. The first bolts 2″ x 4″ legs inside the corners to the sides with 3″ x 8″ carriage bolts. This is simplest but results in bolt heads showing, Swiss cheese-like corners (in terms of the numbers of holes), and the splitting of the sides, since the bolts do not carry the load well. The L-leg (two 1″ x 3″s nailed at a right angle) has the same problem when bolted inside the corner of the platform, in that the bolts carry all the load.

A post and lintel type leg is a better way to engineer the load support. Here the leg (post) is placed directly below the side (lintel) of the platform, so that the load rests directly on the leg. If the side is 2″ x 4″, then a 3″ x 4″ ply scab (4″ x 12″) may be stapled across the inside of the joint between the side and the 2″ x 4″ leg. The University of Illinois's Krannert Center does this with great success. The staples allow for both fast setup and strike.

A 4″ x 4″ leg with two steel pins that fit into a steel plate on the bottom of the platform is another post and lintel solution. The resulting platforms, though easy to strike, are difficult to move and frustrating when the pins become bent.

We have found a doubled 1″ x 3″ leg to be the best method to date. A 1″ x 3″ leg (post) with a second 1″ x 3″ that is 5″ longer, nailed to the first, is a very simple legging method. (Many shops join the legs to the side of the side of a platform, so that the weight is not compressive. Each leg should be joined in such a way that it is under the side and thus compressive.)

The longer 1″ x 3″ is joined to the side with two 3″ x 16″ stove bolts. (The bolts may be small, since they carry none of the platform's load.) If the holes are drilled with a template, the holes on both stack legs and plat-

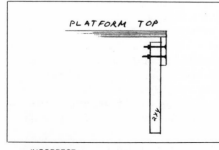

CORRECT—COMPRESSIVE
LEG IS UNDER THE SIDE OF THE PLATFORM.

INCORRECT
BOLTS TAKE THE LOAD.

forms may be re-used. We have found that re-use is possible about 75% of the time; drilling errors and wear are the chief causes of failures.

This legging method again is a chance to use basic tools first (directors usually want platforms as soon as possible). It also uses up short 1″ x 3″ scrap. Modular (up to 5′ long) heights are kept, legs for non-stock heights and rakes become firewood. This is platforming for acting areas, not audience. A careful check of the local code is recommended before building audience supporting levels.

The price per 4″ x 8″ unit depends on local costs and what grade of lumber is used. We try to use ³/₄″ AC interior ply tops and #2 pine sides and legs. The above method is not new but it still has cost and educational advantages for a shop at a liberal arts college.

Sources

TEKS are self-drilling fasteners manufactured by Buildex, a division of Illinois Tool Works, (2500 Brickvale Drive, Elk Grove Village, Illinois 60007).

Originally published in April 1981

Self Adjusting Rake Leg

by Michael Ludwick

Using pipe for platform legging, while initially expensive, is in the long run both economical and easier than standard 2″ x4″ legging. While economics and ease are sound, justifiable reasons for using it, I have encountered several problems with pipe: 1) pipe indentations in the stage decking, 2) a large degree of difficulty when making either raked or counterraked platforms, 3) the labor/ productivity in constructing such legs. Pipe indentation is a prime consideration when operating a multipurpose facility where the space must be shared with

music, dance, and general activities.

I happened on a solution several years ago while working at Missouri Repertory Theatre, in Kansas City. We were building platforming out of 1 ½″ steel tube and needed the platform to counter a raked stage. In addition, the unit had to be struck and stored vertically, which required that the legs be removable. We experimented with cutting pipe to the proper angle and found that along with consuming our time, it was putting deep gouges into the stage decking. We arrived at the solution by starting with a section of ¾″ black pipe inserted into a section of 1 ¼″ tube. A ¼″ hole was drilled through one side of it before this tube section was welded to the platform structure. A ¼″ hex nut was centered and welded over this drilled hole. (Take care here to allow adequate hand clearance for threading a ¼″ eye bolt through the nut.) The pipe was then inserted into the tube and a ¼″ eye hole was drilled through it that corresponded to the hole in the tube steel. When the eye bolt was threaded and inserted into the pipe it acted as the leg's upper locking mechanism.

On the other end of the pipe two pieces of 2″ angle iron were cut to a length of approximately 3″. These angle pieces formed the leg's foot when fitted on either side of the pipe. After it was cut, a ³/₈″ hole was drilled through both the angle iron and the pipe. (When drilling this hole, be sure to allow the pipe to pivot freely when sitting inside the angle iron feet. This free space will allow the platform to counter a rake.) A ³/₈″ heat impregnated bolt was used to withstand the shear forces generated.

We thought these legs held the key to our dilemma, but they had several inherent problems that were previously overlooked: 1) vibration tended to loosen the foot assembly's retaining bolt, 2) the bolt vibrated through the foot assembly, and proved rather distracting during quiet scences, and 3) the stage deck was still scarred by the angle iron.

We solved these problems by visiting a local plumbing shop. To prevent the ambient sound of the bolt through the foot assembly, a piece of ½″ CPVC was installed as an isolator. This required redrilling the holes of both feet and the pipe and inserting the CPVC into this new hole. The nut vibration problem was solved by placing a rubber packing washer on either side of the retaining bolt. The deck scarring was resolved by

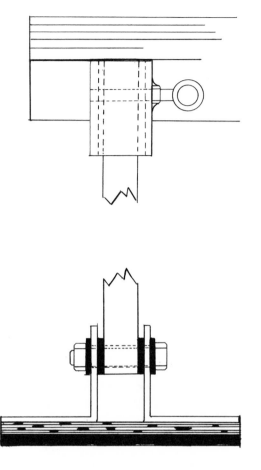

Motorized Turntable

by Stancil Campbell

Mechanized transport of stage platforms and turntables is nothing new. Yet each transport system much be specifically engineered to solve the particular production problems involved. Our recent production of *Oliver* at the University of North Carolina at Greensboro lead us to design and install a motorized transport system for revolving a 20′ turntable.

Early design conferences with the director suggested the turntable as a viable means of staging the play's numerous scenes. It was important that scene shifts move smoothly. The director also insisted that these shifts be accomplished in full view of the audience but without visible stagehands. As the design developed, the turntable clearly solved the problem. Four scenes could be set up on the revolve's various sides. When used in combination with a downstage drop, each of the two acts could be staged with no need for a stagehand on the set.

Our next step was to determine the motorized turntable's exact specifications. The foremost need from the director's viewpoint was selecting the revolve's speed. After several rehearsals and a discussion with the technical staff, the director settled on a speed of between one and two revolutions per minute (rpms). While this is a considerable span of variability, any speed within that range could be worked into the play's action and scene shifts.

The second construction factor was the power necessary to turn the revolve. The weight of a 20′ turntable is considerable. A third consideration was the limited space available under the revolve. Top platform height was limited to one step for the actors. While this would normally be 8″, we stretched the height to 9 ¼″ to give us as much space underneath the revolve as possible with our stock 4″ casters (which have an overall height of 5″). Advantageously located traps were not available to increase that height. A fourth consideration was that the final transport system had to be remote controlled from offstage to ensure that the

operator was masked from view. The control also had to be able to stop the turntable at precise spike marks for each of the many scenes.

The final engineering consideration was our limited budget. The technical staff agreed that $300 was the limit for the entire mechanized unit (budgeted separately from the scenery). With these restricting factors clearly laid out before us, our next step was to find solutions that would fall within these guidelines and requirements.

The agreeable solution had the advantage of relatively simple construction. We decided on a contact wheel-drive track system that used an electric motor/speed reducer linked to a rubber-tired contact wheel that pressed against a 4″ wide circular drive track attached to the underside of the turntable.

The turntable was built in a conventional way using a 2x4 framework with a ½″ plywood decking covered with ¼″ jute carpet padding and muslin. The circular drive track was cut from ⅝″ particle board using the same outer radius as the 20′ turntable. Although particle board has little structural strength, it proved ideal for our needs because it was highly resistant to compression under the contact wheel's pressure.

After the track was cut out, we added shallow grooves about ⅛″ deep and about 1″ apart across the width of each section. This scoring helped give the contact wheel a better surface for gripping. The track was then glued and nailed to the bottom side of the turntable frame. Special care was taken to ensure that the track's full width was supported by the frame. Where gaps existed, extra 2x4s were added to provide the necessary support.

Swivel casters with 4″ wheels and an overall height of 5″ were then lag screwed directly to the underside of the 2x4 framework. The center pivot's male part was also lag screwed to the 2x4 frame. The assembled turntable was then turned over and guided into the female pivot already attached to the stage floor. With the turntable in position and resting on its casters, we had a 4 ⅜″ clearance between the stage floor and the drive

epoxying a piece of ¼″ plywood with rubber gasket material to the bottom of the angle iron feet. When the leg assembly was reinstalled on the platform, our problems were gone. The legs withstood approximately 20 changeovers. We discovered no real problems, besides having to re-epoxy the plywood to the bottom of the feet.

This leg and foot assembly can be adapted to any current system of steel platform legging either by using speed rails, Unistrut, or standard tube. Of course, the top rigging mechanism will vary from system to system. When computing the platform's height, raked or level, you must account for the foot bottom's distance and the foot padding's thickness. Once a system and jig is constructed the foot assembly can be used repeatedly on whatever lengths of pipe the platforming design requires.

Originally published in October 1984

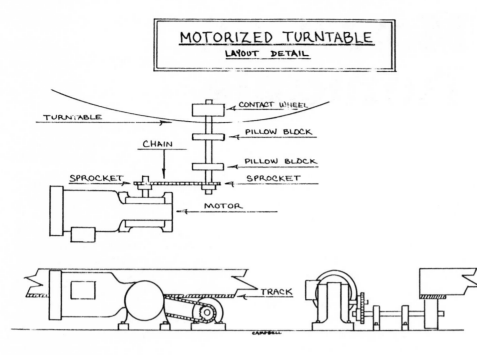

MOTORIZED TURNTABLE
LAYOUT DETAIL

TURNTABLE
CONTACT WHEEL
PILLOW BLOCK
CHAIN
PILLOW BLOCK
SPROCKET
SPROCKET
MOTOR
TRACK
CAMPBELL

track, and an overall height of 9 ¼". We were then ready to calculate the motor drive's exact specifications.

To determine the motor size, gear reduction ratio, and contact wheel diameter, we worked in reverse, basing our calculations on the desired final turntable speed of one to two rpms and the turntable's given weight.

We first purchased a 4" rubber-tired caster to use as our contact wheel. This was the largest standard wheel that would fit under our drive track. Unfortunately the caster had a ball bearing center axle that we could not use. The bearing was removed and replaced with a specially machined plug with a ¾" center bore. (A local machine shop provided this service for a $14 charge.) The contact wheel's circumference was 12 ½" or about 1.046 feet. Calculations indicated the turntable's circumference to be 62'10". By dividing the turntable's circumference by the contact wheel's, we found that about 60 contact wheel revolutions would yield one turntable revolution. Since the turntable's final speed had to be one to two rpms, our contact wheel had to turn between 60 and 120 rpms.

Our next problem was determining the power needed to rotate the turntable. Output power of electric motor/speed reducers is listed as torque, measured in inch pounds. Torque is measured as the force needed to move an object multiplied by the distance from the point of rotation at which that force is applied. We

determined the force needed to move the turntable by attaching one end of a spring scale (similar to ceiling hung produce scales, with a 300 lb capacity) to the drive track. We pulled the other end until the turntable started to revolve and noted the scale measured 175 lbs. The torque we needed was the force necessary to move the turntable (175 lbs) times the radius of the contact wheel (2"). This radius is equivalent to the distance at which the force is applied (surface of the contact wheel) from the point of rotation (center of the drive shaft). The required torque of the electric motor/speed reducer was 175 lbs x 2", which equals 350 inch pounds.

We were then ready to shop for the power plant, calculating that we needed a motor/reducer unit with a final speed of 60 to 120 rpms and an output torque of about 350 inch pounds. When we found a dealer who could supply our needs, we learned an interesting fact about motor torque ratings. He informed us that because most motor/reducers are intended for continuous operation, the listed output torque is generally much lower than the units' actual capacity. Motor manufacturers invariably underrate their products to prevent users from expecting continuous peak-load operations. The dealer said that since our unit only needed to operate sporadically over *Oliver*'s 2 ½ hour running time, we could easily get by with a unit rated anywhere between 250 and 350 inch pounds of output torque.

He supplied us with a unit made by U.S. Electric Motors called a Syncrogear Motor. It was a 208 volt, 3 phase, 1750 rpm, ½ horsepower electric motor combined with a 17.5:1 speed reducer, all in a single housing. The final output speed was 100 rpms with a rated output torque of 277 inch pounds (in later static torque tests we found the actual peak output torque to be about 800 inch pounds!). The unit was perfect except that the output drive shaft was 1" (compared to the ¾" bore in our contact wheel) and the shaft height was too high to place the contact wheel under the drive track as planned.

Time did not allow us to order a unit that fit our requirements more exactly. Consequently, we devised a chain and sprocket power transfer system that entailed extra expense but provided more flexibility. We found that the contact wheel's 100 rpms rotated the turntable at just the right speed, though it was comforting to know we could easily adjust that speed by mounting larger or smaller sprockets as needed. With the unit mounted to the stage floor and wired to an offstage switch, we were ready for the initial testing.

The first time we switched the motor on, to our great pleasure, the turntable jumped to full speed almost instantly, rotating at our predicted speed of about 1 ½ rpms. Even with all the scenery mounted in place, the turntable continued to turn at the same speed; the extra weight had little effect.

Spike marks were made on the turn-

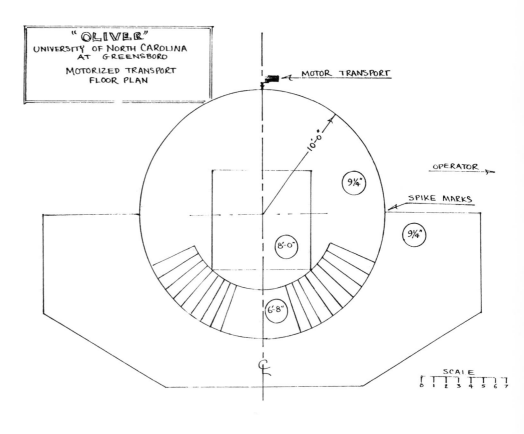

"OLIVER"
UNIVERSITY OF NORTH CAROLINA
AT GREENSBORO
MOTORIZED TRANSPORT
FLOOR PLAN

MOTOR TRANSPORT

10'-0"

OPERATOR

9¼"

SPIKE MARKS

9¼"

8'-0"

6'-8"

SCALE

table's edge in full view of the offstage operator but hidden from the audience. With a few rehearsals, the operator was able to anticipate the turntable's brief coasting rate after the motor was switched off, and could hit the spike marks with amazing accuracy.

Although this account might project the image of an instantly successful, flawlessly operated motorized turntable, we did encounter problems. The swivel casters were noisy and hard to roll. We should have used fixed casters, and would have had we had them in stock. Secondly, the chain between our sprockets broke twice, although the repair was easily made. In addition, a section of the drive track was inadequately supported and broke apart. With only 4 ⅜" clearance, this problem took more time and was difficult to fix. Our most serious problem involved the turntable's extremely unbalanced load.

Most of the heavy stairs and platforms were located on the edge and to one side of the turntable. Because this particular transport system depends on constant pressure between the drive track and the contact wheel, the more the weight over the track the more the friction on the contact wheel. When the stairs were nearing or directly over the contact wheel, the turntable rotated beautifully. However, when all that weight moved past the contact wheel—especially when the stairs were directly opposite the wheel—the friction and pressure between the wheel and track were so greatly

reduced that the turntable slowed down and sometimes actually stopped. When it stopped, the contact wheel continued to zip along at 100 rpms.

Ideally, this load problem should have been corrected during either the turntable's design or construction stages. Stage weights could have been attached to the 2x4 frame before the plywood was nailed down. This extra weight would not have affected the unit's operation. Unfortunately, we did not realize the problem until tech rehearsals. At that point, a major correction was impossible. Our solution was to use stagehands and actors to assist the rotation. When shifts took place behind the act curtain or the downstage drop, we placed stagehands strategically over the revolve's "light" side, adding the necessary weight to provide enough pressure on the contact wheel. When scene shifts occurred before the audience, we used actors instead. This solution worked resaonably well although it entailed some reblocking. We were most grateful to have a cooperative director who understood the problem.

For the most part, everyone was pleased with our efforts. The actors rode the turntable like a fascinating amusement park attraction, the director was happy with the continuity of action that the turntable provided, and the audience was

thrilled to see a 20' turntable loaded with scenery, props, and actors move on and off as if by magic.

BUDGET
½ HP Syncrogear motor $254
Switch for motor $30
Contact wheel (including machining) $20
Drive track (1 sheet ⅝" particle board) $5
Pillow blocks and drive shaft $28
Sprockets (2) $14
Chain free
Total $351

Motor specifications: 2087VAC, 3 phase, ½ HP, 1750 rpm, 277 inch pounds torque, gear ratio 17.5:1

Originally published in October 1984

Steel Tubing Revolve

by Peter Bendevski

As a follow up to Richard W. Durst's "Steel Tubing Construction" (*Theatre Crafts* November/December 1979), here is an example of steel tubing construction involved in making a 24' revolve that was manually turned by two technicians while supporting over a ton of gross weight. Although the initial cost is slightly higher than a wood constructed revolve, we felt we could justify the cost since we could offset some of it by renting the revolve and reusing it over several years. Another reason for using steel tubing rather than lumber was the difference in relative strength. The manufacturer rated the 18 gauge 1" steel tubing at 4,500-5,000 psi, much higher than construction lumber.

Materials and equipment

The revolve was built for a production of *Private Lives* at the George Street Playhouse during the 1979-80 season. We had several construction ideas, finally deciding on modules that could later be easily bolted together. We estimated we would need 600' of steel tubing. A cut list was made, and we manually cut the different lengths with a Milwaukee Sawzall and a miter box. To weld them together, we used an oxyacetylene torch. Since we already had all the equipment, our only cost was filling the tanks with gas.

The modules were drilled and bolted together into a 24' piece. This was elevated on metal milk crates, so that we could get underneath and attach the caster plates and casters. The cost of steel plates was prohibitive, so we used 5/4" white pine lumber instead. The central plates were 9'6" long; in between them were 6'6" plates. There were four 3' plates around the pivot. The plates were all drilled, and casters were bolted on them at 2 1/2' intervals. Our procedure was to attach a plate to a section of the revolve, then bolt the casters before going on to the next plate. Working nonstop for about three days, two technicians were able to complete the process. Ratchet sets were invaluable in speeding up the work, since there were so many bolts involved.

For a pivot point, a 2" steel pipe was lag bolted into the theatre's floor. It came through the center point of the revolve and was later disguised by the set designer's dressing. The steel frame was then covered with 5/8" CDX ply. The 4' x 8' sheets were screwed into the frame, so that after the show's run ended, they could be taken off easily and reused. The plywood was covered with 1/8" masonite so the designer could paint a tile floor. Again, the Duofast pneumatic stapler was invaluable.

For theatres such as ours, where storage is a problem, the modular revolve is a particular boon. It can be taken apart and put back together again with relative ease and at almost no cost after the intial investment. Even on quite an uneven floor, such as the George Street Playhouse's, the revolve turned quite easily. Later, when the walls and furniture were loaded on, after a running start the revolve spun around smoothly. The cost of a mechanical mode of revolve was much too high for the production budget, but two or three technicians were able to make it revolve with relative ease.

BUDGET

1" 18 square steel tubing—600' $348
5/8" ply CDX—20 sheets $316.80
5/4" #2 white pine—ten 12' $126.16
1/8" untempered masonite—20 sheets $76.80
52 4" casters $452.40
1 oxygen/acetylene tank $30
Welding rods $25
Bolts and screws—50 5/16" machine; #8 1" wood screws—100; #8 2 1/2" sheet metal—500 $60
Miscellaneous (grinding stones, wire brush, goggles) $25
Total $1460.16

Originally published in October 1984

5" CASTERS BOLTED ON PLATES

5/4" WHITE PINE

4 OF THESE WERE WELDED AND BOLTED TO MAIN STRUCTURE

4 PLATES AT 6'-6"X 8"

4 PLATES AT 3'X 8"

4 OF THESE WERE WELDED THEN BOLTED TO MAIN STRUCTURE 6'X 11'

THEY CAN EASILY BE UNBOLTED AND STORED FOR FUTURE USE AS A REVOLVE OR AS PART OF A WAGON OR JUST PLATFORMING

Scenic Construction: Tricks and Techniques

Two Solutions from the Vassar Shop

by Bryan H. Ackler

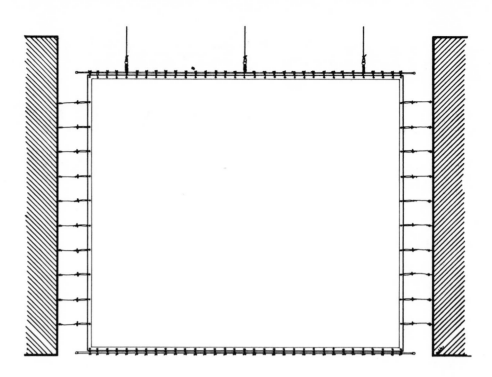

No backstage space. Twenty-five feet to the grid. Wrinkles. Torn hems from pins. Wrinkles. Never enough cyc off left or right. Wrinkles.

A simple inexpensive solution is to turn the cyclorama into a trampoline. This is how Vassar College's Drama Department solved the problem of what kind of cyc to purchase as a replacement.

The old filled scrim cyc was replaced with a muslin and scrim cyc. The innovative difference is in the manufacture of the two cyc pieces. Instead of the normal top webbing, side hems, and batten pocket, Premier Studios of New York webbed and grommetted all four sides of the new pieces. Grommets are set on 1' centers top and bottom and on 30" centers on the sides. The new cyc is attached to 1¼ in. pipe battens on the top, 1 in. pipe battens on the bottom and the sides are tied to 12" pieces of ¼" elastic shock cord. These shock cords have loops on the cyc end for the tie lines and small metal hooks on the wall end. Eye bolts are set at 30" intervals down the wing walls for these hooks. This allows the cyc to be hung under constant tension, wrinkless. If a cyc background is desired in an asymmetrical arrangement the cyc can be quickly unhooked, untied and shifted onto curved pipe additions to its battens. Again no batten pocket or impossible wrinkles to remove. When the cyc is not in use, it is quickly unhooked, tripped and flown out.

This arrangement has proven to be successful in minimizing set-up time, reduces wear and tear on the cyc, does not require constant attention to maintain smoothness and allows the flexibility of using the scrim elsewhere on the stage without any more work than a normal drop.

One of the annoying problems in almost every shop is where to store sheet materials such as plywood and Upson Board. Vassar College's Drama Department has solved this problem by combining a heavy duty work table with a sheet storage rack.

The table consists of three 2 x 4—4 x 4 lap joint frames secured with 9¼ x 96" strips of ¼" plywood which form the bin sides and at the top with 2 x 10's which form the work surface. The entire unit is glued, nailed and the swivel casters are secured with 1" x ¼" lag screws. The top can be left planked or partially surfaced with Masonite to provide a seamless area.

Rectangular handy boxes mounted on the middle frame, connected by ½" thinwall conduit, equipped with two duplex receptacles and a 14/3 S pigtail provide a sufficient number of plug points for hand power tools. The major benefits of the electrification are the elimination of extension cables running across work surfaces and floors and the time saved not having to fool with the cables.

In actual use the tables prove to be heavy enough not to need stops to restrain their mobility but light enough, even fully loaded, for one person to move.

Originally published in May/June 1976

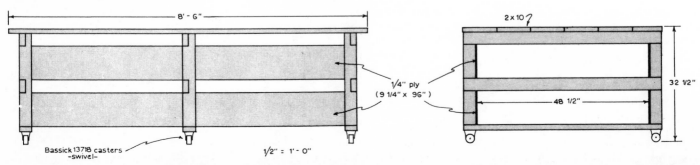

8' - 6"

Bassick 13718 casters
-swivel-

1/2" = 1' - 0"

2 x 10

1/4" ply
(9 1/4" x 96")

48 1/2"

32 1/2"

Building a Practical Door Unit

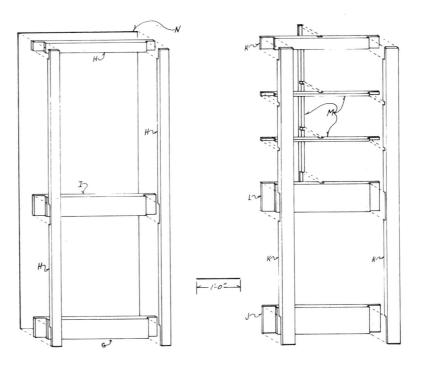

The half lap joint is the basis of the door unit built at Lewis and Clark College. Cutting away the thickness of each of the joint's pieces to half the width of the other allows them to be joined at a right angle (diagram, top left). The unit is built starting with the door and working out (top right).

by Leon Pike

The design and construction of door units have posed problems for generations of technicians. Traditional methods of construction often result in door units that do not hold their shape, and doors that, when closed, do not sound like doors. In the scene shop at Lewis and Clark College, we built a door that can be adapted to any one of several styles, along with a door unit that can be secured easily in the door flat and as easily removed. It withstands heavy use, maintains its shape, and can be varied to suit many set designs. One key to the building of this door unit is the half lap joint.

Constructing a half lap joint

To make this joint a table or radial arm saw is used. The dado blade saves time, but multiple cuts with any saw blade work as well. To join two pieces at right angles, half the thickness of each is cut away to the width of the other. This means that all the pieces are cut the full length or width of the finished product. Since the resulting surfaces will not be perfectly smooth, 1/32" extra is left on each one. Before joining, they are smoothed with a rasp or sanding block.

After the pieces have been cut and rasped, they may be glued together with Tite-Bond, white, or hot animal glue. Clamps, nails, staples, or screws are then used to hold the joint together until the glue sets. A great time-saver is the air stapler with 5/8" staples.

Once the thickness piece is finished the facing may be made. Each side piece is

cut to length—6'9" plus the width of the facing lumber (approximately 7'1"). One end of each side piece and both ends of the top are now half-cut. The width of these cuts has to be as exact as possible. Joints that do not mesh exactly cause a serious weakness in the piece, and this is possibly the most perfect joint you will ever need to make.

Once the joint is cut, glued, and dried, the facing and thickness may be put together with 6d box nails, or finish nails, if you prefer. You may want to glue this joint. We do not, because we sometimes change the facing width—to 1" x 6' for instance—and thus dramatically change the unit. Molding may be added to any facing for additional texture and richness.

Now the strap hinges are added to the sides of the unit. This pair of hinges, one on each side, has the lower leaf screwed to the side of the unit. As drawn, the hinge is at a slight angle and the bottom edge is about 3/4" from the facing. Before the unit is set into the flat, the top leaf is raised. Once through the opening the leaf is dropped and pushed against the inner stiles of the door flat, locking the

top part of the unit in place. The bottom of the unit is locked in place when the front sill iron is dropped behind the saddle iron in the door flat.

There is a 7/8" x 3/16" notch on the bottom of the thickness piece in front of the front sill iron. That notch is for the saddle iron. The door unit may now be securely locked into the flat, yet it may be removed in seconds by lifting the strap hinges and pushing the unit back through the flat. Someone is needed there to catch it.

Building the door unit

To build the door unit start with the door and work out. The standard 2'8" x 6'8" door is used when possible, because the finished unit fits easily through a 3' x 7' opening in a door flat. The thickness lumber is cut from 1" x 6" stock as follows: two sides, each 6'9"; top, 2'10". When the door is assembled this leaves a space of 1/4" on each side and at the top, and 3/4" at the bottom. At this point the bottom of the thickness is secured with two sill irons made from 3/16" x 3/4" x 48" strap iron. These have to be heated and bent into long U's with 90° angles and exactly

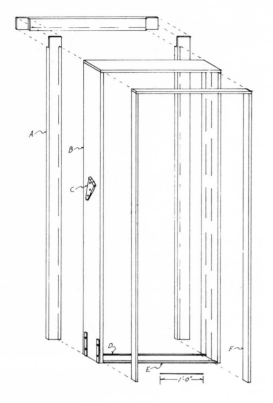

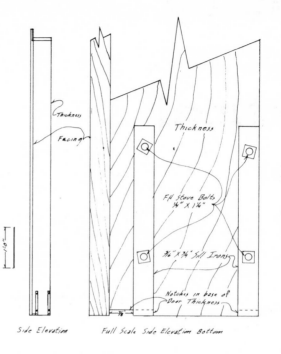

Side Elevation   Full Scale Side Elevation Bottom

2'10" between the two 7" uprights. The front sill iron is placed ⅞" behind the front edge of the thickness piece and is countersunk into the bottom of the sides. The back sill iron, also countersunk, is placed at the back of the thickness piece.

Styles

If you are going to make doors, styles are endless. Unless the design calls for something extraordinary, 2'8" x 6'8" doors will serve many sets. A solid or hollow core door can be built of ⁵⁄₄" x 3" and ⁵⁄₄" x 6", which is very light construction. It is then covered on the front side with a door skin ⅛" x 2'8" x 6'8". The middle ⁵⁄₄" x 6" board is placed with the center 3' above the bottom, so that the knob and latch assembly will fall within it. A two panel door can be built with the upper panel divided into small panes, which could be filled with clear or colored plastic or backed with glass cloth. Plywood could be tacked over the back or molded into the bottom section. Without the ⁵⁄₄" x ⁵⁄₄" bars it would be a regular two panel door. Plastic screen in one or both sections would create a screen door. With a center upright it could become a four panel door. Adaptations are endless.

Four 1/4" x 1 1/4" stove bolts hold the two 3/16" x 3/4" sill irons in place (top right). These secure the bottom of the unit. If a standard 2'8" x 6'8" door is used, the finished unit fits easily through a 3' x 7' opening in a door flat (top left).

Originally published in February 1983

Multi-Purpose Pylons

by Bryan H. Ackler

Twelve foot tall, two foot square, castered, lightweight and more importantly, stable. This describes the multi-purpose units used by the Vassar College Drama Department.

At first glance these units appear to be four flats nailed together, but upon closer examination it is revealed that they are designed and built to be exactly what they are; periaktoi, jacks, masking, or scenery. Wood framing covered on all four sides by muslin that can be nailed to or painted for whatever the situation demands.

Built completely from 1 x 3 stock except for a piece of ¾" plywood and four pieces of 2 x 4 in the base; the pylon is covered as you would four standard flats. Immediately above the piece of ¾" plywood in the base, 1 x 3 has been incorporated in the same arrangement as one of the toggle sections. This not only adds some weight but also acts as a protective edge if weights are added for some reason. The base, however, should not require any additional weight to maintain the remarkable stability.

Four swivel casters bolted in the corners of the recessed base should protrude approximately ¼" below the framing. They can be shimmed out with ¼" plywood if necessary.

Top, bottom, side and section views are all that are necessary for construction since the bulk of the structure is simple rectangular framing nailed together as shown. Based on an 8:1 slenderness ratio these units should be able to be built sixteen feet tall and still maintain an excellent stability. At that extreme height they may require a single stage weight as ballast.

A single 1 x 3 toggle on one side near the base will allow the addition of a top hinged flush trapdoor for weight placement. The pylons require no set-up time and only require a coat of paint and a spike mark to be whatever is desired.

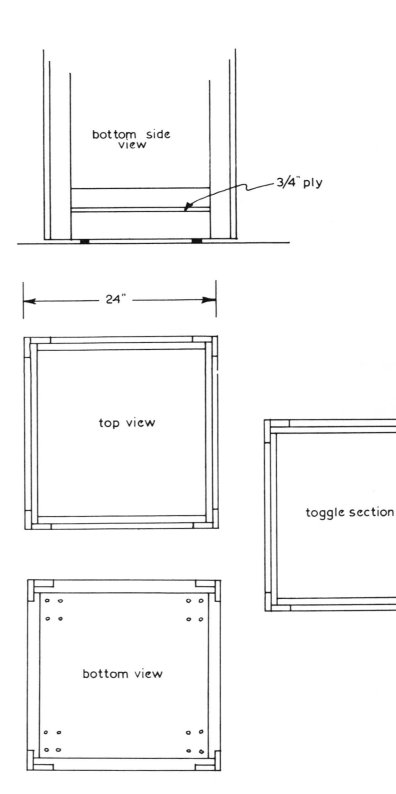

bottom side view

3/4" ply

24"

top view

toggle section

bottom view

Originally published in October 1978

Foolproof Corner Block

by Michael Glenn Ward

It seems that no matter what the expertise of the personnel in your scene shop, a common recurring problem in scenery construction is the corner block. There is always the chance of someone running the grain of the plywood parallel to the crack of the joint between the rail and stile. This renders a ¼" plywood corner block virtually useless, even if glued. Our plant relies on people who have little or no experience in scenery construction. Therefore, this problem is compounded.

The solution is obvious! Run the grain of the plywood parallel to the hypotenuse instead of parallel to a leg. No matter which leg of the corner block is pushed up, the grain runs across the crack.

But doesn't this cause a waste in material and more time spent in ripping the corner blocks? No. Follow the instructions outlined below. This method actually requires less effort and results in little or no waste of material.

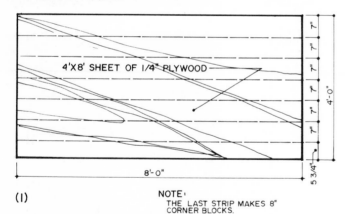

(1)

NOTE:
THE LAST STRIP MAKES 8"
CORNER BLOCKS.

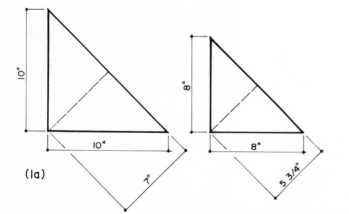

(1a)

(1) On a radial arm or a table saw, rip a sheet of ¼" plywood into 7" wide pieces with the grain parallel to either straight cut. IMPORTANT! Make sure that dimension is 7" instead of the normal 10" dimension used for a standard 10" corner block. This dimension will bisect the 90° angle and be perpendicular to the hypotenuse of the finished block. (see illustration)

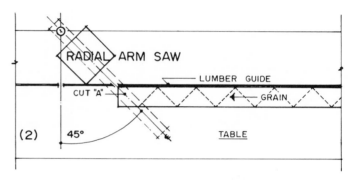

(2) Now set your saw guide at 45° and make cut A.

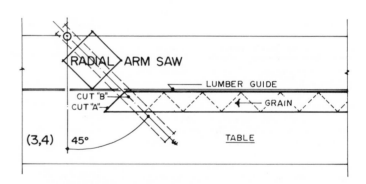

(3) Turn the strip over and make cut B.
(4) Turn the strip again and cut. Repeat until you have finished cutting the entire strip (5).

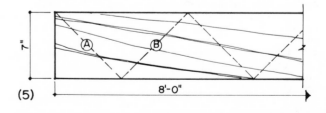

(5)

Save any leftover end pieces to be used in places where a regular corner block is too large to fit, but the support of one is desirable.

This method saves time in construction and valuable dollars of the construction budget are stretched by cutting out the cost of labor in time consuming corrections and the reduction of construction time. It does not, however, sacrifice any strength inherent in a ¼" plywood corner block or any methodology in construction format.

Originally published in October 1978

Dissenting on the Universal Corner-Block

True, "universal" corner-block described in "The Foolproof Corner-Block" by Michael Glenn Ward in your October issue, removes the possibility of error, but it also hides a fact about ¼ ply that the wood-worker needs to understand. When a corner-block can be applied "any-which-way" the true nature of ¼ ply's strength and weakness is obscured and the tyro carpenter can easily conclude from this experience that *all* ¼ ply cutouts can be used "any-which-way." We know how far from the truth this is. Mr. Ward's clever suggestion stems from an understanding of the essential fact that ¼ ply has inherent weakness, and his knowledge of this reality problably developed, as mine did, through an incorrect use of the material, from a mistake, a negative learning experience. What would have happened if he had been saved from making that mistake? The wood-worker in the theatre must be a craftsman, not a "clone."

PHILLIP A. GRANETO
Assistant Professor,
Glassboro State College

A Board Stretcher

by Leon Pike

For years the theatre staff at Lewis and Clark College have cut construction lumber into shorter and shorter pieces, until it eventually went into the scrap bin to be thrown out. In the process much valuable shop space was wasted to store short lumber that was seldom used. Recently, after getting the bill for a set, I decided that some changes had to be made. A finger joint seems to be a partial answer. The idea came from an article in *Fine Woodworking,* an excellent magazine for anyone who works with wood. A finger joint is the closest thing I have found to the mythical "board stretcher," and can be made easily by anyone with a table saw and a dado blade.

The first step was to construct a jig. Two 24" long 2" x 4"s were glued and air nailed (screws would work as well) across the outside grain on two sides of a piece of 24" square ³/₈" plywood. This became the front and back of the jig. A hot glue gun was used to secure an aluminum strap to two ³/₄" wood strips. The combined height of these two items just cleared the table top when laid in the table grooves. If you have ³/₄" wide hardwood strips available, the correct height could be reached without the aluminum strap. When the combined strips were in the grooves and lined up with the near end of the table, we heated them with a torch—so that the glue would not set too fast—and laid a good bead of glue along the top of each. With the blade retracted, the jig base was then lined up with the near edge of the table, centered, and firmly set onto the strips. After the glue had set for a few minutes, the jig was pulled back and the dado blade raised to cut through the plywood. The jig was now complete except for the "adjustable board" (figure 1).

Figure 1

Figure 2

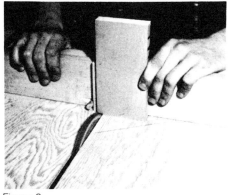
Figure 3

The adjustable board is a piece of 1″ x 4″ about 24″ long. We first placed it on the jig face down and slightly to the right of center, and cut a ³/₈″ x ³/₈″ groove across the board. (We made a ³/₈″ wide finger, so the ³/₈″ measurements would change if you were to make a different size.) This groove would later hold the "spacer," which was cut from a piece of fir and measured ³/₈″ x ³/₄″. Immediately to the right of the groove, so close that the edge touched, we drilled a ³/₈″ hole as near to the bottom of the board as possible. A 1¹/₂″ length of ³/₈″ dowel then was fitted into the hole. The adjustable board then was C-clamped to the back of the jig, so that the groove just cleared the right edge of the dado (figure 2). Next, the dado was raised to make a ³/₄″ cut. This distance is arbitrary: a ³/₄″ long finger seemed adequate without sacrificing too much lumber length. We now were ready to cut the first joint.

Since the edges of the finished board must be in line, it is important that the ends be slightly different. For the first cut, the board was placed against the spacer and run through the saw (figure 3). The spacer then was removed, and the kerf moved to cover

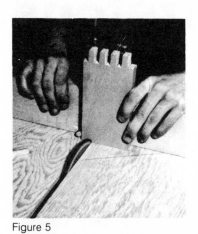

Figure 5

Figure 6

Figure 7

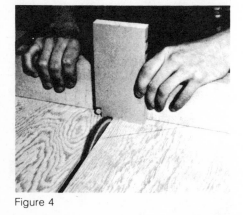

Figure 4

the dowel and again run through the saw (figure 4). The rest of the fingers were made by straddling the dowel with the last kerf. The first cut on the other end of the board was made without the spacer by moving the board to the right until it touched the dowel (figure 5), moving it through the saw, and then cutting it just like the other end.

After using glue from a squeeze bottle, we decided to thin the glue, put it in a large container, and dip each end of each board. This is a little messy, but shop floors are not supposed to be spotless.

To snug them up, we laid several boards that had been roughly interlocked in a line, with one end against the wall. With a scrap of 2″ x 4″ and a heavy hammer we then snugged the whole line at one time (figure 6). It is a good idea to go back then with a

block and hammer and give each joint a solid rap so that all boards are even. Once the new board had dried, it was ready to be cut into small pieces again (figure 7).

Jig materials list

2 2″ x 4″ (24″ long)
1 ³/₈″ plywood (24″ square)
2 ³/₄″ wide wood strips
2 ³/₄″ x ¹/₈″ aluminum strap
1 1″ x 4″ (24″ long)
1 ³/₈″ dowel (1¹/₂″ long)
1 ³/₈″ x ³/₄″ x 4″ spacer

Originally published in April 1981

Each unit of the modular scenic system is numbered to facilitate inventory retrieval and set up. Guide channels are provided in door plugs to allow partial insertion of panels, full insertion of panels with door hinged on one side, or full insertion of panels with doors hinged on outsides (photos and diagram, left and below).

A Modular Scenic System

by Wayne Kramer

Goal: To offer the tools and materials necessary for design students to experience the methodology of theatre design. Problem: Typically, a heavy production season (six mainstage productions, eight thesis-level productions), a limited budget ($600/mainstage production, $50/thesis production), limited faculty time (split between classroom instruction and production supervision), and a small student body (limited crew activity). Solution: A modular scenic system. The system is designed to relieve the strain on money and personnel in laboratory productions while at the same time giving design students a chance to work with design elements such as line, form, mass, balance and movement.

 Rather than beginning with the typical academic design track (stagecraft, mechanical drawing, draftsmanship, history of stage design), our design students are introduced to play analysis as the first step in conceptualizing. The focus is on the "design response"—how a designer reads plays, what he looks for, how he

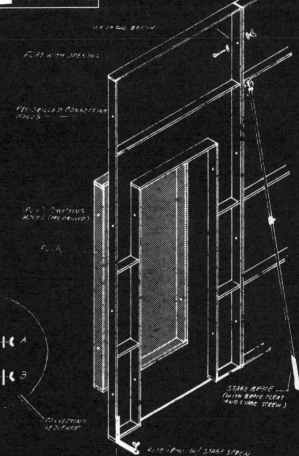

reacts contextually, how he visualizes, and how design elements are manipulated. The modular scenic system is basic to this approach as a practical tool.

The modular scenic system developed at Hampshire College, Amherst, Massachusetts, seems applicable to the many smaller academic and community theatres which suffer those same constrictions. Our solution could be adapted easily to the particular needs of a program or season and offer production values which are not repetitive, uninspired, or debilitating. The modular scenic system was built under a materials/supply budget of $607. The budget was held in line with raids on the scrap lumber and hardware left over from the last strike of the preceding season.

The system consists, basically, of a series of media-construction flats (¼ ply facing and 1″ × 3″ on-edge framing, sometimes called Hollywood flats) with various plugs and inserts (windows, doors, etc.). All units are part of a permanent inventory, designed to be used over and over again. The system necessitates careful pre-planning and experimentation. All units are coded on backs and stiles for ease of inventory check and retrieval. All units are interchangeable and pre-drilled to facilitate attachment combinations.

During practice runs, we found that a typical interior set could be assembled by two people in less than three hours, not including painting and surface ornamentation. One person could do the same setup in approximately four to six hours. This means a set could be put up and dressed for a given production by two people in two weekend sessions. Rehearsal time and theatre space were left free. The student designers could enjoy the sense of realizing their designs without the compromise usually associated with the "cubes and blocks" inventory normally reserved for laboratory productions. However, by limiting the student designers to the established inventory, they were forced to isolate design elements that reflected the specific script and concept intent. Designers could feel a greater sense of investment.

Basic inventory

Six plain flats (4'w, 10'h, 3"d)
Three flats with interior door openings (2'6"w, 6'6"h)
Two flats with exterior door openings (3'w, 6'6"h)
Three flats with arch openings (2'6"w, 7'9"h)
Four return flats (18"w)
Five "bookfold" corner units (5½"w per leaf)
One pylon (18" sq., 10'h)
Six pylons (18" sq., 5'h)
Two practical window plugs
Two exterior framed door units
Two interior framed door units
One French door unit (three-way door)
One practical casement window
Plain plugs for all flat openings
Five modular chair/sofa units
Eight blocks (various dimensions)

Problems of flexibility and very limited storage space resulted in some specific, practical solutions. One example was the construction of an exterior plug framing unit which easily could become a French door, a double paneled door, or a single paneled door. This was achieved with sliding panels inserted into the door unit channels, ornamentation, and a stretcher batten.

All units are pre-drilled for ¼", 2½" round-headed or flat-headed stove bolts. Plain flats have brace cleats attached for stage brace use. The modules are designed for ease of assembly/strike, structural integrity, and minimal surface dressing. By manipulating the various components, designers can create a wide variety of periods and/or styles. Student designers are encouraged to consider and construct additions to the inventory under the prescribed construction guidelines and within the given production budget.

Restrictions

Because the units are designed for long-term use by various groups with varying levels of competency, the following restrictions are imposed for lasting protection of the units.
1. Units are to be spray painted only with a solution of ⅓ to ½ water and latex paint to avoid excessive pigment build-up. Light colors may need a primary or base coat to achieve proper coverage.
2. Units are not to be covered with textures, fabrics, etc.
3. Units are not to be cut, drilled, nailed, or altered structurally.
4. Units are to be assembled using provided and designated hardware. Adequate equipment and flexibility have been provided commensurate with maintaining unit integrity. Stiles, rails, and toggles cannot be changed.
5. Do not dutchman units with traditional muslin/glue techniques.
6. Do not assume anything. Ask.

So far, the units have been used for laboratory experiments in design classes, for practical use in beginning acting/directing classes (how to use doors for entrances/exits, blocking patterns, visual tension, etc.), for playwriting class (creating an environment for themes), and for workshops. The response has been so positive that the units are now scheduled for split use between classroom laboratories (where they are not dressed, but used as architectural units), laboratory productions, and even an occasional mainstage production. One initial fear—that design students would react to the system as design-by-number—seems to have been unwarranted. The units are accepted with their possibilities and limitations in the same way that casein paint, #2 pine, and muslin are accepted. They become the raw material of line, mass, and balance experimentation.

The anticipated savings in time, energy, and money, the high level of acceptance by the student designers, and even the way our directors and playwrights have been talking about design elements, has convinced us that this system is both practical and creative.

Originally published in November/December 1979

Platform Clamps

by John T. Howard, Jr.

Faced with the problem of joining platforms of equal height, many theatres use "C" clamps. They are faster than bolting and do not make swiss cheese of the platform sides. Properly done they are as strong as bolts. Our theatre hasn't the money to purchase "C" clamps in the numbers required. The answer is to make them; we call it a "Would" clamp.

Our design is simple. A ⅜" carriage bolt draws together two pieces of ¾" plywood. Wooden spacer blocks below force the plywood to close above the bolt on the sides of the platform. The masonite between spacer boards is to allow for a ⅛" pad placed between platforms to avoid squeaks. The spacer blocks are nailed together but not glued. A piece of masonite holds the carriage bolt head in place. We use wing nuts so that a group of platforms can be put together "finger tight" first and then tightened with a crescent wrench. We use scrap plywood so they are inexpensive. They are simple and quickly built.

The top of the bolt 6" above the bottom of the "Would" clamp so that the clamp may become a 6" leg. Obviously these clamps cannot be used if the platforms are lower than 6".

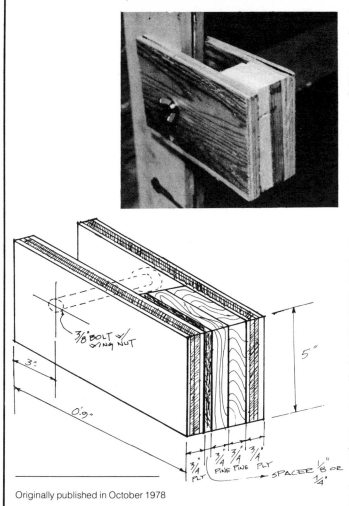

Originally published in October 1978

Hexel Honeycomb Panels

by John Priest and Pierre Cayard

A mechanized mirror cyclorama, created to reflect stage action, as well as the self-reflecting nature of the characters, posed a special problem for us when constructing the set for *Thais* at the San Francisco Opera. Designed by Carl Toms, *Thais* was the premiere production of the 1976 season.

Conventional materials and methods used to construct the ten panel sections of the cyc would have far exceeded the 900 lb. live load limit of the Opera's counterweight sets. Instead, we found a strong, lightweight aluminum panel system manufactured by Hexcel that solved the construction problem.

The panels are composed of a low-density aluminum core of similar configuration to the walls in a beehive. The core is bonded with adhesives between thin aluminum skins. The

panel's edges are sealed with extruded aluminum channels, also bonded between the skins.

Normally, we would have applied aluminum foil or aluminized Mylar over ⅛" plywood to create a mirror, but both materials have a tendency to wrinkle. It would have been especially difficult to achieve a smooth surface on the mirrors for *Thais* because of their size—individual panel sections varied from 21' to 29' long and 18" to 24" wide. In addition, the plywood sections framed with 1" x 2" lumber would have been too heavy to be suspended from the motor-driven yokes used to position the scenery.

We discovered that the use of the bonded honeycomb panels would reduce the weight of each mirror section by 25% to 40%. The mirrored Mylar finish, developed by Hexcel for use in solar panels, is only available on special order. However, its high quality and durability (as compared to stretched Mylar) offsets the extra cost. Hexcel also manufactures panels composed of non-metalic materials, such as paper and nylon.

Because of the need to preserve the smooth texture of the mirror facing, we couldn't use bolts to attach the plywood frames and wire mesh decoration to the panels. So, for set construction on *Thais,* wooden hinge plates on the backs of the panels were used to attach metal ties which held the individual panels in position. Removable hinge pins allowed disassembly of the panel sections.

The manufacturer suggested a room-temperature-curing epoxy adhesive to bond the hinge plates to the panels. To prepare the surface areas on the panels for the epoxy, we first cleaned them with acetone and steel wool. The adhesive was fully cured and at maximum strength within 6 hours. The epoxy bond turned out to be stronger than bolts.

We found the material as easy to use as most others commonly employed in scenic construction, especially since Hexcel supplied the panels pre-cut and edged to our specifications, which saved time.

Hexcel panels can fold and be cut using a "slit-scoring" method, resulting in mitered corners, exact curves, and cylinders, if desired. A sabre saw or heavy knife can be used. Painting and finishing the panels is easy; they can be painted with latex (one coat), wallpapered, carpeted, or stuccoed. Any exposed edges can be finished with tape or snap-on plastic molding (available in 12' lengths from Hexcel).

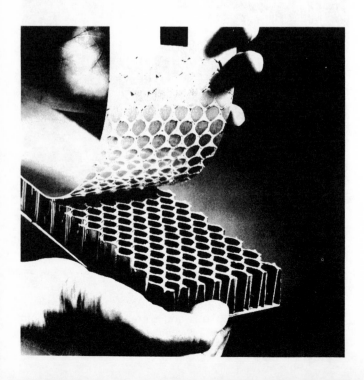

Tested strengths

Allowing for such variables as type of adhesive used in construction, thickness of the panel's core, and thickness of the surface "skin" material, the manufacturer has provided these assurances:

1) Compared to plywood panels of the same weight, the Hexcel bonded honeycomb panels are 30 times stronger and 6 times stiffer.

2) The ratio of strength to weight is higher than any other material used for construction purposes.

Cost and size

The prices for Hexcel panels range from $1.00 per sq. ft. for the paper panels (suitable for flats) through $5.00 per sq. ft. for the aluminum panels used in *Thais* to $8.00 per sq. ft. for some custom-made panels. Hexcel panels are available in thicknesses of ½" to 2" and lengths ranging from 96" to 144".

The manufacturer can be contacted for more information and supplying of honeycomb panels:

Hexcel
11711 Dublin Blvd.
Dublin, CA 94566
(415) 828-4200

Originally published in November/December 1977

Actor-Proofing Furniture

by Patrick Reed

For a recent production of *The Passion of Dracula*, performed at Southern Illinois University at Carbondale, the director, Joe Proctor, and I discussed using a Victorian chaise longue as a major furniture property. After further discussions with technical director Lang Reynolds, we realized that this particular chaise probably could not be purchased or borrowed. The chaise had to fit the design concept, be a period piece, and, most importantly, it had to be actor proof. This was essential because of all the energetic activity that centered around it.

Construction

The project began with research into Victorian furniture. After finding suitable photographs, a prototype was selected and a 1″ square steel tube frame was designed. Pieces were cut and welded together. The welds were then ground smooth and a ⅝″ plywood seat was cut and fitted into place.

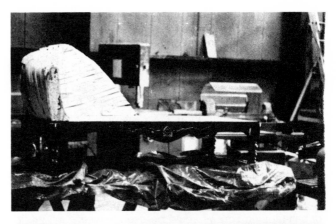

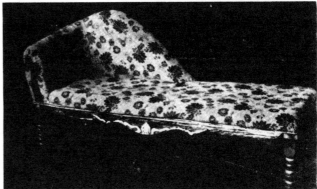

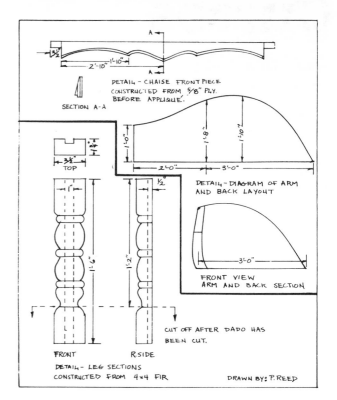

A chaise lounge (right center) for a production of *The Passion of Dracula,* at Southern Illinois University, had to fulfill three requirements: fit the director's concept, be of the Victorian period, and withstand a lot of "energetic activity." From a prototype chaise, a 1″ square tube frame (top, above) was constructed. A 5/8″ plywood seat was then cut and fit to the frame, as were plywood spines (center, above). Strips of 1/8″ fir were soaked and molded (above) over the spines. The chaise's five legs (right top) were each 4″ x 4″, cut in half, grooved, and glued around a steel leg (diagram, right, with details of other sections).

Plywood spines were laid out according to the back and arm curves that had been determined in draftings. After being firmly attached, the spines were covered with strips of fir. These strips were cut from a 2″ x 4″ (⅛″ was found to be the best thickness), soaked in hot water for two hours, and immediately attached to the spines.

The next step was to construct the chaise's woodwork. Five legs were turned from 4″ x 4″, leaving both ends square. The legs were cut in half on the table saw, and a groove ½″ x 1″ was cut into each half on the shaper. The square end on the leg's bottom was cut off and the two sections were glued together, sandwiching the steel leg in between. Our fit was secure enough that no other methods were employed to keep the legs in place. If need be, bolts or self-tapping screws could be used to insure a tight fit on the steel leg.

Next, the front, back, and side sections were made, using several laminated plywood layers all cut to basically the same shape. Each piece was made smaller than the previous piece. After four or five layers were glued together the sections were beveled on the table saw, to suggest the twisted wood decorations on most Victorian furniture. The front decoration was cut from 1″ pine and routed. The woodwork was then bolted onto the steel frame. After sanding, the wood was painted with a high gloss brown latex; gold trim was painted on using bronzing powder with Future floor finish as the binder. The entire unit was then covered with several coats of urethane finish.

The completed chaise after upholstery weighed around 75 lbs. It survived the pressure of over 600 lbs. of actors jumping on it. The set crew checked it every night after performance, and the chaise never moved from its spike.

Budget

Steel	$20.00
Wood	15.00
Foam	30.00
Fabric	30.00
Hardware, glue, and miscellaneous supplies	10.00
Total	**$105**

Originally published in May 1982

Creating Laminated Curves

by Allan Fanjoy

Often the curves and sweeps that make such a natural contribution to the stage picture can be maddeningly difficult to produce. For small units, of course, it is easy to lay out the curve on a piece of plywood and cut it out with a sabre saw or band saw. But this can be terribly wasteful, especially if you cannot completely nest your shapes on the sheet.

For instance, suppose you need a semicircular arch 4′ in diameter, 3″ wide, and ¾″ thick. My current cost for ¾″ ACX is $22 per sheet, or 70 cents per board foot (bd ft = L′ x W″ x T″). Depending on how you value oddly shaped remnants, that 4′ curve will consume a little less than half the sheet and so cost approximately $10. But there is only about 1 ½ bd. ft. of lumber in the arch itself 1x3x6′). This gives you a $1 value for the mere cost of $10!

The frustration is compounded when we need a 12′ semicircle. Now there are joints to consider as well as the optimal arrangement of several segments of the curve on one or more sheets of ply. Curves cut from solid stock also have inherent strength deficiencies since the grain's direction cannot follow their "length" throughout.

I have been quite pleased with curves produced using the following techniques, borrowed from the modern plywood manufacturer's industry and the antique skills of shipwrights.

Bending Beams

It is no secret that when a beam is bent, the stresses within it tend to compress the material inside the bend and to stretch that on the outside. In the beam's center is a neutral plane that is unstressed (neither compressed nor stretched). The farther from the center, the greater the stress. Each layer away from this neutral plane tries to assume a length different than its length before bending. If the wood cannot accommodate this internal length change, the beam breaks. Since stress rises with curvature and distance from the neutral plane, a thin beam can be bent more easily and can conform to a tighter curve than a thick beam.

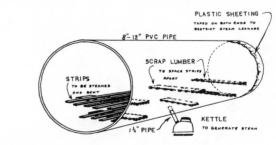

STEAMING APPARATUS

Bend this magazine into an archway with the front cover inside the curve. Notice that the back cover falls short of aligning with the front. It is easy to bend the magazine without breaking it because you are actually bending 100 very thin pages rather than a single ¼″ thick unit. Each page is a separate beam with such a short distance between surfaces that minimal stress is created. If the pages were laminated together, the tendency to change length would have accumulated from page to page until the structure differed in length by ½″ from the back cover to the front. Conversely, if the magazine's pages were laminated together while they were bent, the magazine would be equally rigid to flattening forces.

Substitute strips of lumber for sheets of paper and you have a strong, curved wooden beam. You will not be limited by your stock's width—no one will be able to tell whether you made a curved 1 x 12 of strips originally ripped from a 1 x 12 or from four 1 x 3's. If necessary, you can also make a curve longer than the original stock. When a strip ends in a particular layer, just lay in another strip butted to its end to continue the layer. Be sure to stagger these joints from layer to layer to maintain consistent strength.

Since wood is not uniform—due to knots and grain direction—it is wiser not to align the curve's strips in the same orientation that they had in the original stock. Turn some strips over, spin

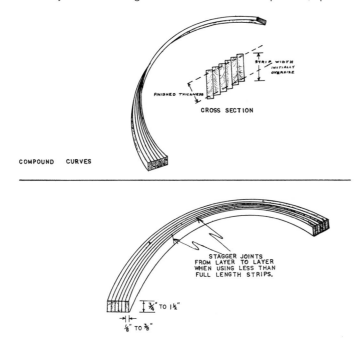

COMPOUND CURVES

LAMINATED WOODEN CURVE

some end-to-end, and intersperse some from one piece of stock with those from another. Local flaws will be less noticeable and consistent strength will be improved.

Realize, too, that wood is elastic. It remembers its shape and when a bending force is relaxed, springs back to its unstressed shape. To minimize this tendency, try to make each strip's natural shape match as nearly as possible its shape in the finished curve before gluing the unit together. Each strip will be easier to bend and more prone to retain its bent shape if it is heated first in steam. This softens the fibers and connections between wood cells. Form the wood while it is flexible and it will harden upon cooling into a shape close to the position in which it has been held.

Designing Curves

I generally rip strips roughly ¼″ wide from D or #2 white pine. Use better, thinner strips for tight curves and thicker, cheaper ones for broad sweeps. I draw the shape I want to form on the wooden deck and lay clear plastic sheeting over it to catch excess glue. Nail down blocks of scrap lumber at the outside of the proposed curve (the convex face). Across a gap about ½″ larger than the piece's intended width, nail corresponding blocks inside the curve. Cut the strips and lay out the form 1′ or so beyond each end of the finished piece. Cut a few extra

strips in case some break while being forced into shape. Do not be too discouraged when you discard some strips that fall apart at knots—think how much waste cutting from plywood can cost!

I generate the steam to soften the wood in a teapot over a gas camp stove. I have fit the spout with a short length of PVC pipe that also fits a hole in the center of a larger horizontal plastic pipe (8″-12″ diameter). Arrange the strips in this larger steaming pipe spaced apart by scrap wood to allow the steam to freely circulate throughout the pipe and to all strip surfaces. Taping plastic sheeting on the ends restricts steam leakage. Take sensible precautions to eliminate fire hazards. Calculate how long to steam by testing extra strips in your form. The steam volume, strips thickness, and degree of curvature will influence your judgement.

When the strips seem soft enough, work quickly to fit them into your form of blocks on the floor. I often steam strips ¼″ thick x ¾″ wide for 40-60 minutes. As I work them into the form, I notice them stiffening in less than a minute. Break several 3″ long unused strip scraps. Drive these between the inner block and the strips at the curve's center to press them

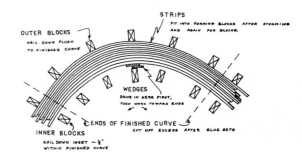

FORMING THE CURVE

tight against the carefully placed outside block. Work out from the center, driving wedges from the loose end of each inner block toward the solid center. I usually let such a set cool, dry, and harden for about four hours. Less time might be sufficient, but the set must be thoroughly dry before proceding.

Remove the strips from the form, retaining their positon relative to one another and to the form. Spread glue at each layer and return the strips to the form, driving in wedges as before.

If you really want to get fancy, you can use this method to produce compound curves. These are shapes that, in addition to their major curvature, also bend out of that curve's plane. One example is the helical shape of a curved bannister. No piece sawed from rigid flat stock can retain this shape on its own.

When producing such shapes, cut the strips out of stock slightly thicker than the finished piece. You will find that in making compound curves, the corner of each strip will protrude slightly from the face of the finished piece. You will want to have enough material to plane and sand the final surface without reducing its dimension below that desired.

Hopefully, these ideas will make some difficult jobs easier and cheaper for you. If your curiosity is piqued, I would appreciate analyses of critical curvature as a function of steaming time, if anyone plans to conduct such statistical experiments.

Originally published in November/December 1984

Shoestring Sliding Doors

As is true of many stock companies on a small budget, we at the Brooke Hill Playhouse in Wellsburg, West Virginia, use flats almost exclusively in our productions. In *Not Now, Darling*, a wonderful British farce calling for the requisite number of entrances and exits, we decided that sliding door panels would be fun for the audience, as well as blending in perfectly with the paneled decor when closed. The solution to this design problem is both effective and inexpensive.

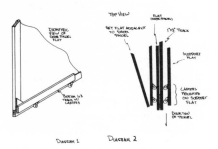

1 The flat used for the door panel must be at least one foot longer than the part you wish to show. This extra foot offstage allows the support casters to retain control when the panel is closed.
2 Two 1" x 3 must have two non-swivel casters attached to its bottom edge. The track is then fastened to the panel, low enough so that the panel clears the floor and rolls freely. The upper track is fastened at or near the top of the panel.
3 The door panel will be sandwiched between casters mounted on two support flats. These casters should also be the non-swivel variety. The four casters in back of the flat —two at the top and two at the bottom—must rest on the tracks and should be positioned accordingly. The four casters in the front should simply rest on the rails of the door panel.
4 The two support flats are then positioned and secured to sandwich the door flat so that it rolls along a straight line.
ERIC ZUERN
Wayne State University
Detroit, Michigan

Laminating Curves for Scenic Construction

by Thomas J. Corbett

Occasionally a production comes along that presents an interesting challenge that allows the stage technician to explore new materials and processes. The design for a recent production of *Twelfth Night* at the University of California, Santa Cruz required curved walls and towers.

A conventional construction method would have been to build all the walls and towers from upright boards attached by plywood sweeps over which Upson board or untempered masonite could be curved. Some of the towers in the final model, however, were 26' tall and would have required huge quantities of 2 x 3s and plywood. An even greater concern was the time needed for layout and cutting.

As technical director, I knew of colleagues who were using Hexcel Feather Panel (see Product Report: Hexcel Honeycomb Panels, *Theatre Crafts* November/December 1977) instead of the traditional flat. The sandwich panel of heavy Kraft paper surfaces contains an interlayer of hexagonally shaped interior cells. As in solid laminating the interlayer "spreads" the outside layers apart (to a maximum of 2") and gluing holds them rigid.

The interlayer can be ordered in varying cell size. The smallest cell is ⅜" while the largest available cell is 1½". The smaller cell size makes the surface more practical while the larger cell size makes the panel lighter and conceivably more flexible. Kraft paper facing ranges from 80# to 207# for paintable surfaces. I thought the panels might work very well for our curves and towers.

Senior scene technician Jack Neveaux and I visited a manufacturer who uses the cellular interlayer to form residential walls. Panel-Tech of Redwood City, California laminates the cell "sheets"

between wood interior paneling and either Masonite exterior panels or aluminum siding to form single system walls. We watched the process of gluing and sealing the completed panels under vacuum pressure to assure a solid bond within the sandwich

The manufacturer's handbook on free standing scenery outlines the possibility of forming curves by backcutting the feather panels and handling the sheets much like conventional plywood. We ordered singlesided sandwich panels which are 4' wide and can be cut to any length up to 12'. Ten feet was chosen to keep our shipping cost within reason.

Twelfth Night's setting rested on a 230° thrust stage. The cellular process was used to form the concave cylinder and the convex column stage left. Conventional wood construction was used to form the stage right curves and the large circular tower stage left.

The architectural column adjacent to the theatre was used as a form for the conventional plywood lamination. The cellular lamination was similar to this process. The center arches were formed of laminated ¼" plywood; four thicknesses were glued together and placed around an architectural column used as a form for the lamination process. Long stock 2 x 4s were used to hold the assembly in place while it dried; compression was achieved by tightening ⅝" hemplines rigged with trimming hitches. Each arch section was then cut down to a 9' tall x 4' 6" wide finished size.

To form the concave cylinder of Hexcel- and Upson the architectural column was also used as a form. Sheets of ⅛" x 4' × 8' Upson board were first painted on their non-watermark surface with a solution of wheat paste and a polyvinyl glue like Elmer's. This adhesive was strong and had enough bulk to attach the cells to the inside surface material.

After the adhesive was applied to the Upson using paint rollers, the sheets were placed around the column shape, watermark to the inside as it was to be the finished surface. Panels of single-sided cellular board were then placed directly against the glued surface, stacked to a finished height of 13' 4". To prevent weak joints, the column was assembled with the seams staggered. Long stock 2 x 3s were then placed

around the assembly and drawn together by 4 ¼" sash ropes rigged with trimming hitches.

Lay-up time was approximately 2½ hours; drying time was 24 hours; finished weight was less than 50 lbs. The finishing process for the cylinder was quick and easy: the column was laid down, a chalk line was used to snap vertical edges, and these lines were cut with a saber saw equipped with a knife blade. Since this shape had to join its reverse shape, the edges were severely back-cut.

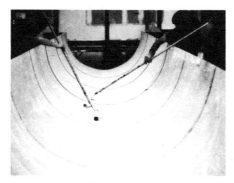

Construction of the large convex column of Upson and Hexcel first required building a form out of ⅜" particle board with five half-circle 5' diameter cut-outs. The sheets were cut simultaneously,

then notched for 2 x 3s. The sweep forms were then tacked to saw horses and the 2 x 3s set in. The column was formed of 6 sheets of ⅛" Upson taped edge-to-edge to make an 8' x 24' sheet. The sheet was placed in the form, watermark surface down. The underside was to be the scenic surface. The adhesive formula was then applied to the inside surface.

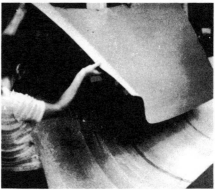

To complete the convex column, the sheets of Hexcel were placed vertically into the form. Two sheets placed side by side filled out the 8' Upson surface since the curvature resulted in a few extra inches for the inside material. One edge was determined the finished edge by lining up the materials along it. After stacking the bottom 2 sheets, we smeared adhesive onto the top Upson panels and placed the upper celled backing layers in place.

The cut-out sections of the concave forms were then trimmed slightly (to approximately the thickness of the cell sheets) and used to press the cellular material into place. The inserts fit adequately and helped hold the interlayer in place—especially in the haunch of the arch. Scrap stock was also placed into the shape to help press the unit while the glue dried (48 hours). Additional adhesive was poured into the edges to further strengthen them. This slowed the drying time since the unit could only dry by passing moisture through the skin of the shape. The column was moved onto the stage and trimmed by a saber saw from an air lift ladder.

The concave and convex columns were set in place and openings were traced and cut out. After cutting, the edges of the cellular material were "filled" by covering them with gaffer's tape. The Upson seams that were not completely flat were filled with spackling, sanded, and painted. Both columns were braced by attachment to each other and existent scenery by gluing additional light boards to the inside of the columns and then screwing through other units and through the columns into these boards. One joint was accomplished by stripping the facing and cells away and stapling the fiber-paper backing to the adjacent flat.

The difference in cost (both materials and time) between the cellular construction towers and the conventional frame towers was quite large. Even taking into account Hexcel's minimum order and/or set-up fee, the total cost for 4' of height was only $8.50 (includes Upson). The results achieved with the cellular lamination process were excellent and the cost factor and ease of construction make this a highly recommended manner in which to build curved shapes for stage use.

Originally published in May/June 1978

Flame Texturing Wood

by Keith Arnett

John D. Cosby's technique for flame texturing raw wood with a propane torch (*Theatre Crafts,* May/June 1977) is quite effective in obtaining a high-contrast, one-dimensional treatment of the wood surface. In order to achieve a more "weatherbeaten" and three-dimensional looking finish, I have discovered that using an oxyacetylene torch and a wire brush can produce excellent results.

The process entails burning the wood surface with the torch, and the softer

A "knothole" burned into a pine plank and portions of the grain carbonized.

parts of the grain will carbonize. After burning, the residue can be removed with a wire brush, leaving the edges and corners rounded and producing a time-worn effect. Knotholes can be highlighted easily and new knotholes can be created wherever desired. The finished surface can be further distressed by use of chains or other metallic objects and clear sealers or finishes can be applied to protect the final surface and to protect

costumes.

Advantages of this technique: 1) the three-dimensional effect produced 2) greater speed than the propane method because of the hotter flame and 3) it can be used on painted, as well as raw, wood. I recommend testing a small block of the painted wood to see how it reacts before you apply the torch to a set piece. Note: avoid using wood painted with 3 or more coats.

Additional considerations: pieces of wood that are ½" or thinner may warp from the heat. Thicker pieces will also warp with prolonged exposure to heat. Oxyacetylene flame texturing is not recommended for wood with a high sap content. Burning sap will give off acrid black smoke and interferes with the wirebrushing.

As in any shop operation, proper safety precautions must be taken. Make sure that you can handle and control the torch. Have a water fire extinguisher at hand. Use insulated gloves and goggles. A dust mask is recommended when brushing away the carbonized

The finished plank after wirebrushing away the carbonization. Smooth edges and rounded corners help to produce the realistic weatherbeaten effect.

wood. The ideal work area is outside, but torch flame texturing can be done anywhere if you are careful.

The cost of the oxyacetylene torch apparatus and fuel is more than the propane materials. However I have found the ease of application, the time saving and the realistic worn look make it a bargain for any theatre.

Originally published in March/April 1978

Contoured Hills

by Stancil Campbell

Key Exchange is about three cyclists who meet on eight consecutive Sunday afternoons in New York's Central Park. Each character brings a bicycle on stage, and depending on the nature of the set, might even ride them during the show. My design for Edmonton's Phoenix Theatre production in winter 1983 demanded a contoured hillside with a bike path cutting through it. The design allowed the director to block the actors actually riding their cycles around the paths on the set, while also providing grassy hills for conversation and relaxing between rides. With the model complete, we approached Scenic Arts Associated, Ltd., of Edmonton to construct the scenery.

Our only real problem was how to construct such contoured hills on our shoestring budget of $3,000, a figure that included all materials, labor, and a small profit for Scenic Arts. While the easiest and least expensive method was to haul in truck-loads of earth and sod, this was an outright impossibility—northern Alberta is frozen under several feet of snow and ice in February. After a few phone calls to area sod farmers who couldn't help but laugh at our request, we knew an alternative had to be found.

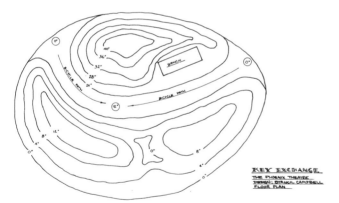

KEY EXCHANGE
THE PHOENIX THEATRE
DESIGN: STANCIL CAMPBELL
FLOOR PLAN

Several possibilities were investigated and evaluated. Urethane foam was ruled out because of strict government controls on its availability and use, a problem that would be of much less concern in the States. Sculpted Styrofoam was considered but ruled out because of excessive material costs. Other potential solutions, such as skin surfaces, were ruled out because of the necessary underframing costs. Scenic Arts' final solution was to use inexpensive corrugated cardboard. Before you jump to the conclusion that I am referring to a hex-core type of cardboard construction, let me quickly point out that the hills were not an open core construction, but solid laminated corrugated cardboard.

The first step was to locate and haul in several loads of the material. This particular batch of cardboard was bundled in large units consisting of individual pieces that measured about 1' x 4'. This was a convenient size since the highest parts of the hillside rose only 1' in elevation above its base level. The set also had to be built in units small enough to transport to the theatre across town. Frames were con-

structed at 1"x3" to contain each cardboard hillside section. The frames served not to strengthen but merely to contain the cardboard. They were built as perimeter frames with one internal support and without tops or bottoms. The cardboard was cut to fit within the frames and was pre-contoured on the bandsaw. The dozens of layers were glued together side-by-side and fit into the frames. Once the frames were filled, they were laid out in their final configuration and further sculpted with a hand grinder so that the contours melded nicely together from one framed unit to the next. After final sculpting, the result was a strong, lightweight hillside ready to be set up and covered.

The set-up went quickly with a minimum of labor as the separate contoured cardboard hill units fit together with ease and simplicity. Covering, the next step, was a little more difficult. To simulate real grass, the surface was covered with a layer of artificial grass carpet. While the carpet had a definite weave pattern, on stage the pattern resembled that of lawn mower cuts running parallel, upstage to downstage. Forcing the carpet to follow the contour's form was not easy either. The carpet had to be cut away in several places so that it would dip into a hole or run over a bump. It was glued and then stapled to the cardboard. The particularly vulnerable

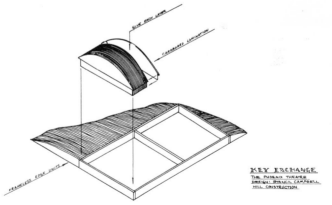

GLUE EACH LAYER
CARDBOARD LAMINATION
FRAMELESS EDGE UNITS

KEY EXCHANGE
THE PHOENIX THEATRE
DESIGN: STANCIL CAMPBELL
HILL CONSTRUCTION

seams were attached more carefully in hopes that no problems would develop over the three-week run. A final painting added texture and life to the otherwise flat, artificially green carpet, and the set was complete.

The construction results were basically very good. The cardboard hills were quite strong and did not sag down during the production's run. Minor problems with some of the seams and some of the carpet cuts were easily mended. Our only real concern was the bit of squeak heard in certain spots as the actors moved about. This noise was minimal and was not noticed by the audience during the show. It was one of those subtle annoyances the production team notices simply because they search for precisely that type of problem. All in all, this approach was an excellent solution to the problem of constructing contoured hillsides on a low budget. I highly recommend it as a construction technique for any theatre since no special equipment, tools, or specially trained labor is involved. Give it a try. I think you will like the results.

Originally published in November/December 1984

Tapered Fluted Columns

by Mark Freij

For a production of Purcell's opera *Dido and Aeneas* at the State University of New York (SUNY) at Purchase, we needed three, 16' tall, tapered, fluted columns. The problem, as always, was to build them with the right combination of speed, economy, and the correct look.

We decided early on to make them from white styrene foam because it is easy to carve and can readily be given the aged, pitted look that designer Mary Angelyn Brown wanted. The difficulty was keeping the taper and size of each flute consistent. Our specific columns tapered from a 1'6" diameter at base to a 1' diameter at the top with each flute at a consistent 3" radius. We needed 12 flutes per column at regular 30° intervals.

Faculty technical advisor Alan Kibbe offered a basic solution. He suggested that each column be mounted horizontally so that it could pivot freely on its axis. It would then be a relatively simple matter to construct a guide to the correct taper, and the column could be rotated to cut each individual flute.

Our specific process, carried out by technical director Chris Parrietti and his crew, follows:

1) Boxes of foam 1'6" x 1'6" x 16'0" were made by laminating the foam onto a center box of wood. The wooden core was used for strength and stiffness, and later provided a simple means of fastening the completed column to the floor.

2) The edges of the foam boxes were cut off with a handsaw—giving it an octagonal shape—simply so that we would have less foam to cut through later.

3) Temporary squares of wood were centered on each end of the column. A hole was drilled at their centers to serve as a pivot point and the squares were marked at 30° increments indicating each flute to be cut.

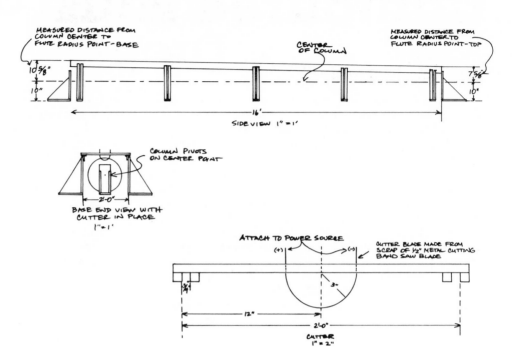

4) The block of foam was then mounted between two identical brackets, pinned in such a way that it could be rotated freely.

5) It was then necessary to construct the taper guide. First a full scale drawing of the column base was made so the actual distance from the column's center to the flute's radius point could be measured. It was unnecessary to do this for the top since we knew the column radius tapered exactly 3" in 16'.

6) Guide boards were then mounted parallel to and on either side of the column·in such a way that one end of the board was our "center-to-flute-radius-point" dimension above the pivot point, and the other end was 3" lower. We were now ready to cut the foam.

7) A cutter was made that could be slid along the guide boards, tracked by a piece of 1" x 1" on either side. The actual cutting blade was a scrap of ½" metal-cutting bandsaw blade carefully centered on the cutter and mounted to give us the 3" flute radius. We picked the saw blade instead of the traditional hot "wire" because it would better hold its shape.

8) The actual cutting was done by passing an electrical current through the blade to heat it and then sliding the cutter along the guide board. We used our arc welder for the current, but any controllable source of electricity could be used. (Note: The fumes given off by the melting foam are dangerous. It is extremely important that this cutting happen in a well-ventilated area, and that crew members wear respirators.)

9) It was then simply a matter of cutting each flute at regular 30° intervals, rotating the column as we went.

10) We distressed the finished columns with carving and acetone, protected them with glued on cheesecloth, and they were painted.

We learned a few, not instantly apparent points as we went along: it worked better to cut every other flute. Otherwise, one side of the cutting blade was passing through more foam than the other side and it began to distort. Even cutting alternate flutes, the blade eventually distorted. We simply replaced it every few passes. The guides need to be well lubricated to slide easily. We found that a bar of soap worked as well as anything else.

By varying the dimensions, this method can be used to cut columns with any height, taper, diameter, and number of flutes. Only the flute radius must remain consistent from top to bottom.

Originally published in August/September 1984

Rigging and Roll Drops

Endless Line Rigging

by Thomas J. Corbett

The endless line is most often used for pulling the main drape or a curtain traveler. Slight modification in the traditional endless line, however, overcomes a problem involved in flying the traveler, and keeping control of the traveler horizontal movement. Also, the technique adds new dramatic possibilities.

The endless line principle was used for the Seattle Repertory Theatre's production of *A History of the American Film* to fly the Virgin Mother character across the stage. The flying rig consisted of a simple platform on which the actress stood. This standing platform was hung from a group of nylon carriers in a Unistrut track which was attached to a counterweighted pipe batten. The counterweight raised the actress to a pre-measured height while a continuous line enabled the platform to trolley left and right along the batten.

A normal endless line would fall slack when the batten was raised, or stack up on the floor when the pipe was lowered, presenting problems in achieving smooth operation. Therefore, the endless line was strung from the carriers, along the batten, and through an idler (or diverting pulley) placed at the grid as well as the floor block.

In operation

With this rigging, the batten can be flown freely from the floor to the grid without loss of control-line tension. If the operator moves the arbor, the endless line will run through the grid and floor pulley freely and the actor (load) will move up and down, but not left or right. When the actor is vertically positioned, the operator pulls the endless line to move the actor left or right. If the endless line is held in position while the batten is raised, a diagonal movement would result. The vertical movement supplied by the arbor and batten is translated into horizontal movement by the arrested endless line.

Instead of using breasting and spotlines, picking up a performer or object, moving it from one point over the stage to another, and then setting it down with control is possible. Moreover, the weight of the load is not on the flymen. The weight of the performer is at all times entrusted to the carriages running within the Unistrut channel and the counter balance of the counterweighted line set.

A variation of this rigging was used for a dance, choreographed by Ruth Solomon, mounted at the University of California, Santa Cruz, in the summer

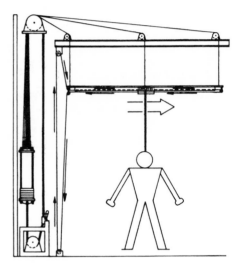

For a Seattle Repertory Theatre production of *A History of the American Film*, the endless line principle was applied to fly a character across the stage. The arbor carried her weight and moved her vertically, while the endless line moved her along the pipe batten (top, above). A variation of the setup flew roll drops (top right), used as screens during a dance performed at the UC, Santa Cruz theatre. Sliding glass door replacement rollers, the least expensive noiseless rollers stocked in hardware stores, were bolted onto an aluminum channel to make the pulley block (right center). A floor pedestal for the offstage end of the pipe batten had a pulley eye-bolted to the platform (right).

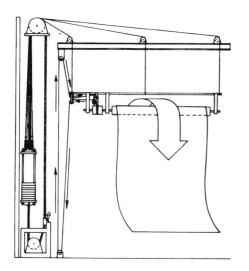

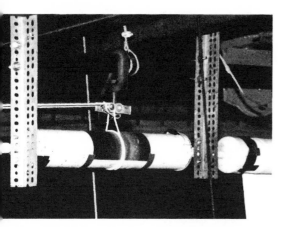

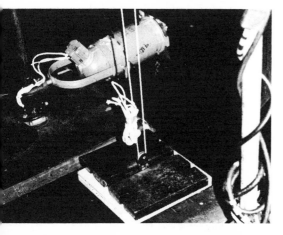

of 1980. The design demanded multiple slide projectors and screens; and the screens had to fly in during the dance and also fly back out. If there had been a full height fly-tower, there would have been no challenge—the panels simply could have been spaced onto battens and hung in the loft for appropriate use. However, although counterweighted battens exist, the borders in the Santa Cruz theatre can only hide about one-third the vertical travel of the pipe.

The solution was to hang the screen panels as flying roll drops, using a variation of the endless line control. Rather than traveling carriers along Unistrut, the endless line wound around a roll made of 4″ HDPE plastic sewer pipe. The middle of the endless line (¼″ sash cord) wrapped the plastic pipe 1½ times, passing through a pulley block hung under the batten. The pulley block was made from grooved nylon sliding glass door rollers bolted onto aluminum channel. The purchase line on the rollers was threaded through an idler pulley at the grid and a floor block on the stage floor.

The two ends of the operating line were then tied together—spaced so that the knot would travel from floor pulley to grid-mounted pulley while the batten with the roll drops traveled from the upper limit of the grid to the lower limit of the pipe batten's travel.

If the endless line was stopped by the fly crew while the batten was moving, the roll of the screen panels would happen two times faster than merely pulling the batten up and unwind at twice the speed of the ascending batten.

The rigging proved very effective. During the dance the screen panels actually had to be pulled far out onto the thrust stage by the dancers and therefore were required to have more than the two-thirds (or 20′ of length) that the simpler travel would have provided. The panels also could fly at different rates of speed in the same battens and ascend or descend independently with regard to timing, speed, and extension.

Whether combined with roll drops or coupled with tracks and carriers, the endless line rigging application shows considerable flexibility.

Originally published in March 1981

The Traditional Roll Drop

by Allan Fanjoy

In a recent production of *Annie Get Your Gun* at the University of Delaware, we experimented with a refinement of the roll drop—a traditional, but much neglected, method of rigging drops. I was surprised to discover how little specific advice is available on this technique in the standard technical manuals. If more appreciated and better developed, the roll drop has the potential of restoring a valuable option to designers and to furnish technicians with a solution to the problem of limited fly space.

Roll drops were very popular at the turn of the century and throughout the vaudeville era as oleo drops. These played just upstage of the house curtain, or in place of one. They were painted either with advertisements for patrons and upcoming shows or with general scenes that suited in-one or crossover scenes. Roll drops are sometimes used for period authenticity. But it is also unexcelled as a way to fly a full stage drop stretched flat and store it in a minimum of fly space. While a simple framed flat stores in its own height and a tripped drop stores in a half to a third that height, the roll drop requires only about 1' of vertical storage space in the flies.

Roll drops work much like a porch or window shade in which a series of slats is rolled up on a bottom core. The roll drop differs from the shade essentially in size and in that the control lines must not obscure the face of the drop. The lines must hoist the rolling core at its ends only—beyond the drop's edge and out of audience sightlines. These lines wrap around the core from behind and the drop wraps around its face. The lines and drop form a cradle in which the core is supported. The drop supports half the

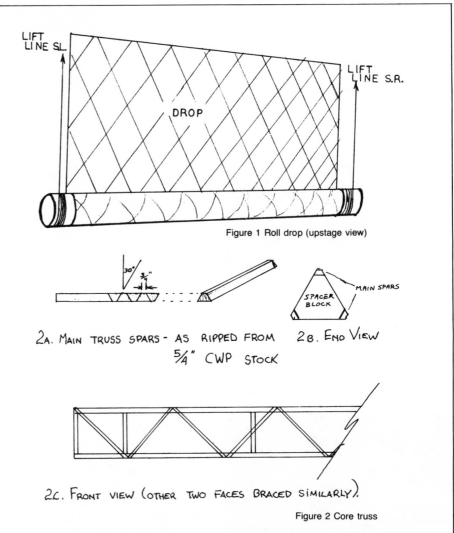

Figure 1 Roll drop (upstage view)

2A. MAIN TRUSS SPARS - AS RIPPED FROM 5/4" CWP STOCK

2B. END VIEW

2C. FRONT VIEW (OTHER TWO FACES BRACED SIMILARLY).

Figure 2 Core truss

core's weight and is stretched tightly as it bears this weight while the control lines support the other half. As the control lines are lifted, the core rolls off them and climbs up the drop. This arrangement provides a mechanical advantage of two. The control lines must be purchased twice as far as the drop rises, but with a force of only half its weight.

An ideal roll drop should be light for ease of operation. The core should be rigid under both flexing and torquing forces so that the drop will be stretched evenly and operation will be smooth and reliable. It should be neither so large as to require excessive storage space, nor so small as to require a great number of revolutions to traverse its height. (This would tend

to magnify small errors in alignment and roundness which might cause control lines to wrap off the core ends, or into the drop, or might distort the drop.) The possibility of purchasing the two control lines unequally and jeopardizing safe operation should be eliminated. If the natural mechanical advantage is not ideal in a given application, it should be easily modified.

For *Annie Get Your Gun*, the designer wished for an oleo to be rigged as a roll drop both for period authenticity and for its old glory of working in a restricted flyspace downstage. The following describes the particular version I designed and built for our theatre based on the above criteria: drop width, 36'; core length, 38'; playing height, 18'; total drop height, 22′; maximum counterweight travel (if employed) 21′. For economy, lightness, and durability, the drop was made in a standard fashion (horizontally seamed, webbed, and grommetted with pipe pocket and skirt) of 140 thread count muslin. This fabrication and the generous allowance of excess height to wrap onto the core will facilitate its use as a stock drop for future applications.

Some past practices for constructing the core were considered but found lacking. Some consist simply of 1″ x 1″ wood strips around a series of circular spacers. These are light but not very strong. They can flex and twist too much to permit smooth, reliable operation. Cardboard tubing (like that from carpet rolls) is usable for small drops but was again considered insufficiently strong in this case. Sonotube (concrete forming material) has adequate strength but is prohibitively costly and heavy. It might also be difficult to splice together standard 14′ lengths to obtain the required length.

For lightness, strength, and ease of construction it is hard to beat a wooden trusswork. Such a frame was used as the basis for a 1″ x 1″ cage. The main members of this truss were made of $^5/_4$″ C white pine (recommended in spite of its cost for lightweight consistent strength). The truss used was triangular in cross section to resist twisting. Main longitudinal members were ripped to shape. The outside edge was only $^3/_4$″ wide to match the surface of 1″ x 1″s to be added later to complete the cage. The sides tapered out at 30 degrees not only to give greater strength than a square cut 1″ x 1″, but also to provide a surface to attach bracing on each face. Sections of these longitudinal members were mitred and cut to lengths so that when three 38 foot lengths were made their scarf joints would be staggered and evenly spaced along the core's length for consistent strength. These pieces were nailed and glued to triangular spacer blocks at each scarf joint. Several additional spacer blocks were added to provide frequent support for the final cage of 1″ x 1″.

With these spars joined to spacers to form an open triangular prism, each face was then braced. One inch white pine was ripped into $^1/_4$″ thick strips. These were mitred to 45 degrees at

each end and were attached with tacks and glue to the long spars. The prism must be kept straight as it is braced since any errors will be locked in by the bracing and the final trussed core will be practically impossible to straighten. The shape at this stage resembles a radio tower and is extremely resistant to both torque and flexing stresses.

The final step of rounding the open cage was accomplished as follows: Curved spacer segments were notched to accept 1″ x 1″ and were nailed and glued to the inner triangular spacers. Joints were again scarfed and staggered as the 1″ x 1″ lengths were fitted in.

This core design proved to be a superior one as the final weight of the 38′ long unit which was 9″ in diameter was only about 75 U.S. and, when supported only at the ends showed a

strain of only about 1$^1/_2$″ at the center (a deviation of less than 1%).

In rigging, a single counterweighted hemp purchase line was used. Restrictions on the counterweight travel necessitated defeating the mechanical advantage inherent in the roll drop. A double purchase tackle was employed. The two control lines that wrap on the core were actually two ends of the same piece of $^1/_8$″ wire rope. Along this length was placed a cable clamp which joined the purchase line at a heavy duty swivel to prevent twisting and fouling. The use of a single cable and clamp arrangement allowed precise leveling during set up. I was quite satisfied with the one man operation of this roll drop. Ease, speed, reliability, and appearance were all well satisfied by a device so useful it will be in service as a stock piece.

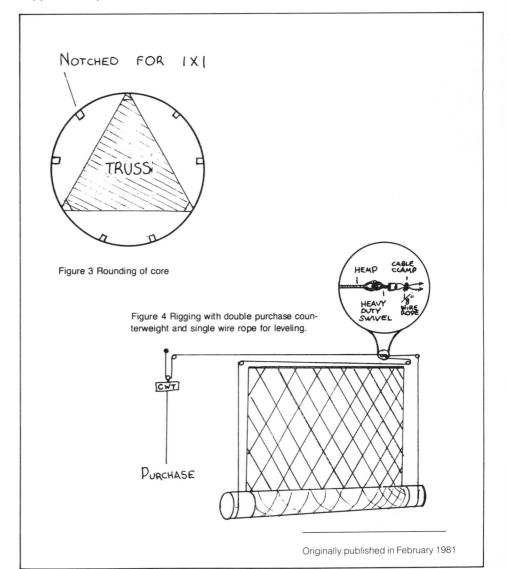

Figure 3 Rounding of core

Figure 4 Rigging with double purchase counterweight and single wire rope for leveling.

Originally published in February 1981

A Variation on the Roll Drop

by James Fay

No theatrical shifting device enhances the American melodrama any better than the roll curtain. This same device still proves to be invaluable in facilities with limited or restricted fly space. However, the aesthetic appeal of scrims and various translucent drop materials is somewhat altered by the appearance of bulky bottom roll. Here is a variation on the roll drop that can be built with materials on hand. It utilizes a top-mounted roller that is easy to rig and resists center sagging, thus eliminating the bottom roller. The supplies listed and the process outlined are for a 24' wide roller.

Materials

24' of 1" x 8" utility grade lumber
200' of 1" x 3" utility grade lumber
White glue
8d box of common nails
Two C-clamps with yolks
Two 6" pieces of 2¹/₄" pipe with flanges
Two 2' pieces of 1¹/₂" pipe with flanges
Eighteen 1¹/₂" lag screws
50' of ¹/₄" sisal rope

Construction

1 Cross cut the 1" x 8" lumber into 34 7¹/₂" square pieces. Put the remaining 1" x 8" aside for later use. Next, cut 45 degree angles across the squares to form octagonal spacers. (Figure 1)

2 Take the 34 spacers and glue them into 17 pairs, with the grain of the wood running perpendicular as in plywood veneers. Take two pairs of spacers and drill center holes 1¹/₂" in diameter through each. Set these aside to become the end spacers.

3 Take two other spacers and attach the 2' x 1¹/₂" pipe to the centers with lag screws. These spacers will become the first internal support pieces on each side. (Figure 2)

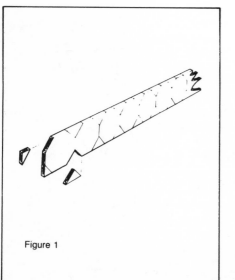

Figure 1

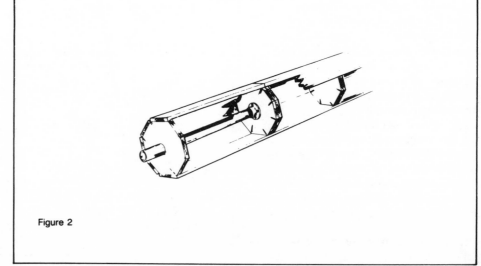

Figure 2

4 Stand the spacers vertically in a row on the floor at 18″ intervals, with the pipe sections protruding out each end.

5 Attach the 1″ x 3″ sweeps along the outer perimeters of the spacers as illustrated. Pieces should be precut at long lengths divisible by 18″ so as to intersect at the spacers. All joints should be nailed and glued to assure uniform strength. No more than two sets of sweeps should begin or end on any single internal spacer.

Once assembled, the rigging of the unit is relatively simple. It is designed to hang inside units assembled from the C-clamps and the remaining 1″ x 8″ lumber with 2¼″ center-mounted pipes. When rigging, make sure that the length of rope looped around the roller is equal to or greater than the length of the drop standing.

Roll drops with widths greater than 24′ may require additional spacers in the center, or thicker sweeps, or the insertion of an inset pipe. If the drop itself has been painted with ordinary scene paint, it might crack and chip. This can be avoided by adding small amounts of glycerin to the paint while mixing, or by using synthetic-based paints, such as acrylics applied in thin coats.

Originally published in February 1981

The roll drop below is a variation of the more traditional roll drop.

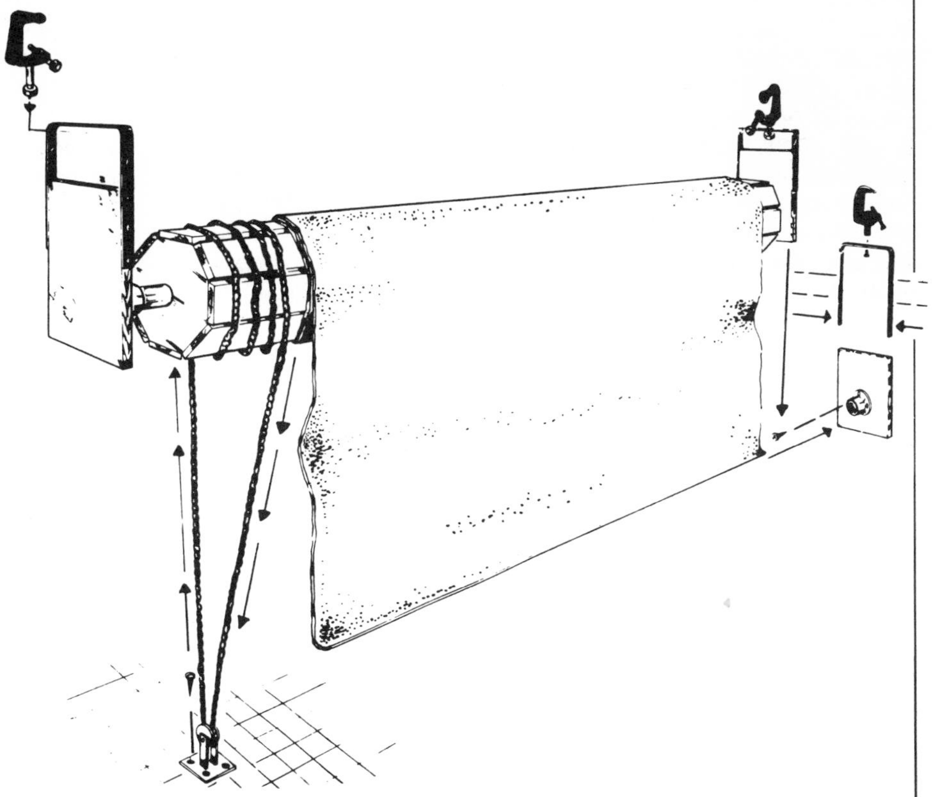

Figure 3

The Versatile Cut Drop Stages a Comeback

by Barry L. Bailey

Today in technical theatre there is candid discussion concerning avant garde production means. Scenic and lighting design have become more technical and mechanical, but unfortunately, often less meaningful to the production. Not every play can be "modernized" and mechanized. Furthermore, many community and educational theatres do not have the budgets for new mechnical wonder effects or the space to accommodate them. Most of these theatres are far from large cities where the new methods are generally available. And, when they do decide to rent or buy, the problem of finding knowledgeable operators arises. The non-professional theatre is seemingly "left behind" where the new methods of presentation are concerned.

As a result, a return to older, more simple methods is taking place. One of the many ideas that has seen a rebirth is the cut drop. The cut drop is one of the most versatile and least talked about pieces of scenery. In its pure form, it can recreate the theatre of gas light, when the cut drop was in its heyday. Used in conjunction with contemporary staging methods, it can help produce even more exciting and spectacular effects. It can be used with all kinds of projections, three dimensional scenery, revolving and moving stages, and other advanced technical scenery.

Ideal for stages with limitations of depth, wing storage or limited fly space, and more versatile than a hard profile piece, the cut drop can be flown with minimum effort. It can be tripped if the grid is not of sufficient height. Parts of it can appear to be free floating.

Choosing materials

The actual construction of a cut drop is almost easier than building a simple flat. Virtually no carpentry is involved, which makes it ideal for theatres with few skilled technicians. Because of scarce information we, at the University of South Carolina, had to experiment with materials and construction.

The most difficult problem was in finding the proper materials. Jack Shirk, then the technical director of U.S.C., spent weeks locating what was needed. Net is used to reinforce a solid canvas or muslin drop, allowing parts of it to be cut away, creating a profile or silhouette effect. The net covers the entire area of the drop including the solid portions. Fish net is the basic material for the usual cut drop, but no theatrical supply house carried it. Scrim, bobbinnet, theatrical gauze, or even cheese cloth can also be used, but they cause a hazy effect. A visible net responds to light the same way as a scrim. Fish net, or an extremely open weave net is transparent with only a slight grid visible.

The most important thing to look for in buying fish net for a cut drop is the "weave." The proper net for cut drops is made with the edges of the square holes in a straight line so the sides hang vertically and horizontally when held by the knots on any one edge. Some fish net is made on the bias with the corners of the squares forming the sides of the net. This will hang on the bias and is useless as supportive backing on a cut drop.

The kind of drop being made and its intended use determine the size of the opening of the net. One inch square

A simple cut drop of red felt letters glued to decorator fish net which was stretched on a batten (above), was used to set the mood for *Canterbury Tales* at Boston's Northeastern University in 1971. The sign was flown out after the audience entered, leaving behind a leaf border and forest scrim traveller to be used as the basic scenic background for the rest of the show.

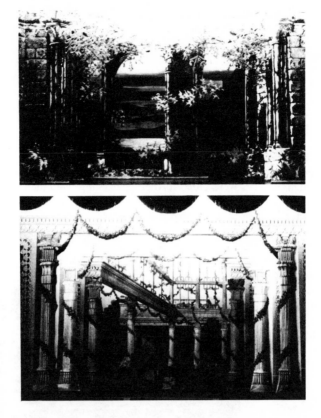

Cut drops (left) from the early 1900's indicate the long tradition of this scenic solution.

hole fish net is most often used. A rule of thumb is that the more delicate and detailed the edges of the solid portion of the drop, the closer the net weave should be. If the cut edges are extremely delicate and involved, scrim or bobbin-net might be required.

Cotton fish net is the most practical type. It is much cheaper than nylon and it takes dye and glue well. Its dull finish usually disappears under proper stage lighting. Small pieces of cotton fish net can be purchased at some marine stores, or novelty or gift stores. Decorator fish net can be found in sizes approximately 6 feet by 15 feet. Larger pieces for a full stage drop can be purchased in New York. We used a bundle of fish net 30 feet by 300 yards and had only a few yards left after our sets for Giradoux's *Ondine*.

The solid part of the drop can be any flexible material that might otherwise be used for soft scenery. Scenic canvas, muslin, scrim, felt, foam rubber can be used with great success. The material applied to the net must be lightweight so it does not stretch the net, or bulge and sag.

Construction of the basic cut drop

A muslin drop several feet larger than the design is stapled to the floor face up and base painted. If the drop is base painted after the design is cut out, the surface will curl. When it is dry, a grid is laid down and the front view design transferred to the face of the drop in chalk, allowing approximately one foot of extra drop on each of the four sides. The staples are then removed and the appropriate portions of the drop cut away. When all the cut-away areas have been removed, the entire drop is flipped over onto its face and fastened again to the floor at the remaining outside edges.

Wire nails are tacked around the perimeter of the drop every three inches or so, in order to stretch the fish net square and hold it in place for glueing. When all the remaining cut muslin pieces have been placed carefully in the proper position on the floor, a large piece of net, cut to size and dyed to match the background is placed over the design back and hooked onto the nails around the edge—like an old fashioned curtain stretcher.

After the muslin pieces are checked for position, the stretched net is snapped from the center of the drop to equalize tension in all directions. The muslin underneath is checked again for positioning and the net snapped again.

Then, the muslin portions are glued to the net. White glue (in a one-to-one mixture with water) is painted over the parts of the net where the muslin shows through. The glue is allowed to dry overnight. The next day battens are placed on the top and bottom of the drop. Some battens can be fastened to net and muslin while the top batten holds only net.

Battening down

Cut drops are always held in place by at least one batten. Full stage drops that touch the floor across the entire stage usually have two battens. A full stage portal cut drop can be made with legs that reach to the floor on each side and a large opening in the center. These need a separate batten on the bottom of each leg. Free hanging drops that do not reach to the floor, such as leaf borders or signs, need only one batten at the top as the bottom edge is often irregular and cut to show as little of the net as possible. Seldom is it left in a straight line, as that would be more noticeable to the audience. Any net that is not needed to hold up portions of the drop, or to hold the shape of the drop can be cut away. But the more use and travel for which a drop is intended, the less net should be cut away.

Construction of silhouette drops

A much different construction is used for a silhouette drop (where the front surface does not show) or on a drop which would be enhanced by piecing, such as a leaf border. Because this kind of drop has more cut away portions than solid one, it can be constructed from muslin scraps rather than from solid cloth.

For a silhouette drop, white butcher paper a few feet larger than the drop is taped to the floor. This paper is blocked off in grid sections onto which a rear view cartoon of the design is sketched with a marking pen. Scraps of muslin are placed on the cartoon, traced through, and cut out. When all the muslin pieces have been cut out to complete the design, they are placed in position on the cartoon master and the net applied.

For the University of North Carolina's production of *Ondine* an underwater silhouette was constructed. The muslin was mostly cut away and the net stretched fairly tight to make the large open net areas remain taut enough to support the muslin. On a lightweight, very porous material such as scrim, the grid has to be laid out right on the floor or other solid surface, because the glue when applied comes through

and fastens the paper cartoon to the face of the drop. Some drops can be face-painted black to emphasize the silhouette effect.

Mistakes to avoid

In experimentation with several types of cut drops, the worst and most time consuming error occurred during construction of the first drop. Fearing that the cut muslin sections of the drop would shift out of position before they were glued to the net backing, we glued the drop sections that would remain and then tried to cut away the correct portions after the glue had dried. In many

places, however, the glue ran or was brushed over the cutting line and we found ourselves carefully pulling each separate string away from the 36 foot header archway drop so we could snip the correct parts away. The minor shifting that the muslin does is not usually worth the extra effort of overall glueing. Also the risk of tearing the net in pulling it loose is very great.

Some professional designers are using the cut drop. But this devise need not be restricted to the union scenic studios. The small professional and semi-professional theatre is just as capable of producing maginficent effects through the use of the versatile cut drop.

Originally published in November/December 1972

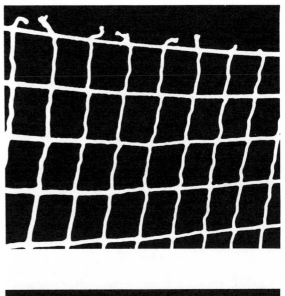

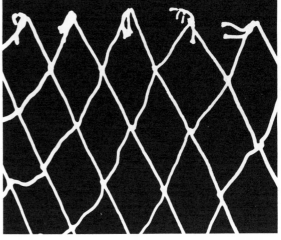

While at the University of South Carolina, Barry Bailey designed cut drop sets for Giradoux's "Ondine," (facing page) and "The Pirates of Penzance." Two full stage, lighted cut drops for "Pirates" (left, top and bottom) create a feeling of depth in about 7 feet of actual stage depth. Net is cut out of the three largest windows in the drop to permit entrances from a platform. Fish net woven on a bias does not provide the supportive backing for cut drops that square netting does (illustrations, above).

Check Your Rigging

by William Lord

Stage rigging is, perhaps, the most important equipment found in any theatre. Yet too often it is taken for granted until a problem arises. Because of its constant load—curtains, scenery, and lighting—rigging should be professionally checked for safety's sake at least every five years.

In between these checkups, you can do a great deal of inspecting and minor adjusting yourself. Should you find an obvious problem, then start a repair program or contact a professional to do the job. Here are some things to look for, from the simplest to the more complicated.

Checking curtain tracks, turnbuckles and pulleys

Although made of stronger materials and formed in a slightly different manner, stage curtain tracks are heavy duty relatives of the traverse rod variety found in homes. This track channel must be parallel to the floor and should be kept clean and dry.

Watch the bottom corner of the lead edge of a traveler curtain. It should always stay the same distance off the floor throughout its travels. If it doesn't, the track channel should be adjusted in height. To do this, lengthen or shorten the supporting lines. When no mechanism is provided for this task, you can make minor adjustments by loosening the track clamp a little and tapping it to one side. This will effectively shorten its supporting chain or cable.

Turnbuckles exist for this purpose. Once properly adjusted, the turnbuckle should be through-wired. Take a soft wire, such as bailing or stove pipe wire, and weave it through eye/center-loop/eye and back again. This prohibits the turnbuckle from winding either in or out.

If the curtain pulls hard, it is not necessarily a rope-to-metal friction causing the problem. Usually difficult operation is the result of one or more defective carriers, a line becoming jammed where it passes through some metal part, improper line tension, or a jammed pulley wheel.

Pulleys

Pulley wheels, or sheaves, are found at the single-wheel (or dead end) of the track, at the double-wheel (live end), and at the take-up block at the floor. To check the operation of any of these, raise the pulley in the floor block—to loosen the operating line—then spin the wheel. It should turn freely.

Today, almost all stage pulleys, as well as the carriers themselves, are ball-bearing equipped and should not cause problems. If they do, however, it is possible to remove the offending part and flush its bearing area with a solvent. Then use some light, durable lubricant—sparingly—and reinstall the device.

Units without ball bearings have self-lubricating bronze bushings and do not require further treatment other than cleaning. Over time the lubricant often mixes with dust, forming a glue-like material. If cleaning and minor lubrication do not clear your problem, contact a professional rigger. Never oil or grease any part of a track system.

The dead hung

The least complex support system used on a stage is the dead hung: supporting battens which are fastened in some manner to the ceiling or structural components above the stage. This system provides no way to raise or lower supported items without a ladder or scaffolding.

When checking this type of rigging, look for: any indication that the supporting devices might be unanchored, evidence of wear where connection is made between items, and loose bolts.

Rope line sets

Technically, a set of lines, or set, is all of the items required to move a pipe vertically and to secure it at a given level.

If you have a rope set, that includes the batten on which everything is hung, the lines themselves, some loft blocks (single pulleys on the ceiling), a head block (a multiple groove pulley at one side of the stage ceiling), a tie-off cleat to secure the free ends of the ropes, and perhaps some sort of counterweighting—such

as a sandbag, clip-on carriage or arbor with weights on it, hanging from a clew or trimming clamp.

Rope sets are the most common, because they are inexpensive to install and provide a flexible, easily handled support material. The rope set is also probably the favorite do-it-yourself project for smaller theatres, since the materials are readily available from the local hardware store and the installation looks simple. But be warned. Store-bought materials are not always of sufficient quality to be safe and home-made installations often lack proper engineering.

The rope itself should either be sash cord or hemp. Sash cord looks like, but is much stronger—and more expensive—than clothesline rope. It was designed for continued service: holding the sash weight at the side of a vertical operating window and running over a small diameter pulley with an equal weight at each end. Clothesline should not be used onstage, since it has relatively little strength, will stretch, and is unreliable.

Manila or hemp ropes are woven strands of longer vegetable fibres, typically used for nautical purposes. Hemp, however, is gradually being replaced in both theatres and marine use by the newer plastic lines.

Whichever type of rope you have, examine each individual line, inch by inch. Look for breaks in the strands or evidence of abrasion or wear. Test the pliability of the material, and, in the case of the nylon or plastics, make sure there is no melting together of strands. As a general rule, if the diameter of a line is affected—either smaller or larger than it was originally—the line should be replaced. When the line diameter is smaller over a long length, the line has been over-loaded and should be replaced with the next larger size.

Obviously, most abrasion occurs from rubbing on an immobile surface such as a stuck pulley or a structural element too close to the line. Find the cause of the abrasion if possible, then clear it either by moving the line or repairing any defect.

Cotton and hemp lines do dry out after

a while. But they last longer in air-conditioned theatres, as the humidity is more constant. Once they have become brittle to the touch or tend to hold a sharp bend when folded, they are reaching the end of useful life. If you can chip loose fibres of the hemp with your fingernail, it is no longer safe.

Other pieces of the rope set, made from either wood or metal, must be checked for any rough surfaces which might cause premature wear to the line passing on or over it. With good light and a piece of gauze, you will find most of these spots: light will quickly show many problem areas; gauze rubbed over a surface in all directions will reveal an imperfect surface.

If any of your sets are equipped with sandbags, the canvas should be checked for rot, either dry or wet. The sand should occasionally be removed and replaced. Pay special attention to the rope saddle around the bag. This ring always stays in the same place, thus putting the greatest stress on that portion of the rope.

Loosen any knots in your rope lines and inspect the section of rope within the knot. You may have to move the knot along the rope or even shorten the rope to remove any stiffened portions of the line.

Winches

The winch, a mechanical means of lifting or driving loads, is a gear-driven mechanism which allows a small-effort/fast-movement to turn into a large-effort/slow-movement, just like the pedal/rear-wheel configuration on a bicycle. For safety reasons, most theatrical winches will not run down—that is, allow the reel to turn without operating the handle.

If your winch has enclosed gearing, there is probably some lubrication instruction on the case. Otherwise, a good axle grease or wheel-bearing grease will work. Although grease lasts longer, paraffin or Vaseline can also be used as a lubricant. Besides, these can be replenished more often and will cause fewer stains on the materials with which they come into contact.

It is best to have a professional inspect electrically-driven winches. These complicated devices usually have several surfaces—such as brakes, drive faces and clutches—which cannot have any lubricant on them.

Check the mounting of your winch. If it is welded to a steel surface, look for any obvious cracks in the welds. For bolted mountings, check to make sure the winch is still tight against the mounting surface. The bottom bolts are subject to the most stress in a vertical pull winch, so give them special attention.

Hopefully, your rigger will have used specially hardened bolts rather than the common hardware store variety. There is a way to tell the difference—by the coding on the bolt's head—but if you have any doubts, call in a pro.

If you can reach the nut securing the bolt, lower your set—allowing its weight to rest on something—and start tightening or replacing the mounting bolts one by one. If you can't reach the nut, as is true of many winches mounted in concrete walls, leave the analysis to a professional rigger.

Some of these walls are actually cinder block, and the normal stress and movement of the winch will slowly disintegrate the block's interior—causing further loosening of the mounting. In addition, some of the anchor devices used in cinder blocks have less strength than the bolt and can be overtightened to the point at which they will fail.

After lowering the load on a winch, check the anchoring of the cable into the winch drum. Often, anchoring is done with a cable clip (a u-shaped bolt with a saddle and two nuts), which can be tightened. Check carefully for any evidence of fraying or kinking. There is usually just a single cable wrapping the drum.

The upper end of the drive cable is often terminated at a clew, which will then have several other cables extending from it to the pulleys and load. This clew needs to have all of its fasteners inspected.

One common variety is the "guided clew" which has some sort of guide or spool on the outside edge. Small cables run through the guides to keep the clew from spinning as the winch is operated. Because these guides are frequently lignum-vitae or some other self-lubricating material, they do not need further lubrication.

Wipe your guide cables clean, make sure they are taut and that their anchors are tight at each end. Again—as you always check for a tight fastening—look for breaks or fraying in the ropes.

Counterweights

Stages with sufficient height from stage floor to the upper structure are usually equipped with counterweight rigging. This may be hung under heavy roof members—which means you have to have someone with the means of getting to the rigging to check it—or may be on a gridiron where you can move around to check it yourself.

A counterweight set seems complicated at first glance, but it operates much like a rope set. Better yet, it provides a means of permanently counterbalancing whatever weight is placed on a batten for a performance. Used and maintained properly, this is probably the safest system available.

In this system the batten is the same, but cables are used in lieu of rope. Cables are not only stronger, they don't stretch and are much less susceptible to deterioration. These lines pass through grooved loft blocks and head blocks—the grooves are sized precisely for the cable—while the end of each support cable is secured to a counterweight carriage.

The carriage is a steel frame designed to hold weights which can be easily added or removed, depending on the batten load. Theoretically, the batten and its load should be counterbalanced by the carriage and its weights. The system should not move on its own, even if the remaining parts are deleted.

Your operating or overhaul line is made

from ¾" rope, either hemp or one of the poly materials, and is used to raise or lower the carriage, which in turn moves the batten. This operating line needs to be treated like any other rope—checked for knots, moisture content, and abrasions.

The operating line goes from the top of the carriage over the head block and returns to the operating level, where it passes through a rope lock. The lock is actually a brake or clamp and should be only tight enough to hold, not crush. Most abrasions will appear near the lock if it is set too tight.

Remember to remove all markings when inspecting the operating line. Tape should not be used to mark levels on a set, because it can become lodged in either the lock or take-up block and impede operation. Commercially manufactured trim clamps—knuckle busters—are better for marking.

At the bottom of the run, a take-up block turns the operating line path from down to up, and the line is then secured to the bottom of the counterweight carriage. Your take-up block should be in the mid-point of its run when the operating line is at its proper length. This way the rope may stretch or shrink without causing undue slack or tension. If the block often reaches either limit, adjust your operating line length with the knot at the bottom of the carriage.

Some stages have compound or two-speed rigging systems. These have a second head block at the top of a carriage and a second take-up block on the bottom. Other than that, they operate essentially the same. Any adjustment work on a two-speed system should only be attempted by a professional rigger.

Steel cables used in stage rigging usually have an internal fibre cord designed to keep a lubricant working in the cable as it is moved. Still, steel cables need to be examined for: any abrasion, which often shows up as a shiny surface along the cable; cracked or broken strands; evidence of flattening or kinking; broken strands or looseness at cable end anchors; or excessive rust penetrating the individual metal strands.

If you find any of the above, note the exact location and call it to the attention of someone with steel cable experience. You might have a safety problem.

Originally published in May 1984

Uncle Dunc and Scenic Artists' Techniques

Uncle Dunc's Tipsheet

by R. Duncan Mackenzie

Flat Joint Ideas

Nuts and bolts are fine for permanent connections. But an hour and a half changeover in a heavy repertory situation is a poor place for loose nuts and cross-threaded bolts. The method shown below makes use of those old cross-threaded bolts and concrete form whaler wedges. Although it can and has been used with wooden-framed scenery, it is primarily intended for use with steel or aluminum tubing framed flats.

The rails of the metal framed flat are drilled to receive old, stripped bolts (round heads are preferable, but hex or flat heads will do). The bolts are welded in place and oversize holes drilled in the frame of the adjacent flat rail. Additionally, some tight fitting pins are installed to keep the edges of the flat in plane register.

Connecting the flats is simply a matter of slipping the wedges (commonly called SNAP-TY wedges) over the heads of the bolts after the flats have been mated, and then seating the wedges with a mallet. SNAP-TY wedges are available at most scaffolding and shoring supply houses.

Joe Kaplor, the technical director at Houston's Alley Theatre, had one of these sitting on his desk. Made by the Adjustable Bushing Company, this device is called an Expando Grip Pin. Used as a jig fixture pin or for securing the rotors on helicopters, this device offers quick release capability, high shear strength, and very good pull-out resistance. While Joe had planned to use them in conjunction with a matching sleeve insert for securing temporary seating to a concrete floor, another possible application is shown below. Please note the spacer bushing required to keep the "female" segments from opening beyond their elastic limit.

For more information, contact:

Adjustable Bushing Company
11905 Rose Street
North Hollywood, California 91605

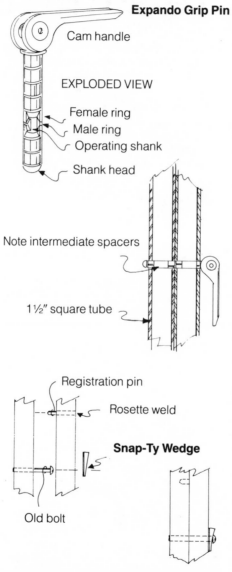

Expando Grip Pin

Cam handle

EXPLODED VIEW

Female ring
Male ring
Operating shank

Shank head

Note intermediate spacers

1½" square tube

Registration pin

Rosette weld

Snap-Ty Wedge

Old bolt

Length determined by tubing size plus a distance sufficient to start wedge

Bubble Film

Here's a process of making black and white slides from negatives I came across in *Technical Photography* (August 1980). I have seen finished examples of slides and microfilm produced by this process and they do live up to expectations.

Writing it up in *Technical Photography* Michael A. Munzer tried Instant Image Film's "vesicular film," activated by heat and sensitive to ultra-violet light.

Munzer explains that "the easiest way to use this material is to make a contact image using a glass slide mount and exposing through a projector. We then ironed the exposed film for a second to bring out the latent image and then re-exposed the film through the projector to 'fix' it."

For information on "Bubble Film" write to Instant Image Films, P.O. Box 520, Maywood, CA 90270.

Originally published in November/December 1982

Uncle Dunc's Cheapo Air Cylinder

Any scene shop that possesses a wood lathe can now make cheap air cylinders which are relatively efficient. Although the detailed diagram is self-explanatory, a few notes should be added.

PVC Schedule 40 pipe, which is used to build the air cylinder, is rated at 150psi to 200psi. I would not, however, recommend using a cylinder of this construction over 60psi. During testing of an experimental air cylinder, the adhesive bond that secured the rear cap of the cylinder failed, sending the end cap flying across the shop at high speed. All subsequent cylinders had end caps secured after adhesive bonding with steel pins heated and then forced into the walls of the cylinder.

In building the air cylinder, the hardwood piston is turned and sanded to a dimension slightly less than the inside diameter of the pipe. Two lands (grooves) are turned into the piston to seat the O rings that seal to the inner bore of the pipe.

When determining what size of actuator rod to use, consider whether operation is to be in tension (pulling the load) or compression (pushing the load). An early cylinder had to be rebuilt when the device it actuated jammed, causing the 5' long ½" cold rolled rod to bend into a permanent semicircle.

Almost any length cylinder (up to 20') can be built using this technique. For those applications that require more force, I would advise using larger bore cylinders to satisfy the load requirement, in lieu of increasing the air pressure.

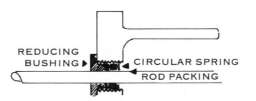

REDUCING BUSHING ▶ | ◀ CIRCULAR SPRING
ROD PACKING

Hand-held Feet/ Inches/Sixteenths Calculator

Muddled by metric? Designing in decimal feet? Or are you one who fervently wishes there were ten inches in a foot because it simplifies calculation? At long last there is a hand-held calculator that will handle feet and inches calculations and conversions from feet/inches/sixteenths to decimal feet or metric measurement. Feet/inches/sixteenths can be added and subtracted directly without conversions and can be multiplied or divided by whole numbers. In addition, the unit has basic trig functions, two memories, and can solve for right triangles in the feet/inches/sixteenths mode. The unit, marketed under the name of JOBBER II, currently sells for $89.95 plus shipping and handling. For information contact Calculated Industries, Inc., 2010 North Tustin, Suite B, Orange, California 92665.

The shaft rod packing is a standard item available at all hydraulic and pneumatic supply houses. It is held in place by an oversize bushing in front and a circular retainer spring in back to prevent the movement of the rod from unseating the packing. It was found that air leaks around the outside of the packing could be eliminated by doping the threads of the PVC reducing bushing that acts as the front cap of the cylinder with silicone sealant.

Originally published in April 1983

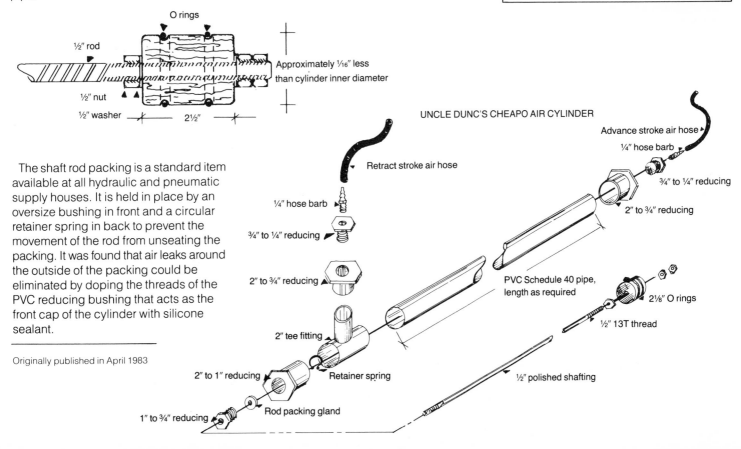

O rings

½" rod

½" nut

½" washer — 2½"

Approximately ¹⁄₁₆" less than cylinder inner diameter

UNCLE DUNC'S CHEAPO AIR CYLINDER

Retract stroke air hose

¼" hose barb

¾" to ¼" reducing

2" to ¾" reducing

2" tee fitting

2" to 1" reducing

Retainer spring

Rod packing gland

1" to ¾" reducing

½" polished shafting

Advance stroke air hose

¼" hose barb

¾" to ¼" reducing

2" to ¾" reducing

PVC Schedule 40 pipe, length as required

2⅛" O rings

½" 13T thread

Uncle Dunc's Pushmi-pullyu Actuator

I can hear all of you out there snickering at this idea. Please do not—I used this on a production of *Blithe Spirit* for some of the effects at the end of the third act.

After a while I tired of stringing trick line to the vases and dishes that are ostensibly smashed by the ghosts night after night. Instead I put together a system using several hypodermic syringes mounted, with hot melt glue, to a 1″ x 3″ backstage. Hard plastic tubing—the kind used to feed water to the icemakers in refrigerators—was run from these backstage master syringes to slave syringes mounted in the set's woodwork. On cue the operator would depress the appropriate master syringe, thereby raising its slave and upsetting a vase or dish. Resetting the system entailed no more than simply depressing the slaves after the end of the show.

It is important when initially charging the circuit that no air bubbles are left in the lines or in the syringes. If there are bubbles the air merely is compressed and no hydraulic force is transmitted. It is sometimes necessary to insert a hypodermic with the needle still attached along side the piston of one of the slave or master syringes to evacuate the trapped air.

Cable-tensioning Device

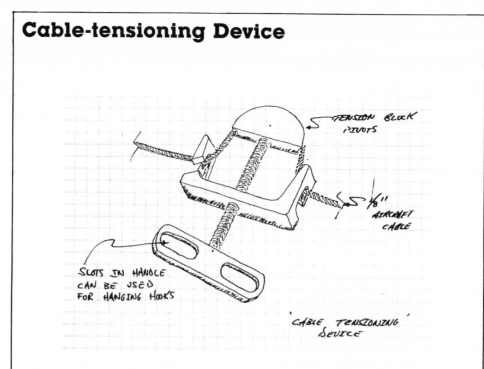

This novel cable tensioning device may save a few turnbuckle-tired wrist muscles. The sample I saw demonstrated was well made and did indeed tension the cable. Although there may be numerous applications in the theatre, I do think that the cable should be used only once, as this tool puts a permanent kink in the cable where it enters the device. For more information and prices contact:
Robert Zukaitis
Ten-Press Engineering
4550 Old Woman Springs Road
Yucca Valley, California 92284

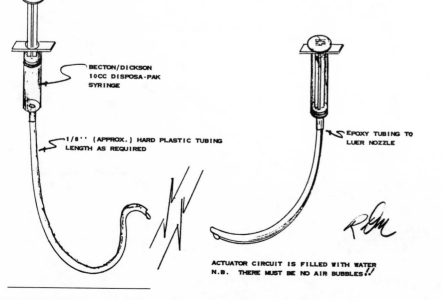

UNCLE DUNC'S PUSHMI-PULLYU ACTUATOR CIRCUIT

BECTON/DICKSON
10CC DISPOSA-PAK
SYRINGE

1/8″ (APPROX.) HARD PLASTIC TUBING
LENGTH AS REQUIRED

EPOXY TUBING TO
LUER NOZZLE

ACTUATOR CIRCUIT IS FILLED WITH WATER
N.B. THERE MUST BE NO AIR BUBBLES!!

Originally published in February 1983

Catalogue Pick

Many of you already have "Fluid Power Components" from the Parker Hannifin Corporation. For those of you who do not, a brief description of this 1,400-page catalogue is in order. Not only is one of the better component lines represented in complete detail, but the operational descriptions accompanying each item are in themselves a lesson in fluid power application and design. Additionally, the compilers of this catalogue have included a 100-page introduction to fluid power design. This design information is packed with useful formulas, application hints, trouble-shooting procedures, and general design considerations. If you are currently using or considering using pneumatic or, especially, hydraulic systems, I urge you to acquire this catalogue—it is free. Write to:

Parker Hannifin Corporation
17325 Euclid Avenue
Cleveland, Ohio 44112
or check with your local distributor.

Air-powered Curtain Tracks

Air-powered curtain tracks were conceived and constructed to replace manually operated ones located in an inaccessible portion of the Inner Below of the Elizabethean stage at the Oregon Shakespearean Festival. The manual method entailed a complicated operating-line muling scheme that ran the lines offstage to a concealed stagehand. Unfortunately, lines would become fouled or break (usually during the pre-show checkout), and performance reliability was a marginal, ulcer-inducing nightmare.

To build air-powered curtain tracks, a 3' stroke, 1½" bore air cylinder was fitted with a dual sheave assembly, and a 12' Kirsch Double Duty track was reeved. Line muling was accomplished with small diameter (2"), delrin-bearing sailboat blocks fitted with deck mount plates. The assembly was mounted on 1" x 3" wooden tee as shown.

The cylinder ports were equipped with flow controls, providing full flow during the power stroke and controlled flow on the exhaust. In this manner, a degree of speed control was possible. Since the reeving was at a 2:1 mechanical disadvantage, very fast draw speeds were possible. Backstage at the stage manager's panel, a four-way air valve was installed. Control and operating pressure was provided by regulated 20# CO_2 cylinders.

Although the system worked beautifully (and is still in use to my knowledge), a few refinements were added in subsequent years to enhance the operation of

Originally published in November/December 1983

the device. Ordinary cotton curtain sash cord (which wore out very quickly) was replaced with ¼" nylon parachute cord dyed with dark brown shoe dye. After experimenting with several commercial exhaust port mufflers, the noise of the valve exhaust was finally controlled by the simple expedient of piping the exhaust ports to a remote location in the building.

While on the subject of small curtain tracks, the bane of every TD and prop person's life, here are some hints regarding restringing the little devils—an event that invariably takes place at three minutes to curtain.

A small piece of copper braided shielding from scrapped microphone cable or RG-59/U co-axial makes a good tension sleeve (Chinese finger trap) to aid in butt splicing a broken line to a replacement one when re-reeving. Although it is flexible enough to run over the tiny sheaves, it is a good idea to secure it to the new line with a drop of hot melt glue.

Nylon parachute cord makes excellent operating line for small tracks, as it does not wear out as readily as cotton cord. It can be dyed and its ends can be melted to form non-fraying points that will easily pass through those tiny tie-off slots in the master carriers.

Keeping a small length of black iron stove wire in the dead tie hole of the live end sheave assembly will save time trying to find something to snare the operating line through the master carrier's tie-off slots.

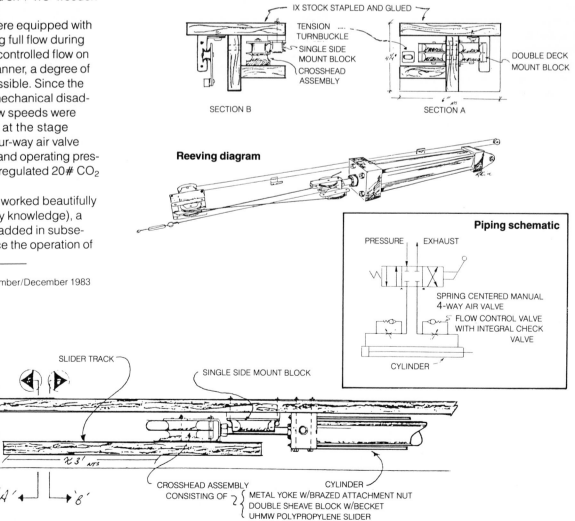

SECTION B

SECTION A

IX STOCK STAPLED AND GLUED

TENSION TURNBUCKLE

SINGLE SIDE MOUNT BLOCK

CROSSHEAD ASSEMBLY

DOUBLE DECK MOUNT BLOCK

Reeving diagram

Piping schematic

PRESSURE   EXHAUST

SPRING CENTERED MANUAL 4-WAY AIR VALVE

FLOW CONTROL VALVE WITH INTEGRAL CHECK VALVE

CYLINDER

Side view

DOUBLE DECK MOUNT BLOCK

SLIDER TRACK

SINGLE SIDE MOUNT BLOCK

TENSION TURNBUCKLE

CROSSHEAD ASSEMBLY CONSISTING OF

CYLINDER

METAL YOKE W/BRAZED ATTACHMENT NUT
DOUBLE SHEAVE BLOCK W/BECKET
UHMW POLYPROPYLENE SLIDER

Screenwire Panels

by David Glenn

During the early design meetings for a recent production of Eugene O'Neill's *Ah, Wildnerness,* Tom Haas, Artistic Director of the Playmakers Repertory Company told me the Monet paintings, specifically "The Lunch" and "Poppy Field" had the feeling and colors that were right for the show. In order to create this quality for the entire production, we decided to change the setting from three interiors and one exterior to a single exterior set that would be redressed from scene to scene. This change was due, in part, to the limited size of our stage, but more importantly, we felt that in one environment we could create the feeling of a wondrous world of youth, of hot summer days and cool nights, in effect "Ah, Wilderness."

When I began thinking about creating the Monet effect, I remembered a set I had seen at the Long Wharf Theatre that used a crumpled screenwire cyclorama to create a cloudy sky. What struck me the most was the way the screenwire took the light. If there was a way to use the screenwire to create a "Monet" garden onstage—complete with trees, flowers, bushes, and sky through scene painting and lighting—we might get the look we wanted. As it turned out the process of construction and painting of the screenwire panels was relatively simple. However, lighting the panels effectively proved to be more complex.

We first painted the trees and shrubs on the screenwire with undiluted clear vinyl paint tinted with aniline dyes. After the paint dried, we crumpled the screenwire randomly in the leaf areas and in long creases following the lines of the tree trunks. We then hung the panels, using sandwich battens, one behind the other going upstage in a layered pattern to make a grove of trees. After hanging the panels, we cut away some of the unpainted screenwire in the downstage panels, just as one would a

cut drop, but left large areas of the upstage unpainted screenwire in place. This created a bold and striking downstage area that became softer and hazier the farther you went upstage. The final look was one of an endless forest that just faded out to no detail but did not go to black.

In designing the lighting for the show, my desire was to create a dappled effect that would be similar to Monet's style of brushstrokes. This was done by a heavy use of leaf gobos from the front position in addition to area lighting and bright backlighting on the screenwire panels. We tried a number of different types of instruments as backlights and found that striplights worked the best; they were

the most even. The light through the translucent paint was very alive, it was bright and airy but did not create a "candyland look." On the other hand, by using no backlight, the silhouettes of the trees were quite effective in enhancing the sense of darkness for the night scenes. One surprise that occurred was when certain shades of blue gel were used in the backlights the green dyes in the paint reacted with the color of the light and appeared to be purple or magenta. This was corrected by going to paler and greener shades of blue gel. We also found that as long as the backlight levels were equal to or greater than the front light and the gobos, the unpainted screenwire faded out. In a few

To create the feeling of a Monet background for the Playmakers Repertory Company production of *Ah, Wilderness*, designer Glenn used screenwire panels painted with a vinyl media. The process involved: painting the trees on screenwire on top of Visqueen sheeting (facing page, left) and, when dry, crumpling the screenwire in the leaf areas to give the surface texture (facing page, right). When painting, the holes in the screenwire are completely filled (right top). The panels were then hung on sandwich battens and heavily backlit to produce the desired dappled effect (right).

spots where there was serious spill from the front, we sprayed down the screenwire with flat black spray paint. The overall look of the show was quite striking: the trees were bright, colorful and luminescent, but with a sense of memory—it was a hot summer's day in a different age.

The following is a step-by-step explanation of the method we used. Although we used this process for trees, I feel that it would work for many other subjects and effects (i.e. tapestries, stained glass windows, etc.).

Materials

Screenwire—aluminum (12-16¢/sq. ft.) copper, brass (very expensive)
Paint—clear vinyl, gloss, or flat (Cal Western at $7.15/gallon; Kleer/Vogue at $7/gallon; Flo-Paint at $8/gallon). We tried all these paints and they all act similarily.
Aniline dye—mix 1 tablespoon of dye to 2 tablespoons boiling water to ½ gallon of clear vinyl. It is important that the paint not be diluted, otherwise it will not fill the spaces in the screenwire.
Visqueen sheeting

The process

1) Stretch Visqueen on floor and staple down very smoothly; all wrinkles will show in finished paint job.

2) Lay out the screenwire on top of the Visqueen and staple down, overlapping adjacent panels by one or more inches. The edges will be "glued" together invisibly. Cartoon the panel. For a shiny effect, cartoon backwards so that the side of the screen against the Visqueen is what will hang downstage. The smoothness of the Visqueen plus the fact that the paint settles through the screenwire produces a very shiny effect. For a matte effect, cartoon normally and perhaps use Flo-Paint's flat instead of gloss clear.

3) Mix paint and dye. Large amounts of paint (1 gallon covers 25-36 sq. ft.) are required for a panel of any size. Be sure to test each color on screenwire before painting panels, since color change from wet to dry is drastic. Also, do not use heat to dry panels—the color will be greatly affected.

4) Let dry thoroughly. Be careful when pulling up screenwire since wet paint does not adhere to it.

5) Attach sandwich battens and unstaple. Then crumple areas as desired for texture. Roll up battens loosely.

6) Hang panels and stretch to floor. Do not worry about tearing them since they are quite strong. Cut out areas as desired and touch up with black spray paint to kill any unwanted glare.

Variations on a theme

Rosco imports a transparent liquid plastic from Germany manufactured by Hausmann that apparently has greater "filling" power than the clear vinyls we used. This product might be used with chicken wire or hardware cloth instead of the screenwire. It comes in colors which can be mixed, but I have no idea how easily it can be tinted with dyes. I hope this will give someone a good idea to try out.

Originally published in May/June 1979

Textural Fiber Hangings

by Karen Huffman

The technical problems facing the Seattle Repertory Theatre's shop with the physical production for *Strider: The Story of a Horse* were common ones: the time and budget were limited, the scale was large, and weight had to be kept within a reasonable range for handling ease. It was the aesthetic goal, however, that was unusual.

Both the director, John Hirsch, and the designer, Richard Belcher, wanted to create a non-representational, organic environment for *Strider,* an allegory presented in a story-theatre format. Since Hirsch was particularly interested in using woven textures, from there the design concept evolved. At the shop the idea was translated into a technical problem: how to create a very thick, very dense, woven texture on a large scale. Since no traditional scenographic methods seemed suited to the project, two guest textile artists, Georgia and Jack Becker, were brought in as consultants and artists in residence.

Considering our limitations, the Beckers advised the use of foam strips woven on large wire mesh screens as the basic materials. Bunskin, the trimmed-off outer layer from the foam manufacturing process, and other types of industrial scraps are very inexpensive in volume. Moreover, the foam is lightweight and takes color well. Using varying widths of foam strips would help to create the desired natural, random effect.

After some experimentation it became clear that we should pre-color individual strips of foam for weaving, rather than try to overpaint them after the sculptural work was done. The approach compares with that of painting a drop—do the base coat and lay-in as quickly as possible, then

A backdrop made of fiber hangings was the principal component of Richard Belcher's set (facing page) for the Seattle Repertory Theatre's production of *Strider.* The fiber hangings were made of dyed foam strips (above, top) and woven through wire screens (above).

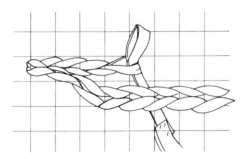

The fiber hangings were chain stitched together (diagram, above, center). Strings, ropes, and scrap foam pieces were added for texture (top). Photos: Mike Boulanger.

Variations on Foam Core Construction

Inspired by Richard Moore's article, "Large-scale Foam Core Construction," (Nov/Dec. '79) I adapted similar techniques to solve a stability problem inherent in the design of one of the major scenic elements for a recent production of *Blood Wedding* at the University of Connecticut.

The main element was a three-fold unit comprised of arches. The entire unit had to be free-standing and linked with double-action hinges to allow for various ground plan configurations of U, Z and delta. The units were approximately 12′ tall, 5′ wide and 3″ thick with legs that tapered to 3″ wide at the base. Hybrid construction consisted of a framing technique using 1″ x 3″ stock covered with 1/8″ paneling on both sides for the lower "leg" portion of the arch. The paneling sandwiched the styrene for about 18″ before stopping, helping to distribute stress to the top stress skin portion of the arch.

I opted to use gray bogus paper which we already stocked as a paint supply instead of rosin paper. The bogus paper was ripped into manageable sections, wetted down, and applied over a coat of polyvinyl glue which was brushed over the styrene and paneling. Additional glue was brushed over the wet bogus paper. Wetting the paper prevented bubbling which occurred when trying to glue dry paper. The wet paper also absorbed the glue, improving tensile strength—ideal for the stress-skin. Seams were overlapped and each layer was allowed to dry completely. Three layers were used, taking care to stagger seams which were always ripped edges.

Bogus paper covered both faces of each piece and carried around the edges, dutchman fashion, to totally enclose the styrene. This protected the fragile edges and improved the strength at the rabbet joint on each sandwich.

Final texturing was achieved by spraying a half-strength coat of polyvinyl glue over the arch and sprinkling Zonolite insulation. One final coat of the cut polyvinyl glue sealed the texture, which held up rather well during handling. The resultant stress-skinned units proved structurally sound and the light weight was appreciated by the actors who shifted the scenery a vista. Piecing the bogus paper did not seem critical—at least in this application. This experience leads me to believe that even newspaper could be used as an inexpensive covering material in this process if the layers are increased and flameproofing assured.

JACK NARDI
Emerson College, Boston

increase interest and depth with successive semi-transparent layers.

Next came the most difficult part of the process: organizing people and materials in the most efficient manner. During our first week of physical work, a team of artisans wove during the day, and Belcher and the Beckers worked out design elements and introduced other materials in the evening. By the second week the team, reduced in numbers, was working on the subtle, more time-consuming finish work—responding to the initial lay-in and working closely with the designer to achieve the desired effect.

Procedure

1 Fasten appropriate size wire mesh screen to batten and hang in an accessible location

The wire mesh used in this project was 6" square-gauge welded wire. Care was taken in determining the finished size of the textural hanging. If it had not conformed to the mesh spacing, some cheated alterations on an off-stage edge of the wire might have been necessary.

We cut the wire mesh screen into panels of the desired length and width. Initially each panel was hung horizontally so that we could work woven rows in long runs quickly, adjusting the working height as we went. The foam was left overnight to dry (pipe battens were required to support the wet, working weight), then the panels were rehung vertically for the finish work. In the shop our panels were hung on spot lines from the shop roof supports, in the same relative positions as intended for the stage—an ideal set up.

2 Cut and strip foam

The foam sheets were purchased in varying thicknesses, from ¼" to 2". Our cut widths also varied, from approximately 3" to 6". (The thicker the foam the narrower we cut the strips.) We stripped the bunskin off the foam strips, which doubled our volume of weaving material and added another variation to the overall surface texture.

3 Mix paint

In order to mix large volumes of paint and dye, we used metal trashcans, which were sealed to prevent leaks. The design determined the number of colors used. We used eight basic colors. The paint was mixed to a thin consistency, because the foam could be easily dipped and wrung out, and it would dry faster. We used casein paint and analine dye with Swift's flex glue for binder.

4 Dipping foam and skins

We dipped only as much foam as we could use in one day: the foam becomes too brittle to weave when it dries. We discovered that the foam took both dye and paint well, but the skins of the foam took only the dye well. After the dye or paint had dried, the glossy bunskin had the look of tanned leather, while the painted foam read very much like suede and soft rope. We used the variable surface qualities to our advantage.

5 Weave foam using chain stitch

This part can go very quickly, if the materials are assembled and the work force is organized. For our project one person—the designer or project coordinator—supervised the choices of color and texture, and the sizes and shapes of color areas. Two weavers worked from the front. Two staplers worked from the back, fastening foam strips together with plier-type staplers, to keep the weavers supplied with the necessary lengths of foam, and patching tears. Two workers kept the paint stock mixed and dipped foam. We rotated jobs during breaks to avoid the monotony of routine work. At the end of each work day, the staple guns were thoroughly cleaned of paint and dye.

6 Add center of interest with texturing

The material possibilities and design choices here are limitless. Belcher and the Beckers chose various sizes of rope, sisal, and cargo nets from a collection of scavenged materials. They used bundled foam sheets, which we had previously used as work floor mats, to help absorb all the wet paint. The mats were beautifully mottled and worked in bundled forms as major centers of interest in the hangings. The ropes were looped loosely around and over the bundles, creating a visual line that ran across the panels.

Contrasting colored foam and erosion cloth were interwoven to break up large blocks of color in the base coat of the weaving. These also helped emphasize the texture.

Depending on the design, various lengths of strings and nets could be woven into the hanging. For our design, the "hair" was part of the dense, animal-like, organic quality of Belcher's set. We used small diameter sisal, cotton string, and raffia in 3' to 5' lengths, dipped to appropriate tones and tied on in groupings, which accented and softened the other design elements.

7 Overspatter with thin dye wash

We recommend that any final overspatter be tested, because too much or too opaque a spatter will disguise the heavy texture you have worked to create. In order to be effective, the combinations and placement of the original dipping colors should be as close to the finished look as possible.

8 Flameproofing

Dipping apparently washes out the factory flameproofing of the foam. The problem possibly could be solved, however, by mixing the flameproofing chemicals directly into the paint solutions. Also, latex paints would be worth experimenting with on a similar project.

After our project was completed and hanging in the theatre, flame tests were made on the scrap foam. As it was obvious that some flameproofing was necessary, we sprayed on a commercial chemical, Flamort CP, recommended for fabrics. Spraying in the theatre was messy, and we would try to incorporate a flame retardant in an earlier step (perhaps, as noted, in the paint mixing) in a future project.

Tools and equipment

Plier-type staple guns
Hog rings and ringer (for fastening very thick foam)
Foam cutter
Scissors and mat knives
Scaffolding (for work at heights)
Battens and line

Work force

1 designer
2 guest artists for one week
3 full-time artisans for two weeks (one as coordinator)
4 jobbed-in workers for three days for basic weaving
1 miscellaneous scout for one week to do primarily phone research
1 foam cutter for one week

Originally published in August/September 1982

Stained Glass

by Leo Gambacorta

Designer Bill Mikulwicz's set for last season's production of *The Show Off* at the Arizona Theatre Company called for the creation of realistic stained glass windows on a small budget. The materials I chose were as inexpensive as you could wish: five sheets of 2' x 4' x ⅛" pebbled Plexi @ $2.00 a sheet, two tubes of non-adhesive black caulk @ $1.75 per tube, and, to color the glass, transparent watercolor mixed with a clear latex tile seal. Since the paint came from the theatre's stock and the art supplies were my own, the cost to the company came to $13.50.

For each of the four windows, an outline was scaled out of brown paper. Next, the Plexi was placed over the outline, with the pebble side up, and the outline was traced on the Plexi with the caulk, which was flattened and smoothed out when dry to simulate the frame of the glass pieces. Finally, the Plexi was turned over and painted with water color and tile seal to match the paint elevation. Two of the windows had to be pieced together, because their dimensions were larger than the Plexi sheets.

Using the downstage plane of the glass for the outline and the upstage plane for the pigment gave depth to the glass, leaving the audience with an impression of realism in keeping with the production concept.

Originally published in May/June 1980

GINA BIAMONTE

For a production of *The Show Off* at the Arizona Theatre Company, Leo Gambacorta created realistic stained glass windows (below) with pebbled Plexi, non-adhesive black caulk, transparent watercolors, and clear latex tile seal.

Elegant Etched Glass

In a recent production of *A Doll's House* at Western Virginia University, director John Whitty and I used a traditional folk art motif, emphasizing airiness and light colors. One large upstage center entrance—filled with etched glass doors and side panels—became the focus of the stage. Behind the doors was a glassed-in vestibule, in which entering and exiting characters could be seen subtly through the etched glass.

Materials for the etched glass include:

1 Plexiglas, preferably sealed in paper on both sides— ⅛" for large windows; ¹/₁₆" for small windows. Plexiglas costs about $80 for a 4' x 8' sheet. You may find it necessary to coat one side with plain contact paper on which to draw the design.

2 Frost spray. I use No Vue Window Frosting, a Nybco product, No. NV9, available at hardware stores for about $3.25 per can.

3 A sharp X-acto knife.

4 A full-sized cartoon of the design.

Materials at hand, what to do next?

1 Cut all windows or panels to fit the spaces for which they are designed. Preposition them using precut screw holes to install, or some kind of frame; then remove them.

2 Make a full-scale cartoon of the design on butcher paper, taping the design to the plain paper adhered to the Plexiglas.

3 Cut around the entire design with the X-acto knife. Do not bear down too hard.

4 Peel away *only* the portion that is to be frosted. Leave intact all the pieces that are to remain clear.

5 Frost. Observe no smoking and ventilation procedures for your shop, as the spray is toxic. However, a fan is NOT recommended, as the spray needs to settle on the Plexiglas surface. Spray about 4" to 5" from the surface just until it looks thoroughly wet. Frost one entire surface without stopping and allow to dry in a horizontal position for about 30 minutes.

6 Remove the remaining paper pieces by lifting corners with the knife and peeling them away. The areas covered by paper during the spraying step will now appear clear and shiny. To dull some of the shine, if necessary, apply a dusting of frost spray over the completed work. Take care not to apply too much, or it will look spotty.

W. JAMES BROWN
West Virginia University
Morgantown, Virginia

Flat Black Solution

Flat black latex paint is one of the most commonly used paints in regional theatre. It's also great on floors, except that it picks up dust and looks grey. Well, if you wet mop the floor with an acrylic floor wax, you can solve this problem. You lose a bit of the flatness, but the floor will remain a nice, dense black even after people walk on it. And the black paint will last longer. A must for black boxes.

SCOTT KOUE
Designer/Technical Director
Davis, California

Styrofoam and Canvas

Recently I needed a platform top that would have little resonance, but had no carpet, padding, or other material normally used under the top layer of platform top covering. We did, however, have many sheets of ¾″ styrofoam which I used over the platform tops with a final top of ⅛″ masonite and covered the whole thing with canvas. It turned out to be very effective, resilient, and resonance-free.

MARC L. RUBENSTEIN
Lighting Designer University of Akron

50 Cent Beams

For a production of *Deathtrap* at the Barn Theatre, we constructed heavy beams for about 50¢ a linear foot. Insulation Styrofoam measuring 2′ x 14″ x ¾″ was ripped to form the three visible sides and ¼″ ply was ripped in 8′ lengths to form the support (or offstage side) of the beam. Styrofoam glue (Fullers MAX Bond) in tubes was applied with a gun and gave a very sturdy structure. The Styrofoam was carved and spackling compound applied to give texture. Then the beams were painted. These were attached to the flats with machine screws through the back of the flat into the beams' ¼″ ply support.

RICHARD DESILETS
Kenvil, New Jersey

Solutions for Painting and Plumbing

by Phillip Grayson

Painting with tank sprayers; updating the process

The tank, weed, or garden sprayer has been proven an efficient tool for the scenic artist. Lynn Pecktal, Ned Bowman, and Harold Burris-Meyer and Edward Cole all refer, in their respective texts, to tank sprayer scenic painting. Sizing, base coating, and spattering can be more easily and quickly executed with a sprayer than with brush techniques.

The primary limitation of the tank sprayer is the frequent pumping needed to maintain air pressure. It is common for beginning scene painters to have inconsistent results from failure to maintain air pressure or to end up with paint rings on the drop from the bottom of the tank while pumping up air pressure.

The problem of pumping can be overcome by modifying the basic sprayer. Ned Bowman in *Handbook of Technical Practice for the Performing Arts* (Inter-Galactic Serial Shop Cookbook, available from Scenographic Media), shows a sprayer which has been modified by adding a tire valve to permit filling the sprayer from an air line with a tire chuck. This practice requires that the air supply be carefully regulated. Sprayer manufacturers test their tanks at pressures far above those reached by hand pumping; even 80-100 psi can be put into the tank without rupturing. However, empirical tests have demonstrated that the hose between the sprayer nozzle and tank will rupture well before 100 psi is reached—resulting in paint gushing toward the grid. In fact, by having the sprayer designed so that the hose ruptures before the tank explodes, serious injury from shrapnel is prevented.

Figure 1 shows a tank sprayer equipped with an adjustable pressure relief valve as well as a tire valve. The adjustable relief valve can be pre-set to any pressure the scenic artist desires. In my experience, 30-40 psi is sufficient pressure for scenic painting. Any source of compressed air can be applied to the tire valve with a standard automotive air chuck. The tank will fill until reaching the pre-set pressure, then the relief valve will vent the excess and the sprayer will be ready for operation.

In order to calibrate the sprayer, first fill the tank approximately half full with water. Then loosen the lock nut on the relief valve and back off on the relief valve adjustment. Apply air at the tire valve until the relief valve triggers, then use an automotive tire guage to measure the pressure in the tank. By tightening the relief valve, the pressure capacity will be raised. After the desired pressure is set, tighten the lock nut on the pressure relief valve. The sprayer can be repeatedly energized to this pressure and since all hand pumping is eliminated, energizing the tank is a short operation. Air pressure can be maintained easily to achieve consistent and controlled paint application.

Water supply on stage; plumbing the depths

Many productions require the use of running water on stage. Just about any show with a kitchen or a bar needs running water to reinforce a realistic style of production. A further enhancement is the addition of plumbing noises. One common approach to onstage

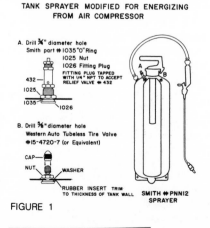

TANK SPRAYER MODIFIED FOR ENERGIZING
FROM AIR COMPRESSOR

A. Drill ¾″ diameter hole
   Smith part #1035″0″Ring
   1025 Nut
   1026 Fitting Plug
   FITTING PLUG TAPPED
   WITH ¼″ NPT TO ACCEPT
   RELIEF VALVE #432
   432
   1025,
   1035
   1026

B. Drill ⅜″ diameter hole
   Western Auto Tubeless Tire Valve
   #15-4720-7 (or Equivalent)

CAP
NUT
   WASHER
   RUBBER INSERT TRIM
   TO THICKNESS OF TANK WALL
   SMITH #PNNI2
   SPRAYER

FIGURE 1

Originally published in May/June 1980

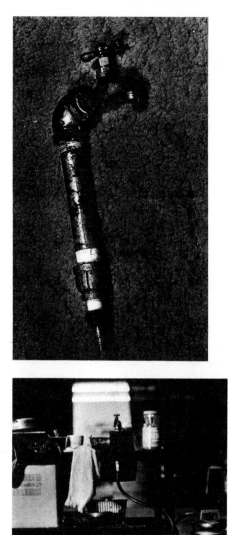

A tank sprayer used as a self-contained pressure water system (above) provided an onstage water supply for a production of *The Effect of Gamma Rays on Man in the Moon Marigolds* at James Madison University. Plumbing fittings were used to adapt a male air line connector to the faucet (top).

water supply has been to run a garden hose to an offstage tap, attaching the other end to a faucet on the set. This approach has often resulted in flooded stages from leaks in the hose, as well as providing the water at too-high a pressure. Another problem with this system is trying to rig a drain to cope with an unlimited source of supply. A bucket under the onstage sink can be filled to overflowing very rapidly when the sink is being supplied from a tap.

A second method of water supply involves the use of a recirculating electric pump such as the type for display foun-

tains. Edmund Scientific Company supplies small, low-voltage pumps which easily can be mounted in a drain bucket to supply a faucet. Problems with this approach are coordinating the switching of the pump with the actor turning the faucet and disguising the pump's electric hum from the audience.

A third variety of water system uses an offstage gravity tank to supply a faucet. As long as the set design includes a wall on which to hang the reservoir, a gravity system can be simple and fail-safe. The output pressure and volume will be adequate and there is no inappropriate pump noise.

A fourth option for water supply on stage involves the use of a tank sprayer as a self-contained pressure water system. Figures 1 and 2 illustrate the arrangement used in the James Madison University theatre production of *The Effect of Gamma Rays on Man in the Moon Marigolds*.

To fabricate this system, remove the weed sprayer wand and trigger assembly from the sprayer hose. Then use plumbing fittings to adapt a male air line connector to the faucet. Finally, the male air line connector is secured to the end of the sprayer hose with a clamp. Fill the tank half full with water, add desired air pressure, and open the faucet.

This system eliminates the limitations of the other three systems and is virtually the only possibility in production situations involving a turn-table or arena or thrust areas. The major advantages of using a self-contained system are 1) the opening of the faucet directly controls the water supply and eliminates cueing problems and 2) there are no water lines running backstage. Also, if a small amount of water is used in conjunction with a large amount of air pressure, very convincing plumbing noises come from the tap when the faucet is opened.

Sources

D. B. SMITH COMPANY
Main Street
Utica, New York   13503
Smith sprayers and parts

SURPLUS CENTER
Box 82209
Lincoln, Nebraska   68501
Adjustable pressure relief valves,
air hose and pipe line fittings,
tire service air chucks

EDMUND SCIENTIFIC COMPANY
Edscorp Building
Barrington, New Jersey   08007
Small water pumps

Spatter Techniques

Anyone who has painted scenery knows that spattering is the most often used texture coat

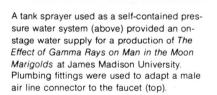

in the theatre. To overcome some of the problems involved in the process, I have developed a technique using a stiff round cleaning brush instead of a paint brush. This has proven to be less tiring and allows for more control.

Instead of snapping or rapping the brush, simply draw your hand over it and the bristles will snap the paint onto the surface. The 8" Sun Brush, manufactured by Wright-Bernet Inc., Hamilton, Ohio, is recommended.

To spatter with the scrub brush, pour a quantity of paint into a shallow container, such as a roller pan, covering to a depth of not more than ¼". Then dip the brush into the paint just enough to cover the ends of the bristles. Scrape or shake off excess paint.

The actual spattering technique can be refined through experimentation, as paint thickness and effects desire will vary. Dragging one hand across the top of the brush while holding it near or over the material works well on both vertical and horizontal scenery. However, as with all vertical scenery, running may occur.

TERRY HAYES
Davis & Elkins College
Elkins, W. Virginia

Scenic Solutions with Fibers

by Carey Wong

The use of fibers and soft hanging goods, such as ropes or woven materials, is not new in scenic design, but in our work with the Portland Opera, we have developed some interesting scenic solutions by utilizing these materials. More and more these days, designers in regional theatre must be concerned as much with the cost of having their designs realized as with the interest and integrity of the designs themselves. Of

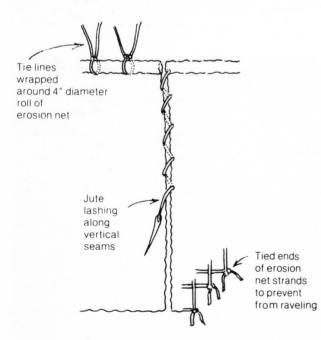

Tie lines wrapped around 4" diameter roll of erosion net

Jute lashing along vertical seams

Tied ends of erosion net strands to prevent from raveling

course, as a rule, soft goods like painted drops or hanging non-practical pieces have generally been less expensive to construct than hard goods like platforming and 3-dimensional scenery. It makes sense, then, for a designer to be aware of the scenic effects that can be created with soft goods.

To create a forest

Probably the best known fiber material with considerable texture and seemingly infinite uses for scenic design is

erosion netting. The material comes in large rolls that are approximately 4' wide in natural taupe or dyed green. For a Portland Opera production of von Weber's *Der Freischütz* in 1974 we utilized a series of cut erosion net drops to suggest the claustrophobic, threatening quality of the German forest which becomes a tangible force in the opera.

Procedure

1. In constructing each erosion net drop, we first calculated the number of widths of material needed which would have to be placed side by side and sewn with vertical seams to create the full size of the cut drop.

2. Next, we lashed together these widths at their edges with thin jute twine using very large needles generally employed in sewing through thick canvas or leather.

3. Instead of using the usual webbing for the top of drops to attach them to the pipes, we decided it would be easier to roll the tops of the erosion net drops until we had about a 4" diameter roll and then to run the tie lines through this roll, thus securing its tightness and allowing the tie lines to have proper placement. The tie lines were placed 6" apart because of the weight of the erosion net.

4. The work on the uneven cut-edge portions of the drops took time. All loose and irregular edges were knotted and hand-tied to adjacent loose strands. If this had not been done, the erosion net drops would have started to unravel. Although this procedure was time consuming, it proved the best way to preserve the frequently irregular outside shape of the drops.

5. After each erosion net drop was constructed, we added tonalities to its basic green color using thinned down mixtures of latex paint and aniline dyes applied by an air-compression paint gun.

6. Once the paint was dry, we began to attach additional materials to the basic drop to create greater density and diversity in each piece. Other irregularly shaped pieces of

Carey Wong's design for the Portland Opera's production of *Der Freischütz* featured a series of cut drops of erosion net to suggest the claustrophobic, threatening quality of the German forest (facing page, top). A spider web cutout drop combined jute roving with the erosion net (diagram above of how to hand-tie the cut edges) to make an actual pattern that further enhanced the structural units and 3-dimensional objects such as trees and rocks (facing page, bottom). Photos: Edmund Keene

erosion net were attached to the basic drop using the same lashing procedure mentioned above. Jute roping which had been pre-dyed in a series of earth colors and fireproofed was attached to the tops of the drops at 6"-8" intervals, and various suggestive macrame-like designs were created by tying and weaving different strands of the rope together. In some cases we attempted to create actual patterns using the rope on erosion net, such as a spider web pattern for a drop which flew in during the Wolf's Glen scene. Again, at the specific points where we needed precise angles marked or created with the rope, the rope was secured to the erosion net using bits of thin jute cord. In all cases, the macrame-like rope patterns were attached at various places to the erosion net drop with bits of jute cord so that the rope patterns would not become inextricably tangled up when the drops were folded or rolled and transported from scene shop to theatre.

7. Additional dyed and ripped rags were added for other effects on some cut drops while for a number of erosion net drops in the final scene of the opera, skeletal outlines of tree branches cut out of burlap were glued to the back side of the erosion net. When backlighted, the shapes of these branches could be seen through the erosion net.

Things to be remembered

Generally, erosion netting is not fireproofed when purchased from a distributor. Like all other fiber materials, it is extremely flammable. Hence, it is important to thoroughly soak the finished drops with a fireproofing agent before using them onstage. Erosion net and jute roving can shed small particles of lint and fiber into the air when moved or brushed against, and such particles occasionally may make it more difficult for singers or actors to perform. One solution is to spray the stage area with a fine mist of water before each act or scene, since this will help settle many of the particles.

Cost and distributor

We purchased our erosion netting from the Charles R. Watts company in Seattle. Each roll is 4' wide and contains 100 running yards. It costs $50 per roll. For *Der Freischütz,* Portland Opera used 15 rolls of erosion netting and from this the scene shop was able to build 10-12 cut drops, many of which were full-stage drops (our stage proscenium opening is 60' x 30').

To create architectural projections with fibers

One step beyond actually using erosion net or macrame-like elements in a setting is to have them photographed and to make projection slides from them. For Portland Opera's American premiere production of Krenek's *Life of Orestes* in 1975 we utilized a series of projections for the entire opera.

Procedure

1. In one location of the production, Athens, the director wanted to suggest the lightness and sophistication of the populace. She also wanted to convey the impression of an eclectic classicism in the scene, so we manufactured small pieces of macrame (all in ½" scale) inside steel rod frameworks to resemble a Greek temple pediment and columns.

2. Once constructed, these pieces were mounted on solid-color velour backgrounds.

3. The artwork was photographed and made into projection slides at Background Engineers in Los Angeles. They produced slides which would withstand prolonged heat from the projectors using a lamination technique in adhering film to glass and also compensated in the photographing for the

For *Life of Orestes* (1975), small pieces of macrame (in ½" scale) in steel rod frameworks were mounted on velour backgrounds. The artwork was then photographed and made into projection slides (below) using a lamination technique that adhered the film to glass. Three projector images overlapped to produce a 60' wide x 30' high image on the backdrop (above). Photo: Edmund Keene

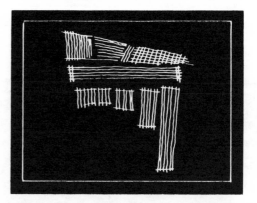

keystone effect encountered in projection.

4. For each scene in the opera, three 5K projector images overlapped to produce an image on the backdrop that was 60' wide and 30' high. Slides could be changed from the stage floor by the stage manager through a switch which activated a slide change mechanism on all three projectors simultaneously.

Things to be remembered

The artwork photographed best, of course, when mounted on dark-color backgrounds. The major problem with any sort of projection on a background intended to create a scenic statement is that as the stage lighting becomes brighter at the front portion of the stage, the visibility of the projections decreases. This is especially true in a front projection situation, such as the one we were using for *Life of Orestes*. The scenes in which projection worked the best for us were those in which moody atmospheric lighting or very specific area lighting were called for on the rest of the stage.

Cost and distribution

Approximately $25/slide from Background Engineers, L.A.

Carey Wong used a vertical rope motif as the central design feature for *La Cenerentola* (1977). Tightly stretched lengths of jute were evenly space on battens to suggest pillars (above and right), as well as topiaries and walls (top, above). Other scenic effects that carried out the motif were a rope curtain in three sections used in front of a painted show curtain at the top of the show (center, above) and a rope rain curtain (top). Photos: Edmund Keene

To create rope pillers, walls, and a rain curtain

For a recent Portland Opera production of Rossini's *La Cenerentola* in 1977, which played both in Portland and Seattle, the director Ghita Hager felt that she wanted this version of the Cinderella story to have a lightness and deftness of touch that was similar to ballet. We decided to place the entire action of the opera on a slightly raked stage and to make as many scene changes as possible in view so that the action of the opera could be continuous. After a number of experiments and trials, we decided to utilize tightly stretched lengths of rope evenly spaced on battens to suggest the walls, pillars, and topiaries called for in the production.

Since the vertically stretched rope motif was the central design feature scenically for our production of *La Cenerentola,* the director and I felt that we should carry this idea even further. A rear rope curtain against a black velour backdrop, imperceptably lighted, played throughout the show, while a front rope curtain in three sections was used in front of a painted show curtain at the opening of the show. In the storm or "temporale" sequence of Act II during which Ramiro travels from his palace to the home of Magnifico to see if the bracelet which the fleeing Angelina left at his palace fits any of its inhabitants, the rope curtain was flown in front of the set for Don Magnifico's mansion and was lighted so that it looked like a curtain of falling rain. While people scurried under umbrellas across the stage in front of the rain curtain, the Magnifico house behind also showed the storm of tempers in the characters with the two stepsisters fighting each other and chasing their father all around the set. It proved an effective theatrical moment which added a further dimension to the utilization of the tautly hung rope strands. Because of the kind of simple scenic effects used, the costumes proved to be a more important design feature in the show with a carefully selected color palette.

Procedure

In constructing all vertically hung rope pieces, the procedure was the same.

1. After experimentation in the theatre using 4-ply jute rope, we found that the best spacing between rope strands was either 3″ or 4″. Less than 3″ spacings made the rope look cramped or crooked if each piece were not perfectly taut, while more than 4″ intervals completely dissipated the effect of the rope curtain, wall, or column feeling that we wanted to convey.

2. All rope was dyed first in aniline dyes to the designated colors and fireproofed.

3. The rope pieces were cut to the desired lengths.

4. The ends of the rope pieces were air gun stapled into one batten and then glued and sandwiched between the first batten and another—all 1″ x 3″s. All of this work, of course, had to be done with care, and after moving into the theatre some of the vertical ropes became a bit limp due to the change in temperature between scene shop and theatre.

5. The limp or loose rope strands were made taut by stapling the excess of rope at the bottom of a loose strand to the batten at the bottom. Usually, this looseness consisted at most of 1″-2″ of rope, so that one small loop of rope stapled to the bottom batten could correct the problem.

Things to be remembered

As with erosion netting and other fibers, fireproofing and the lint situations must be remembered. When using vertically stretched ropes, some care must be used in lighting such scenic pieces, especially when depicting one layer against another. If such scenic pieces start to sway or are lighted improperly, a moire pattern can be set up which will end up distracting the view.

Cost and distributor

The cost of 4-ply jute rope is minimal. We used close to 10,000 yards of it for our production of *La Cenerentola,* and the material budget for it came to under $500. It is available through practically any craft, hobby or weaving store.

In summary, jute rope and materials such as erosion net is as well as other fibers can be useful to a designer for creating a number of novel effects when judiciously used. In comparison to built, dimensional, practical scenery, the material costs are less, as well. But like all other materials, rope and fibers won't necessarily work for all shows. They are merely one more set of items that an experienced designer can pull out of his bag of theatrical tricks to use when time and occasion are right.

Originally published in September 1978

Out of the Hospital and onto the Stage

by Gregg Olsson

At the University of Washington's School of Drama, we developed a technique for "semi-scrim" backdrops and legs for a production of *Uncle Vanya* (directed by Robert Loper, set by Gregg Olsson, and lighting by David Percival). This technique was not only inexpensive and relatively uncomplicated but suggested a great amount of visual depth in a very shallow area.

The problem facing the designers was to combine a Chekhovian forest with the masking and backdrop that enclosed the upstage third of the ¾ arena stage. Because of the design's simplicity and realism, and the proximity of the audience, realistically painted legs and backdrops were not considered. And as there were only 3′ between the back wall of the theatre and the backdrop, 3′ between this drop and the second leg, and 5′ between the second leg and the first, projections and gobos were out of the question. To create the undistorted, come-and-go tree silhouettes, which have more depth than simple cutouts would, a layering of a scrim-like material called Celestra, a Crown Zellerbach product, was combined with opaque painted and paper cutout tree silhouettes.

Celestra is a polypropylene material used for hospital gowns and bedding. It comes in various densities and widths. For *Uncle Vanya* we used one ounce per sq. yard density in the 5′8″ width and ½ oz. per sq. yard density in the 6′8″ width. The wholesale price was $.06 per ½ oz. per sq. yard.

Construction

The steps for creating this semi-scrim forest were simple once initial experimentation was completed. First, because we were using white Celestra (it comes in a limited array of colors), the denser, downstage layer had to be treated with some kind of pigment. To keep the Celestra's translucency, aniline dye was sprayed on in three coats, until the desired shade

"Semi-scrim" backdrops and legs for a production of *Uncle Vanya*, at the University of Washington's School of Drama, were built with Celestra, a polypropylene material more often used for hospital gowns and bedding. When the material was painted and used in two layers, which sandwiched a layer of paper cut-outs (drawing, right), its translucency gave the appearance of variable tree silhouettes (photo).

ISOMETRIC DETAIL
SHOWING CELESTRA LAYERING

DYED 1 OZ. CELESTRA

BOGUS PAPER CUT-OUT OF TREE SILHOUETTES

½ OZ. CELESTRA W/ PAINTED SILHOUETTES

was reached. Using enough binder it would not rub off—although it could be scratched.

The next step was to sew the widths together into the desired rough sizes. To achieve the sharp-edged silhouette of the first layer of trees, bogus paper silhouettes were cartooned, cut out, and glued to the back of the dyed first layer. (Back-painting the tree directly onto the material proved unsuccessful, as the paint bled through.) When gluing the paper on, small amounts of contact cement were used only in select areas, as white glue also bled and puckered the fabric.

Next, we prepared the second layer (the ½ oz. fabric). This was dyed a dark color (to prevent the backlight from bouncing upstage) and sewn into panels. These were stretched onto plastic drop cloths (plastic to keep the fabric from sticking to the floor) before more silhouettes were painted with black latex paint. To mask seams in both layers of the fabric, "trees" were strategically placed. Then both layers were stretched over a 1" x 1" wood frame.

Stretching them 1" apart threw the second layer just out of focus; varying this distance produced interesting effects. For the irregular tree-like profile at the onstage edge, we bent 1" conduit to match the bogus paper cartoon and then connected it to the wood frame.

Onstage

Each leg was lighted with 1,500w 8" Fresnel per color wash. Striplights on the floor were focused onto a bounce drop 3' upstage of the backdrop. Additional depth and texture was created by back skidding gobos.

Since fire was used onstage, the Celestra had to be flameproofed as it would sustain a flame.

Materials

In all, the four legs (two 14' x 17' and two 8' x 17') and backdrop (17' x 33') cost under $75 for lumber, conduit, dye, paper, and flame retardant. We used a total of 436 sq. yards of the one ounce and the ½ oz. Celestra, which came to $52.32 and $26.16 respectively at wholesale. For information on Celestra and where it can be purchased, contact Paul Tomkins in the Non-Woven Fabrics Division of Crown Zellerbach, in Camas, Washington (206) 835–8787.

Originally published in January 1984

Supergraphing Sets and Costumes for The Life of Orestes

by Carey Wong

The use of supergraphics and photo blow-ups in stage design has become increasingly widespread as a method of abstracting theatrical realism and of making a comment on the supposed "realism" of the stage action portrayed. This is by no means a new idea. But the attempt to integrate actual settings, properties, and costumes with supergraphic properties and overlays on costumes and set pieces is somewhat novel. This approach was attempted this past November (1975) in the Portland Opera Association (Oregon) production of the American premiere of Ernst Krenek's *Life of Orestes*. Written in 1928-29, the opera basically follows the plot of Aeschylus' *Oresteia*—yet its musical idiom is a clever blending of late 19th century and early 20th century influences, including echoes of Mahler, Hindemith, Schumann, Schubert, Handel, Puccini, Weill, Gershwin, and Joplin.

The opera is made up of diverse musical and situational elements. Because of this and because the composer intended (as *New Yorker* critic Andrew Porter pointed out) "no evocation of period, whether prehistoric, classical or Hellenic, and no specific local color, only the generalized South-North antithesis," director Ghita Hager and I chose an eclectic approach. One that mixed historical influences from 1000 B.C. to 2000 A.D. into the production design, while also attempting to generalize silhouettes and outlines. Both of us viewed the opera as an interpretation of a timeless Greek story, but with modern overlays and aspects in addition. For us, a geological equivalent to the opera was the image of a mineral bed with layer upon layer of rock formation accumulated over the ages, one on top of the other. The basic Greek story was the base rock or lowest level and in attempting to get to that story one had to burrow through the other historical overlays and interpretations. This lead us to use supergraphics because they could provide visual overlays and visual layers to the set pieces, props, and costumes. They could at times comment on the exaggerated nature of the situations—or at others emphasize significant themes or motives in the opera.

Map panels telegraphed the supergraphic theme and the character of the opera's four major locations.

Setting and concept: 4 locations, 4 looks

The set for the opera consisted of a few carefully selected elements. All action took place on a massive raked stage, painted to resemble a generalized mineral bed. For each of the opera's eight scenes in four major locations furniture and set props (an altar, magic mirror or fair stands for examples) were added as required. A painted backdrop (again suggesting geological textures) behind the rake functioned as a projection surface for slides of sculptural collages. These suggested materials of the four major settings in the opera (stone for Argos, rope and webbing for Athens, stretched hides and skins for Northland, and abstract foliage for the mountaintop). Against this stark and simple format, costuming and fanciful hand props provided the major visual statement and created a kaleidescope of fashion and style. The final elements of the overall design were a show curtain consisting of panels of oversized antique map details, and a complex lighting plot which allowed for a variety of color, tone, and mood during the piece.

In addition to relating one particular type of material (through projection) to each of the four opera locations, director Hager and I also tried to find various groupings of supergraphics that would heighten the distinctiveness of each setting. For "Archaic Argos," (where Agememnon attempts to sacrifice Iphigenia, and where later he, Klytemnestra and Aegisthus are murdered) we chose drawings of warriors from Attic vases, as well as stylized plants, flowers, insects, and beasts. This was to emphasize the blood lust, the mob psychology and relative primitivism of this tyrannical civilization. In contrast, for "Charming Athens," (where Orestes is enslaved for destroying a shooting gallery and is later freed from the guilt of murdering his mother and her lover) all manner of words and abstract symbol diagrams were used for blow-ups. This reinforced the literate, sophisticated, inquiring nature of the enlightened, if slightly irreverent and blasé Athenian citizenry. "Mistic Northland" (where

In "Charming Athens," all manner of words and symbols reinforce the literate, sophisticated quality of the city in which Orestes is enslaved for destroying a theatre (top, and street acrobat, left) and later acquitted of murder charges. He is then lionized by such local civic organizations as the Athens Athletes Club and the 3 Graces Tea Circle (above).

Iphigenia materializes in a moonbeam and Orestes is re-united with his sister) took for its supergraphics pictorial symbols from the arcane and the occult. This stressed the superstitious, introverted, pre-civilized intellect yearning for enlightenment which characterized the inhabitants of this location. And finally for "Nature," (the mountaintop where Orestes ponders his life) Ghita Hager and I chose to make a statement through the very absence of supergraphics. This indicated the one "real" location in the opera. Where protagonist Orestes, away from the various psychological afflictions and affectations of the three other worlds, could make a choice about his destiny and contemplate the world at peace for a moment.

The distinctions set up among these four locales were also carried into other areas of the production. As a general palette for the opera blacks, dark browns, grays, and olives were used for Argos; light ochers, yellows, oranges, and siennas for Athens; dark grays, blues, and blacks for Northland; and mild greens, browns, and grays for Nature.

Each of the four settings also had a distinctive costume silhouette. For the chorus of Argos, it was a pleasant style, reminiscent of the dark, closely wrapped people of today's Cyprus or Sicily. The colors were near black in dark browns, grays, and olives. In contrast, the royal family was richly dressed in gowns, dresses, and tunics of resplendent brocades and silks of blacks, silvers, and reds. Red was reserved for the royal family in this production to symbolize royalty as well as blood lust.

The Athenian silhouettes were alluring and seductive; both as modern and as timeless as Homer and *Vogue*. The women were gowned and draped in pastels of earth and fruit tones, while the men sported fitted pants and tunics. There was an air of stylish frivolity and festivity in these costumes. If not naturally present, the ideals of youth and beauty were achieved cosmetically and there was an air of fantasy about the costumes. The motto of the Athenian scenes could be "All is for show. All is for sale."

Northland's inhabitants wore tunics and dresses in blue and gray fur, suede, leather, and homespun fabrics. The silhouettes were nomadic—Tartar and American Indian. On Nature's mountaintop, the sole inhabitant was a realistically dressed shepherd.

In the shop: problems and solutions

In as much as it was physically possible and dramatically justifiable, supergraphics were painted onto all set pieces, props, and costumes as well as in the projection artwork for this production of *Life of Orestes*. Whether these transferred onto a rock, a flat, or a dress made no difference—the method was the same in the scene, prop or costume shop. A photocopy of the image to be transferred was placed in an opaque projector. Its size and positioning determined and then the outline was traced by hand on the receiving surface.

What did vary, however, were the media used to achieve the best transfer in each case. What follows is a practical explanation of the variations and the problems encountered along the way and their solution.

In general, we found that in transferring supergraphics onto surfaces it was best to do the work in a semi-lighted space, rather than in complete darkness. In the best situations, a light source well behind the opaque projector did not appreciably dim the image but did allow some indirect light. This made

it possible for the person outlining to see which parts were finished and which remained to be done. In complete darkness, it was almost impossible for a worker to distinguish a projected line from an already traced one.

For *Orestes* we only transferred line drawings and graphic works (like engravings and wood block prints) that had a high degree of contrast in their original format. We did not attempt to blow up photographs or graphics with significant gradations of gray—they had no place in our concept. However, we would suggest if photographs are to be used they should be copied or printed to produce a high black and white contrast eliminating as many gray tones as possible.

There seems to be no justifiable advantage for using overhead projectors instead of opaques, although both work. With an opaque projector any picture or graphic can be inserted and traced on the projection surface. With an overhead projector, a transparency of the artwork must be made first. This often reduces the sharpness of the original image. Also with an overhead there is more danger of the artwork slipping out of place.

In our scene shop, the supergraphic images were transferred on to flats and set pieces using liner brushes of various sizes and black latex or casein paints. Because of the distance at which the audience would be seated, precise detailing was not necessary. The supergraphics were painted on first so that later tones and washes in thinned latex or aniline dyes could be done over them yet still insure their visibility. In some cases, like the Argos altar, where background colors of the prop were so dark that the black graphics did not show up, highlights of white, yellow, and light brown were added.

In our costume shop, the labor was greater—we had originally intended that every portion of each costume should be covered with appropriate graphics. For the Argos scenes black graphics were chosen, while for the Athenians the blow-ups were in various multi-colors. On the other hand, the supergraphics of the Northland were painted in metallics—gold, silver, and bronze.

Waterproof, broad felt tip Magic Markers proved to be the most effective medium to transfer the images to the costumes. Unlike a paint which could become brittle and crack off when dry, the marker ink soaked into the fabric without affecting its texture. One problem encountered with the markers, however, was that the ink had a tendency to bleed on certain porous non-synthetic fabrics like the Indian cotton we used for the female chorus in the Athens scenes. We found no way of preventing or inhibiting this bleeding, and luckily the folds and drapings of the women's gowns made the fuzziness in outline of words on the dresses nearly undetectable. The felt-tip markers, however did work well on the majority of fabrics—ranging from chiffons and taffetas to wool blends and synthetics. Another related problem was to keep the marker ink from bleeding through multiple fabric layers. For instance in tracing on a cotton pant leg, the solution was placing layers of thick butcher paper inside the leg to separate the layers.

Finally, when large areas had to be filled in, after the outline had been traced, the rest was filled in under regular lights This allowed for maximum use of the rented opaque projectors and made the work more accessible.

Another problem was transferring designs to dark fabrics. As might have been expected it was also impossible to

Kinetic Leaves

My task as set designer for a musical-ballet adaptation of Grahame's *The Wind in the Willows*, at Southern Illinois University, was to create a kinetic environment using leaves as the major scenic element. In addition to a large mobile leaf, four leaves were suspended over the acting area, creating a sense of falling leaves. These had to be lightweight, maintain a definite shape, and have a texture that provided a good lighting surface.

The hanging leaves were constructed from chicken wire and Peel Filmite—a liquid vinyl used in industry to coat the walls of paint booths. The leaf foundations were built from 1″ chicken wire cut into shapes of flat leaves. With ⅛″ steel rod veins for support, the Peel Filmite was then sprayed on the chicken wire. The best results were produced when the forms were hung during spraying. After the surface dried, the leaves (which resembled cobwebs) were shaped. Continuous application of the Peel Filmite filled in the holes in the chicken wire, creating a semisolid surface of varying textures. These textures allowed for an excellent range of lighting effects. A fantastic look was obtained by spraying a mixture of shellac and bronze powders over a latex base coat.

Warning: Peel Filmite, which becomes a white, light-reflecting film when dry, contains two hazardous materials—toulene and methylene chloride. It has a flash point of 97.3 COC and can be extinguished with foam, carbon dioxide, and dry chemicals. Overexposure can cause headaches, nausea, and giddiness. Therefore 1) use in a well-ventilated space and wear respirators; 2) avoid clogging the spray gun by adding a small amount of acetone; and 3) spray in a space with a temperature of approximately 72° F. For additional information on Peel Filmite, contact DeBois Chemicals, a division of Chemed Corporation. A number of similar substances are available under various trade names.

TYRONE W. G. MARSHALL
Riverton, Wyoming

distinguish traced lines in black or a color on the fabric. In these cases our workers traced in white chalk and then painted the chalk lines in a regularly lighted area of the shop. To produce a visible enough contrast, images were painted in lighter browns or grays for the Argos chorus. For the Northland costume, the chalk lines were painted in metallics. In all these cases a thick acrylic paint proved the most workable. If a fabric texture was rough (as many of the Argos and Northland were) then the acrylic outline of the graphic was rough as well and this rustication merely reinforced the primal quality of both locations. Those costumes painted with acrylic did have a certain stiffness to them, but they served the singers well and there was no evidence during our run that the acrylics had begun to chip or crack.

Director Ghita Hager has suggested that her initial image for the visual production of *Life of Orestes* was that of a compass with four directions pointed to four different worlds that were somehow part of the same cosmos—this is what the production design set out to accomplish. Four unique locations populated by diverse inhabitants yet visually cohesive. In short we devised our own sort of *Gulliver's Travels*—Greek style.

Originally published in September 1976

ROBERT LEPPERT

CAREY WONG

CAREY WONG

ROBERT LEPPERT

Supergraphic patterning overlaid costumes, props, and settings in an attempt to parallel the blending of the various musical idioms with the visual presentation. The supergraphics served the dual function of reinforcing as well as commenting on the themes and situations in the opera. Costumes of the Athenean judges (left, top) were bordered in pertinent words and phrases. A nurse to the House of Atreus found solitude near a two-dimensional cutout statue of Athena (above). From the Northland sequence, the designs for Thoas' coat (top) were first traced in white chalk. These lines were painted with metallaic acrylics which were sprayed down with blue paints and dyes. Aegisthus' cloak (left, bottom) for the Argos sequence was deep pink with black felt-tip pen supergraphic drawings.

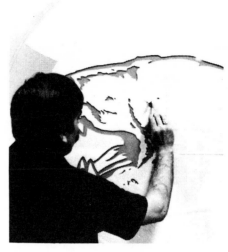

Acrylite Logo

For the Bowdoin Film Society's annual student film awards night, a permanent logo with a glass-like finish was required. Acrylite, an inexpensive acrylic sheet material with a high gloss finish, was selected for the project after testing a variety of materials. Local glass distributors will provide scraps of acrylic for a nominal price, if not for free. In addition to its relatively low cost, a sheet of Acrylite is sold with a protective paper backing which is important to the execution of the design.

First prepare a full scale drawing of the design, preferably on 100% rag vellum tracing paper with a felt tip pen. Although the protective paper backing on the sheet of Acrylite can be used, it is important to remember that the design must be applied in reverse since the high gloss finish is a result of the acrylic face and not necessarily the paint used.

Lay the drawing face down on the acrylic sheet and register its location. Remove it and spray with Scotch 3M spray adhesive. Carefully apply the design to the acrylic backing and smooth out all air pockets and wrinkles. With an X-acto knife cut out the entire design, applying firm pressure to insure that both the rag vellum and paper backing are cut. Do not remove any sections until the entire design has been scored.

Next, determine which of the colors selected is the darkest. With the X-acto knife remove the sections to be painted that color and spray an even coat. Lay the Acrylite sheet face down to spray it, otherwise the paint will seep beneath the paper backing. Allow the first color to dry. Remove the next sections of the paper backing to be sprayed with the same color. Krylon spray paints are recommended because the naptha and propane content of other paints affects the bonding of the Acrylite backing.

Once the other sections have been painted, apply a final neutral color to the entire painted surface and allow to dry before removing the paper backing on the face of the Acrylite sheet. Remove the backing and wash the surface with a 10% solution of mild detergent and lukewarm water and a soft cloth. This will remove surface static.

MICHAEL RODERICK
Bowdoin College
Brunswick, Maine

A Wood Graining Tool

by Richard Slabaugh

There is on the market a rubber squeegee that wipes away wet paint and leaves a smeared pattern closely resembling wood grain. The squeegee has a curved face covered with grooves arranged in a pattern of concentric semicircles. The rubber face removes much of the paint, partially revealing the underlying base coat, while the grooves trap some of the paint, leaving nearly parallel lines. The semicircular arrangement of grooves is designed to leave loops similar to the pattern of cut grain and the face is curved to allow the painter to vary the pattern produced.

This tool would seem to be of great help to those of us who have spent long hours carefully dry-brushing scenery with so-so results. There are serious draw backs, however, which limit the usefulness of these squeegees for painting scenery. First, they are small—intended for use on furniture and household woodwork—and too much time would be needed to grain an entire set. Moreover, the painted pattern, although realistic, is too tiny to read effectively from the stage.

A tool based on the same principle as these small squeegees can be manufactured in the shop simply and cheaply. It can be made big enough to cover large areas of scenery in a reasonable time, and it can be designed to produce the size of grain pattern desired. The shop at Washington State University made a graining tool consisting of a piece of cardboard tubing, either a carpet roll or a mailing tube, covered with Ethafoam rope. The Ethafoam is attached to the tube in a pattern of concentric semicircles, like the pattern of grooves found on the rubber squeegee. Ethafoam is laid side-by-side on the curved face of the

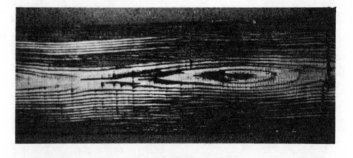

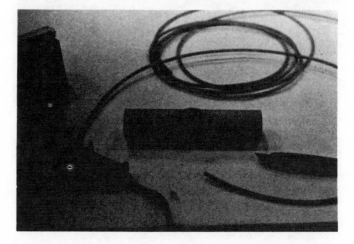

Wood grainers (top) can be made inexpensively using cardboard tubing and Ethafoam rope (bottom). The diameter of the Ethafoam determines the fineness of the grain (center).

tube, creating a scalloped surface that traps the wet paint and leaves smears of paint in the desired patterns.

The effectiveness of the graining tool is due to the properties of the Ethafoam rope. First, the Ethafoam is flexible, so it can take the double curvature needed to form semicircles on a curved surface. Second, the Ethafoam is resilient, so it can effectively wipe up wet paint. Ethafoam rope is a caulking material, a type of basking rod. It is made by the Dow Company and can be purchased from large specialty insulation firms. Many designers know the value of this flexible foam rod in making curved moldings and trim. Ethafoam comes in diameters of 1/4″, 3/8″, 1/2″, and larger. The smaller sizes work well for the construction of this grainer. The size of the grain pattern is determined by the diameter of the Ethafoam used: the smaller the rope, the smaller the grain.

Construction

A cardboard tube is cut to a length from 6″ to 12″. The length of the tube determines the width of the grained pattern and should be the width of one painted plank or board. The diameter of the tube determines, to some extent, the configurations of the grain patterns. The larger the tube diameter the coarser and more theatrical the grain. The smaller diameter produces finer and more realistic grain.

Lines are drawn dividing the tube lengthwise into two equal halves. Only one side is covered with the Ethafoam rope. The center point of one line is found, and this point becomes the center of the concentric semicircles of Ethafoam. To find this point, determine the smallest circle that can be made by bending the Ethafoam. (It will be approximately 1½″ for 1/4″ Ethafoam.) On the tube, draw a semicircle of this diameter with its center at the center point of the line. Lay a bead of hot melt glue along this semicircle, position the Ethafoam in it, and cut it to length. Lay another bead of hot glue next to the first semicircle of Ethafoam,

and apply a second row of Ethafoam, butting the rows together as tightly as possible. Note: the hot glue must be applied to the cardboard, not to the Ethafoam. The temperature of the glue directly from the gun is high enough to melt the Ethafoam. Care must also be taken not to touch the tip of the glue gun to the foam.

Row after row of Ethafoam is applied until the face of the cardboard tube is covered. A screen door handle is attached to the back of the tube, completing the construction of the grainer.

Painting procedures

The material to be painted should be well primed and layed flat so the graining can be done in the horizontal position. The scenery is coated with a base color and allowed to dry. The grain color is quickly applied and immediately wiped off with the grainer. Only the area that can be wiped with one pass of the grainer is painted at any time. The grainer is drawn across the surface with enough downward pressure to wipe off as much wet paint as desired. The grainer is rocked back and forth slightly as it is being drawn along. This rocking motion causes variations in the pattern, creating the wood-like effect. The painter can experiment and learn to control the patterns. The grainer is cleaned of excess paint between each operation by blotting it with rags.

The grainer works best on hard surfaces, particularly masonite. The slick surface of masonite wipes off cleanly, leaving a very distinct grain pattern. Corrugated cardboard produces an interesting effect. The slight variations created by the corrugations leave a check-like grain. Breaks or bends in the cardboard trap the paint and leave splits and cracks.

Canvas-covered flats do not work as well as hard flats, but they can be painted with the grainer. Two problems arise when graining canvas flats. First and most obvious, there is the problem of hitting toggles and diagonal braces. Pressure must be applied to the can-

vas to wipe the wet paint. It is difficult not to leave a blob when a structural member of the flat is encountered. Care and a gentle touch, learned with practice, can minimize but not eliminate this problem.

The second problem is that canvas can absorb paint. If the wet paint soaks into the canvas before it can be wiped off, the grain pattern is muted. Special steps must be taken to prevent the paint from striking in. First, the flats should be well primed with sufficient pigment to completely fill the weave of the canvas. Priming with latex gives a better surface than dry pigment paints or casein, although we have had satisfactory results using casein and then a coat of acrylic gloss. The gloss serves as waterproofing and provides a slick surface that is easy to wipe. The sheen of the gloss is an added benefit if a finished woodwork look is desired.

Another way to compensate for the absorption of the grain color by the canvas is to increase the contrast between the base color and the grain color. Whatever the surface the contrast between base and grain is reduced because the grain color is never completely removed by the graining tool. Thus, the colors used should have more contrast than would be used if one were dry-brushing. When painting canvas flats the contrast should be further increased.

The cost of the grainer is next to nothing. We used approximately 25′ of Ethafoam at 5¢ per foot. The cardboard tube was free. Added to this was the cost of five or six sticks of hot melt glue and a 50¢ screen door handle. A grainer can be constructed in less than an hour. The patterns it produces are amazing. If you have an acre of stage floor to paint as planks or a paneled library to grain you might do well to give this Ethafoam wood grainer a try.

Originally published in August/September 1982

Shop Built Hardware and More Pneumatics

Lift Jacks

by John T. Howard, Jr.

Mounting a lift jack on an individual caster can solve the problem of keeping a wagon stationary. The caster is held down by a trunk-lid type of brace. In building this lift jack, the jack was mounted on the rear of a 4' deep wagon behind a scenic unit. The unit was heavy enough to prevent movement when the rear of the wagon was resting on the floor. The front remained on the caster. These lift jack units do not travel well over bumpy surfaces and are recommended for use during act break changes, where there is time to operate them quietly.

The lift jack (below) designed by John Howard employs a trunk lid-type brace.

Originally published in February 1981

Shop-Built Hanging Irons

by John T. Howard, Jr.

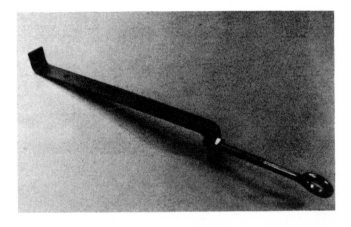

Most cable flying of flats is done with the aircraft cable ending at a turnbuckle attached to a hanging iron. At a cost of about $6 to $8 per line, a heavily flown show can become quite expensive. A shop-built hanging iron at a cost of 80 cents is one solution.

Holes are drilled in a 12" piece of ⅛" x ¾" flat iron for three bolts, to join the flat iron to the flat and for the ¼" eye bolt. The bottom of the flat iron is then bent to go under the bottom of the flat, and the top is bent to accept the eye bolt. The 4" of threads on the eye bolt allow for the adjustment of the line length replacing the turnbuckle.

We have used the shop-built hanging irons for the past five years. Based on stress tests, we have limited the allowable load to 50 lbs. per line.

A D-ring plate (Mutual Hardware #2060) is used to join the cable to the top of the flat. If rope is being used, a ⅛" x ¾" x 6" piece of flat iron is used to join it to the top. The flat iron is bent to allow the rope to slide through and drilled for bolts. The plate and the shop-built hanging iron have an additional advantage in that they do not rattle. They are bolted to the flat with ³⁄₁₆" flat head stove bolts.

To build a hanging iron (above) a 12" piece of ⅛"x¾" flat iron, bent at both ends, is connected to a ¼" eye bolt. Three stove bolts are used to attach the flat. A load of up to 50 lbs. can be supported per line.

Originally published in August/September 1982

Hydraulic Wall Jacks for the Theatre

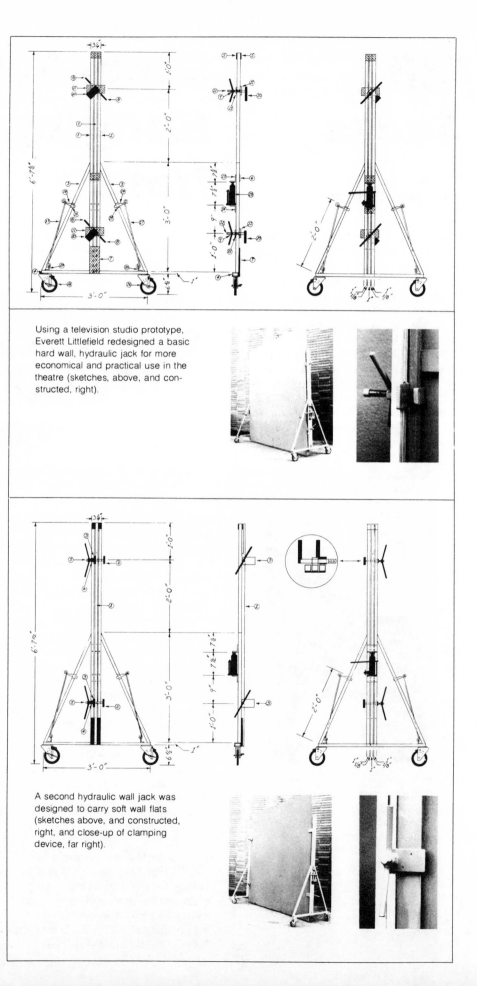

Using a television studio prototype, Everett Littlefield redesigned a basic hard wall, hydraulic jack for more economical and practical use in the theatre (sketches, above, and constructed, right).

A second hydraulic wall jack was designed to carry soft wall flats (sketches above, and constructed, right, and close-up of clamping device, far right).

by Everett Littlefield

Hydraulic wall jacks have long been used by both movie and television studios to support and carry scenery walls. Two types are common but, because both are intended for hard walls, neither is suited to use in theatre, where scenery is more likely to be built with soft walls.

The hydraulic wall jack most often used by the major motion picture studios is distributed by the Matthews Studio Equipment Company and costs $250. Two are needed to steady and move large scenery walls and platforms. Each jack weighs approximately 150 lbs., is 4′ wide and 5′ high, has two 8″ swivel casters, and can raise a wall 17′ 3/4″ off the floor.

For use in a theatre—especially a theatre where students build most of the sets—these jacks are too large. They are also potentially dangerous should they fall over. Moreover, their clamping device would not be effective for use in steadying and moving the soft walls often used in theatre scenery. This jack, then, is practical primarily for professional shops and theatres that construct more hard walls than soft.

The second type of hydraulic wall jack is that used by the television studios. Often these are built by the individual studio for its own use. Although the hydraulic wall jack built at one studio is a better size than Matthews'—56 lbs., 3′ wide and 6′7 1/2″ high, with two 5″ swivel casters and a two-ton jack that can raise a wall 6″ off the floor—like the Matthews jack, it is intended for hard walls.

Soft wall and hard wall jacks

Either the movie or TV industry hydraulic wall jack can be adapted to carry hard walls and platforms in a theatre, but neither would work with soft walls. Since the UCLA Department of Theater Arts scene shop builds mostly soft wall but does sometimes build and use hard walls and platforms, I designed and built two sets of hydraulic wall jacks. One is adapted for carrying soft walls and the other for carrying hard walls or platforms.

Both the soft wall jack and the hard wall jack are based on NBC's hydraulic wall jack. Each weighs 57 lbs. The total cost of materials for a pair of either the hard wall jack or the soft wall jack was approximately $140. Including cutting, welding, and painting of metal parts, it takes about 40 hours to build a pair.

My hydraulic hard wall jack has two new features that improve the NBC hydraulic wall jack. One of these is the clamping device with turnscrew handle, the means by which a hydraulic hard wall jack is attached to a wall. The second improved feature is the locking swivel casters.

The locking levers for the casters are painted red on one side, which when pressed down locks the wheel, and green on the other, which when pressed down releases the wheel. It is important that these caster wheels be locked when the jack is not in use to prevent them from rolling.

The hydraulic soft wall jack is unique in being designed exclusively for carrying soft walls. This jack has the same mechanical and structural features as the hydraulic hard wall jack except for the clamping devices, the center slider, and the positioning of the turnscrew handle and the turnscrew shaft. Instead of clamping onto the end and back side of the upright 1" x 3" stile of a hard wall (as the hydraulic hard wall jack does), the hydraulic soft wall jack clamps onto the front and back sides of the end 1" x 3" stile of a soft wall.

Advantages of hydraulic wall jacks

Safety and convenience are the most important advantages of using these hydraulic wall jacks. Scenery walls and platforms are often assembled flat on the floor into large units, either by bolting the walls together (hard walls and platforms) or by use of mending plates and stiffeners (soft walls). Units assembled in these ways are not only large but also heavy and hard to balance. With a set of hydraulic wall jacks, after a large scenery wall or platform is assembled it can be "walked up" to a vertical position (by a sufficient number of stagehands) and the jacks easily clamped to each end of the unit.

Once the jacks are clamped to the unit and the unit raised off the floor (by tightening the thumbscrew clockwise and pumping the hydraulic jack handle) the unit can be rolled into place by only two people. This eliminates having stagehands manually lift and balance large scenery units that are potentially dangerous should they fall over.

TABLE 1
PARTS AND MATERIALS LIST
Hydraulic hard wall jack
materials list and cost breakdown

A. Basic Frame
1 .065 x 1" sq tubing x 6' (outside vertical supports), 2 pc.
2 .065 x 1" sq tubing x 6' (center slider with two $^3/_4$" holes located 1' from the top and 1' from the bottom), 1 pc.
3 .065 x 1" sq tubing x 39" (A-frame supports), 2 pc.
4 $^3/_{16}$" x 2" x 1" channel iron (base support).

B. Material to tie the frame together
5 $^3/_{16}$" x 2" x 3" flat stock (welded to the outside pieces of the vertical at points 1" from the top, front and back side), 2 pc.
6 $^3/_{16}$" x 2" x 3" flat stock (welded to the center slider #2 on the back side), 1 pc.
7 $^3/_{16}$" x 3" x 6" flat stock (welded to the $^3/_{16}$" x 1" x 2" channel iron base support #4 and the sides of the 1" sq vertical tubing #1), 1 pc.

C. Turnscrew Handles (upper and lower)
8 $^5/_8$" x 5" rd stock welded to a $^3/_4$" hex nut, #9, 4 pc.
9 $^3/_4$" hex nuts that receive turnscrew #12, 2 pc.

D. Wall Clamp, Back Holding Plate and Turnscrew (upper and lower)
10 $^3/_8$" x 2" x 3$^3/_4$" flat stock (clamp welded to the NC threaded rod #12), 2 pc.
11 $^3/_8$" x 2$^1/_2$" x 6" flat stock (back plate welded to the 1" sq tubing—center slider #2), 2 pc.
12 $^3/_4$" x 6" NC threaded rod (turnscrew), 2 pc.

E. Hydraulic Jack, Angle Iron Base, Angle Iron Pusher
13 1$^1/_2$ ton hydraulic jack (welded to the $^3/_{16}$" x 2$^1/_2$" x 2$^1/_2$" angle iron base #14; raises 0 to 4").
14 $^3/_{16}$" x 2$^1/_2$" x 2$^1/_2$" angle iron base (welded to the two outside 1" sq tubings #1).
15 $^3/_{16}$" x 2$^1/_2$" x 2$^1/_2$" angle iron pusher to receive the hydraulic plunger (welded to the center 1" sq tubing slider #2).

F. Wheels
16 5" locking swivel casters (Industrial Caster and Wheel Co. # -48-161-VC), 2 pc.

G. Outriggers/Wall Stabilize Rods (left and right sides)
17 $^3/_8$" x 33" rod with 2" diam. rings on each end, 2 pc.
18 $^1/_4$" x 1" x 4" flat stock (nailers) with a $^1/_2$" hole that attaches to the 2" ring of the $^3/_8$" rod #17. The nailers have two $^1/_8$" holes drilled in each to receive sixpenny doublehead nails, 2 pc.
19 $^1/_8$" x $^3/_4$" x 2" flat stock receivers welded to the 1" tubing #3, 2 pc. The receivers hold and store the $^3/_8$" stabilizer rods when not in use.
20 $^1/_4$" x 3" x 4" holders welded to the channel iron base #4, 2 pc. The $^3/_8$" rod stabilizers attach to these holders by the 2" diam. ring.

H. Turnscrew Reinforcing Plate, upper and lower
21 $^3/_{16}$" x 1" x 2" flat stock (welded to the center slider #2), 2 pc.

COST BREAKDOWN
Frame	$25.00
Miscellaneous Steel Parts	10.00
Wheels	35.00
Total Cost	$70.00

An added convenience is that scenery walls held by hydraulic wall jacks can be left vertical and mobile until they are painted and moved onto the stage. And a vertical wall takes up less storage space.

Limitations

Because it is possible to tip the hydraulic wall jacks over, they should not be used to lift scenery walls that are higher than 20' or longer than 30'. For the same reason, it is necessary to use caution when moving scenery walls outdoors, where wind gusts are a problem.

Leaking and binding up of hydraulic cylinders is another possible problem. A hydraulic wall jack that is used primarily to steady and move scenery walls in a shop will not leak or bind if it is not dropped or used to lift weights heavier than its 1½ ton capacity. The center slider of each type of hydraulic wall jack, however, can bind under certain conditions. For example, when taking a set of hydraulic wall jacks off a scenery wall that is balanced and raised 1" or more off the floor, it is important to have a stagehand at each hydraulic wall jack to lower the scenery wall to the floor. Each stagehand should turn the thumbscrew counterclockwise simultaneously. If these jacks are not released simultaneously, the center slider of each jack will bind.

Operating hydraulic hard wall jacks

A set of hydraulic hard wall jacks is clamped to each end of a wall by the upper and lower wall clamps and secured by turning the turnscrew handle clockwise. That pulls the clamp snug against the backside of the 1" x 3" vertical stile of the hard wall and against the back holding plate. After both jacks are secured to the end of the wall, the hydraulic jack can raise the wall by tightening the fluid key clockwise and then pumping the hydraulic jack handle until the wall is 1" off the floor. The hydraulic jack is welded at its base to an angle iron base that, in turn, is welded to the two outside vertical 1" square tubings.

When the hydraulic jack is pumped, its base remains in position on the angle iron and the two outside 1" square tubings of the frame. Its plunger, however, raises the angle iron, which is welded to the center sliding 1" square tubing—to which the upper and lower back plates are also

welded. Pumping the jack handle raises this tubing—to which the wall is attached—and shifts the weight of the wall onto the base of the metal A-frame supported by the locking swivel casters. When the wall is raised 1" off the floor by the hydraulic wall jacks and the locking casters are unlocked, two people can roll the wall away with ease. If the wall is large and heavy, it is necessary to use the outriggers, which swing out and attach to each side of the wall by two double-head nails.

Originally published in February 1981

High Speed Electric Screw Shooter

by Mike Stair

Once again the theatre industry takes a look into the construction trade and unlocks another secret applicable to the special needs of set construction. This time the look is into the drywall industry and the find is the high speed-electric screw shooter.

Normally the screw shooter is used by sheetrock hangers to fasten plasterboard to stud walls. Its high speed and ability to handle various sizes of fasteners makes it an ideal tool for the quick and sturdy construction needed in the theatre scene shop.

The scenery technician's reasons for using the screw shooter are similar to those of the professional dry wall constructor: speed and holding power. These are two vital concerns of the scenery technician. Because his work must be completed by specific deadlines, he cannot afford to go back over a set piece reinforcing the holding power of the fasteners. Having a tool that is as fast as hammer and nail, but holds better, is valuable—especially when pro-

duction time becomes limited.

Lumber—as most technicians realize, is not getting any less expensive. Therefore, any materials which can be salvaged after a strike can last for many productions. A reversible screw shooter unscrews fasteners at the same speed as it puts them in. The screw shooter can cut strike time by ⅓ and significantly increase the amount of salvageable lumber. If your set is assembled with screws, then by removing the screws, the set is struck and cleaned in one motion. There is no need for prying and splitting valuable building materials, or taking the additional time to pull the nails.

Another reason for utilizing the screw shooter in the scene shop is that screws are ultimately less expensive than nails. The dry wall screw is made from harder steel than a nail or staple and therefore can be salvaged after a strike. The initial cost of screws is higher than nails, but one thousand screws can last for many, many shows.

Most screw shooters have a magnetic tip to which the screws cling. The screw is then placed on the joint and forward pressure is exerted on the gun; the pressure causes the positive drive clutch to

engage. The positive drive clutch is a safety feature which does not allow the screw drive to turn until the operator is set.

The operator then presses the trigger while continuing to exert forward pressure into the screw, and the screw is driven into the stock at speed up to 2500 RPM's. The screw shooter is equipped with a bit housing and depth locator which disengages the clutch when the screw is countesunk.

There are various types of tips which can be used with the screw shooter, but at the Dordt College scene shop finds that a number 2 Phillips works the best. The drywall screw, a necessary investment because of its harder metal content, comes with a Phillips head. The high speed application of the fasteners requires a firm connection which the Phillips head provides.

The drywall screws come in various sizes. Our scene shop stocks the one inch length which is used in flat construction: ¼" plywood to 1" stock. The 1¼" length is used in platform construction—¾" plywood to 2" x 4" or 1"

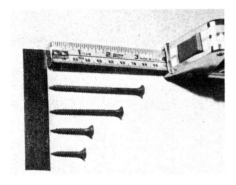

stock. The 2½" is used in joining 1" stock, and the 3" size is used in joining 2" stock. All of these sizes work easily in wood, however it helps to add a lubricant such as soap or wax to the 3" screws.

There are only two problems which we have encountered with the tool. The first is a problem with the tips. The metal of the screw is actually harder than the metal of the tip. This means that the tips tend to be chewed up over a period of time. However, the fact that screws are harder than tips is an advantage because the head of the screw will not deteriorate and the screw can be withdrawn again at strike. The second problem is that there are never enough screw shooters in the scene shop. The tools are a lot of fun to work with, and consequently they are very popular during production time.

Guns usually cost between $111.00 and $138.00. Our scene shop owns a Milwaukee Model 6798-1 and a model 6747-1. The model 6798-1 has variable speeds. Both guns are reversible. The following are manufacturers of screw shooters:

MILWAUKEE ELECTRIC TOOL CORP.
13135 W. Lisbon Road
Brookfield, WI   53005

ROCKWELL POWER TOOL DIVISION
400 N. Lexington Avenue
Pittsburgh, PA   15208

BLACK & DECKER MANUFACTURING CO.
Towson, MD   21204

SIOUX TOOLS
Sioux City, IA   51101

Originally published in November/December 1978

Multi-Purpose Clamps

by R.J. Loyd

Shortly after becoming creative arts center technician at West Virginia University, I set out to solve one problem as soon as possible. The touring dance companies that appeared at the university did not carry their own lights —a common practice. Lighting plots were sent ahead to be pre-hung with our own equipment.

When an equipment inventory was taken, I discovered one major lack. It concerned the side trees that are needed to light dance concerts. The university had the heavy, cast iron bases and vertical extentions, but did not have the necessary side arms. And the side arms in stock were crude and unsafe. I therefore set out to design and construct safer side arms for the university.

After some discussion with David Fiddler, the art department shop supervisor, and Stanley Abbott, theatre design professor, I developed a clamp

design that could be used for many purposes. Using them for side arms was but one. The needed materials are easily found around most theatres and shops, or are available locally. The clamps are quite inexpensive and easy to make, especially if you have knowledge of simple arc welding.

Materials and construction
The materials you will need are as follows: one C-clamp (we used one from Century lighting instruments), one 1½" steel pipe end cap, cutting oil (for drilling), and welding rods. You will also need a drill press with ½" bit and arc welding equipment. If it is not necessary to buy the clamps, then cost is approximately $1.00 for materials and 15 minutes labor per clamp.

Here is how it's done. Drill a hole exactly centered in the pipe end cap. Use the bolt, which is normally used to connect the clamp to the instrument yoke, to attach the clamp to the cap. To strengthen this connection, weld a

Among its many uses, a clamp (above) designed by R.J. Loyd can serve as a lighting side arm, a backstage ballister for handrails (left), or a rigid spacer between battens or pipes for special rigging.

bead between the clamp's spacer and the pipe cap. (I wanted the clamp to be able to slide, to allow for minor adjustments.)

I call this tool the multi-purpose clamp. On the end of an 1½" threaded pipe, it is a lighting side arm. On another pipe, with a flange on the opposite end, it is a backstage ballister for handrails, making handrails for escape platforms and stairways fast and easy to assemble. Or, on each end of a 1½" threaded pipe, it becomes a rigid spacer between battens or pipes for special rigging. And there are dozens of other uses.

Originally published in August/September 1982

Air Cylinders at the Guthrie

by Terry Sateren

During the past couple of seasons at the Guthrie Theater, pneumatic cylinders of various sizes and configurations have been used in many applications. We have found them to be quiet, efficient, and foolproof.

In *The Matchmaker* (designer Desmond Heeley) an 84" cylinder was used for an old-fashioned store elevator on which Dolly made her initial entrance. In *Christmas Carol* (designer Jack Barkla) a 60" cylinder silently and smoothly cantilevered a balcony platform. In *Dr. Faustus* (designer Ralph Funicello) a trap, lowered by a 65" cylinder, became steps as it went down. We have used many small cylinders to trip curtains and activate special effects on sets and props—sometimes using a compressed air tank mounted in the unit. Often these cylinders are used in

lieu of an electric solenoid because they provide more power and don't burn out.

In *The Winter's Tale* (designer Desmond Heeley) a 24' cable cylinder lowered in Father Time in a chariot. In *The National Health* (designer Sam Kirkpatrick) an operating room light (4' in diameter) was lowered in using an 11' cable cylinder. The cable cylinders are manufactured by the Tol-O-Matic Co. in Minneapolis. Depending on the cylinder, loads of up to 7,480 lbs. can be moved horizontally or vertically up to 48'.

In most cases, we have been using standard ¼" I.D. air hose with an air pressure of 100 p.s.i. The other items needed in a system such as this would be lever controlled valves, flow control valves, mufflers and miscellaneous pipe fittings.

The advantages of these systems are that they are simple to operate, they are consistent in operation, there are few moving parts to wear out, and they are quiet and safe. The speeds of ascent and descent can be established and set with flow control valves. When that is done, the operator of the mechanism can open the lever valve full and not have to worry about the speed of travel. The flow controls also help reduce the

"spongieness" of the air in the cylinder.

Another advantage in the pneumatic system is that there does not have to be a large oil reservoir or pump as in hydraulic systems. There is not the danger of a high-pressure oil line rupturing and shooting out oil. Oil systems are less spongy but if one compensates for this in a pneumatic system with the proper size cylinder bore and the flow controls, there is little problem.

On larger cylinders it is best to have cushions built in so the speed of travel is decelerated just before the end of both the in and out stroke. Otherwise they come to a very abrupt stop. Depending on the length of cable cylinders, an automatic cable tensioner should be included as the cable will stretch somewhat with use.

On a cable cylinder system which operates a vertically moving piece, a clew is attached to the cylinder cable harness. Aircraft cable runs from the clew via normal rigging to the object to be flown or moved. On systems using a cylinder with a piston, structure is built for appropriate balance. The cylinder in most cases only propels the piece. The structure (guides, tracks, rollers) assumes the torque and strain of the mechanism.

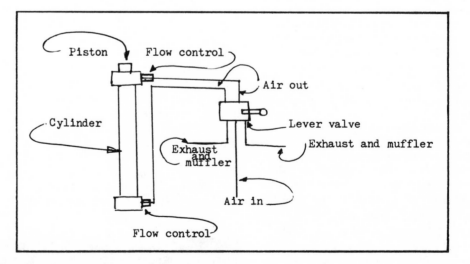

DIAGRAM OF PNEUMATIC CYLINDER SYSTEM

Originally published in October 1977

Upside Down Air-Bearings

by Pete Davis

For the Pacific Conservatory of the Performing Arts production of "Peer Gynt" designer Ralph Funicello wanted a full raked stage with a 17 ft. turntable center. This turntable had to be perfect. To begin with, it had to be silent; there could be no rumble of casters. Secondly, it had to be absolutely solid when stationary; it could not "walk." Next, it had to make ½ and ¾ revolutions in three to four beats. This means we had three to four beats from the time ten to twelve dancers left a solid surface to the time ten to twelve more dancers hit the solid surface. Further, it had to be able to carry five or six people while turning, and finally, the whole raked set had to set up and strike and fit through a 6 x 8 opening in an hour and a half. The solution that Funicello and I evolved was to use air bearings upside down that would lift the table to allow it to turn.

We used eight 12 inch Air Float Air Bearings on a 13 ft. diameter mounted within a structure we called the cobweb. The cobweb would support the turntable above the bearings when they were deflated. The bearings were bolted to a ¾ inch plywood plate, ⅞ inch below the top of the cobweb. When inflated, the bearings would lift the table a quarter inch off the cobweb (see drawing). We chose a 2 x 4 inch frame for the cobweb because 3½ inches allowed plenty of underneath room for hoses, connectors, and the body of the air bearings. (By having the bearings stationary we avoided the twisting air hose problem that mounting the bearings in the table would have produced.) We ran a one inch hose to an eight outlet manifold in the center of the cobweb; from each of the eight outlets ran a ⅝ inch hose, one to each air bearing.

The turntable itself was made of one inch steel square tubing, .049 wall thickness, constructed in a sixteen inch square honey comb pattern. Half inch plywood was bolted to the bottom of the turntable in a donut configuration, just over the radius of the bearings; ¼ inch tempered masonite was then screwed to the plywood. We allowed four inches on either side of the air bearings for the screws in the masonite. This prevented any screw head from actually passing over the air bearings. Then the top of the cobweb and the bottom of the donut were polished, and silicone was sprayed to cut friction. This basic plan worked fairly well.

Our repertory requirements demanded that the table break into four pieces. I broke the turntable so that no two breaks would pass over any two bearings at the same time. My theory was that seven bearings would still keep the table afloat. It was true that the loss of one bearings did not harm the turn-

operated. But we cut this to almost nothing by turning the air on one-half a beat before the "go" cue and turning it off as the cue was completed. Our compressor was a high volume, low pressure Gast 3040 compressor. This was purchased on the recommendation of Air Float so as to keep the on time of the compressor to a minimum. We eliminated compressor noise by running it through a tank and enclosing both compressor and tank in a sound proof box. Our lift pressure was six to seven psi.

The turning mechanism was a cable wrapped around the table to a hand operated winch. The winch had an eighteen inch drum to gain leverage with two handles, one on each side. The winch worked fairly well, but if I had to do it again, I would use an electric motor inside the table, eliminating the cable, various shivs and two people. Then one man could sit backstage with two control boxes: air off and on, motor off and on.

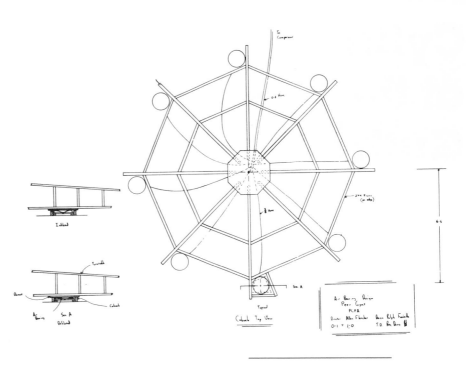

Originally published in March/April 1976

ing motion. The problem, though, was noise. With eight cracks and eight air bearings, the whoosh of the air bearings was almost continuous. To solve this, we simply contact cemented garage door weather stripping between the sections of table over the bearing track. This eliminated the noise and made the table much easier to turn.

The only noise we finally accepted was the bearings themselves as they

Finally, we found we could turn six to ten people on the table depending on their spacing. If they were evenly spaced, ten was not a problem. But with uneven spacing the table grew unbalanced and six was pretty difficult. We also found that two or three could dance anywhere on the table as it turned.

By opening night we had achieved a silent, rock solid, floating turntable that would indeed start and stop on a dime.

The Air-Bearing Caster

by Robert Scales

The air-bearing caster ("air-caster") has many practical applications for use in the theatre. Basically, an air-caster affords frictionless movement of an object by directing a flow of compressed air through a flexible inner tube and out of two or more vent holes in the caster, thereby lifting the object on a "film" of air. During the 10 years I have used them, air-casters have proven to be most effective in the following instances:
1) When moving heavy loads that would be too difficult to handle easily on wheel-type casters.
2) When the height required by use of wheel-type casters is more than desired.
3) When definite setting marks are required in putting up a movable unit.
4) When the floor must be protected from marks, indentations or crushing.
5) When the element being moved must rest firmly and not move about after the initial move is completed.

In order to achieve the best results when using air-casters, keep these items in mind:
1) When air-casters are activated they lift the load. This must always be considered when you are mating moving pieces with other items. Be sure to allow lift clearance above the item you are moving.
2) Air-casters function best when they are parallel with the floor surface; the load on the casters must be distributed in a manner that keeps the casters level at all times. I've learned that the larger the air-caster, the more tolerance it has. Twelve-inch and smaller air-casters can tip easily and are more sensitive to floor irregularities.
3) Three or more air-casters are required to lift a load. I've tried them in combination with wheel-type casters and found resultant problems with lift and balance, friction of casters and pushing the air-casters flat.
4) Air-casters are load sensitive: the pressure required to lift and move the load is proportional to the weight applied. There is some tolerance in this area, but it becomes critical if a great deal of weight is subtracted or added while the air-casters are active. If a constant weight is not going to be maintained in the moving process, you must regulate the air-casters.
5) The floor surface is extremely important when using air-casters. It must be airtight, smooth and level. (Stained and sealed wooden plank floors and painted wooden floors do not allow effective use of air-casters. However, level, sealed concrete floors can be used.) If the floor is level, the portable surface can be added to achieve air-tightness. The portable covering should be strong enough not to wrinkle as the air-caster load moves over it. I have found that .03-thick ABS works very well; it can be rolled with ease, but will not wrinkle in use. And although heavy-duty linoleum makes a good portable surface, ABS is not as heavy to move, or as brittle.
6) Air-casters require air or gas in order to operate and I have discovered that retractable hose-reel arrangements simplify the "feed" procedure. In order to minimize the size of the feed hose required, the regulators operating the pressure should be as close to the casters as possible. Feeding high pressure 100 psi to the air-caster pallet seems to work best. Note: it is very important to have high-volume low-pressure regulators for effective supply to the casters. CO_2 cylinders are an optional way to power air-casters. Just be sure the CO_2 regulator is large enough not to freeze as a result of the volume down by the air-casters.
7) There must be an adequate and continuous volume of air or gas available for use of air-casters. None of the places where I've used them has had a compressor that enabled continuous use of the air-casters. If this is a problem, make moves in steps from caster to caster, allowing scheduled stops for the compressor to "catch up."
8) All air-casters produce a hissing noise in operation. And if the casters wrinkle or the load tips very much or if the floor is allowing air to escape, additional noises will result. This is an especially important consideration if you plan to use air-casters in production. Noise can be masked to some extent, but I have never been able to eliminate it.

The following manufacturers can be contacted for more information and supplying of air-casters for theatrical use:
AERO-GO, INC.
5802 Corson Avenue South
Seattle, WA 98108
(800) 426-8892
AIRFLOAT CORP.
1550 McBride Avenue
Decatur, IL 62526
(217) 422-8365
ROLAIR SYSTEMS
Box 30363
Santa Barbara, CA 93105
(805) 968-1356

Originally published in September 1977

Hydraulic Casters

by Terry Sateren

One of the reoccurring problems in the theater is how to secure scenery to the stage quietly, quickly and be able to move or shift scenic units just as quickly. Wedges, jacks, stage screws, etc., on castered units don't always fulfill this need.

The hydraulic caster unit was developed over the period of a year to solve this problem. It is self-contained in a set requiring no external power source; i.e. air hose or power cord.

The principle of the unit is simple, basic hydraulics; Oil is forced thru a tube at high pressure activating the piston in a cylinder. The cylinder is

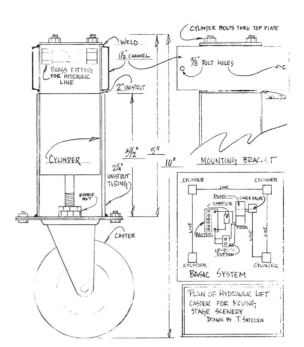

HYDRAULIC CYLINDER AND CASTER

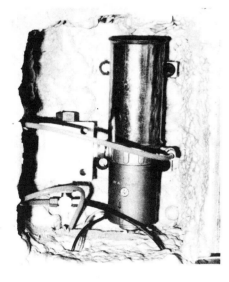

mounted in a guide sleeve which is secured to the set. When the cylinder is activated, it pushes down a caster, thus raising the set unit off the floor. The hydraulic pump can be either AC or DC, or a hand pump can be used. Lowering the set is accomplished either by releasing the check valve (on the hand pump) or reversing the motor (releasing the pilot check valve) on the electric units. The operation is quiet and requires about 3 seconds.

The number of cylinders used varies according to the size and weight of the sets. Each cylinder will lift approximately 300 lbs., in most cases a minimum of 4 would be required for balance. The major disadvantage of the hydraulic caster is that it requires ap-

proximately 10" in height. The advantages over our usual method of moving scenery (i.e. air bearings) is that they don't require a high volume air source, a large pneumatic hose to the unit or a seamless floor.

The materials can be purchased through local mechanism dealers or government surplus dealers. Variations in mountings and substitutions in materials can be made for individual needs. The hydraulic casters were used on the sets for "King Lear," "The Crucible," "Tartuffe," and "School for Scandal" in this past season.

Materials for Hydraulic Caster Unit

Hand Pump	$40.00
A-C Hydraulic Pump	100.00
D-C Hydraulic Pump	50.00
Heavy Duty Battery 12 V.	30.00
Trickle Charger	10.00
Cylinders	30.00/ea.
Check Valve	30.00
Nylon Tubing	7.00/100'
Brass Fittings	1.50/ea.
Casters	15.00/ea.
Sleeve casting material	10.00/per caster

Originally published in May/June 1975

Hydraulic lift caster for moving stage scenery (plan) which was developed by Terry Sateren at the Guthrie Theatre, can be installed in a foam-lined, sound proofed box.
The basic system includes
1. 12 volt battery; 2. D-C electric pump; 3. Check valve; 4. Caster; 5. Mounting and sleeve guide.

Photos: Jim Worthing

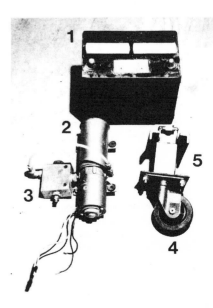

Air Stapler and Scenic Construction

by William Miller

It seems that every time technicians gather at conventions or workshops, the conversation invariably turns to a discussion of new materials. These discussions point up the flexibility of working in plastics, metals, or foams to name a few, but the fact remains that a large percentage of our productions still involve the use of wooden scenery. Scenery constructed in much the same way and with the same tools that have been used since the hammer was invented. The pneumatic staple gun, used in industry for many years, can help the theatre technicians speed up his construction process, and not reduce the quality or strength of his product. While a number of large scene shops already have pneumatic tools, the staple gun is a time and labor saving device accessible to most modestly funded shops.

Since most scene shops already own a small compressor (they can be purchased for under $200) for paint sprayers, a moderate initial investment of $250 will adequately tool-up the air staple gun turning that compressor into a tool as valuable to the technician as his radial arm saw. Air staple guns are available in three main sizes suitable for theatre use. A gun with a ¾″ to 1½″ capacity that operates at a pressure of 60 lbs per square inch is the most versatile. This gun is available for both wide crown and narrow crown staples for under $200. A pres-

Equipment (center) and techniques (top and bottom) used in constructing scenery with a pneumatic stapler.

sure regulator (if your compressor is not so equipped) and enough rubber hose to reach work areas may cost $20. Fittings and couplings to allow you to use more than one gun or a gun with spray equipment may add another $5. The staples themselves cost slightly more than nails. ($5 per box of 2400 for the ¾″ narrow crown). The time saved in various construction phases will quickly repay this initial investment.

Many of the standard construction techniques may be modified with the air stapler. By using ¾″ staples instead of clout nails you may cut flat construction time by more than one third. Additionally, staples will not spilt the rails and styles as clouts will if used improperly. The resulting joint is as strong and much faster to assemble. Further, if the unit is not to become part of the theatre's stock, the corner blocks and keystones may be removed, with little or no damage to the rails and styles, with a ripping chisle or pry bar allowing longer usable lengths of lumber to be recycled than was possible with clout nailing.

Cross bracing and squaring platform legs becomes a simple operation when the braces are fastened with 1¼″ or 1½″ staples since the operation of the staple gun requires only one hand and the units being fastened need not be supported or "footed" as in nailing. Since air pressure drives the fastener, even the less experienced crew members will be able to accomplish any fastening job regardless of strength. Battening flats can be done in place, as can the addition of profile pieces or dimensional units again without supporting the units to be fastened. Additional toggels may be added to standing flats in seconds without supporting the unit. Virtually every operation requiring up to and including 6d nails can be done faster and easier with the air stapler with no resulting loss of strength and with less chance of splitting the material. During strike, staples can be cut off flush to the surface of the lumber with carpenters pincer or removed completely with a pair of pliers.

Originally published in November/December 1975

Robert Scales' Lab Theatre: Hydraulics and Pneumatics

Pneumatics, Part 1

by Robert Scales

Most of us are in theatre because it demands inventive and creative behavior. It is this atmosphere and environment that generates excitement and significance in our work. As a theatre practitioner, I find a great deal of satisfaction in solving technical theatre problems by non-traditional methods, although sometimes my attempts to improve traditional practices create more problems than using a good old fashion solution. I have been accused of never using the same solution to a scenic problem more than once. That is not exactly true, but close.

Solutions to technical theatre problems are infinite. There are almost no absolute ways to solve particular problems, but we must search for the best ways. Everyone involved in the shops and on the stage should be seeking the simplest and most efficient solution to the problems given to us by the production, the designer, and the director. There is always the possibility of discovering—from an experiment—a better way of doing things.

Most theatre practitioners are not secretive about their work. We are all working on very similar, if not the same, problems—independently all over the world. I have never sensed a competitiveness with other technical directors or craftpeople. There is always something we can learn from each other.

There seem to be two basic motivations to acquiring new information and knowledge in technical theatre:

1 You have an immediate problem and you are searching for a solution. "What will solve this problem?"

2 You search for a device, a technique, a material that can be applied to problems you may encounter in the future or that you have encountered in the past. "What problems would this solve?"

Dealing with these two concepts becomes an endless, continuous cycle for technical theatre practitioners. We

remain incomplete, unfinished always moving, changing, searching, evolving, and—on exceptionally good days—discovering.

The series of articles which will appear regularly in *Theatre Crafts* under the title of *Lab Theatre* will seek to present principles and approaches hopefully to stimulate the reader to search for simple solutions to scenic and technical problems. This first series of articles will deal with principles of pneumatics and application of the principles to technical theatre problems.

There is a saying, "Anything can be made to work if you fiddle with it long enough." Unfortunately, in the theatre we are short on time and can't fiddle too long at anything. My experience has brought me to understand that the fewer functions any device is required to perform, the better it can perform those functions. I find pneumatic devices simple, easy to understand, and suited to solving many technical problems in the theatre.

Our modern world is full of pneumatic devices. Many such devices are easy to recognize by the *psst* sound in the exhaust mode, such as a bus door, the automatic doors in department stores and grocery stores, or train, bus, and truck brakes. Banking transaction at the drive-in banks, the soft drink and beer on tap dispensers are applications of pneumatics. Modern industry, manufacturing, transportation, and air conditioning all rely strongly on fluid power.

Fluid power is the term used to cover the use of water, air, gas, oil, steam, and any other liquid for power. I have found pneumatics the least expensive and, generally, the most versatile and easiest to deal with form of fluid power. Pneumatics is using air or gases rather than a liquid. Using liquids is called hydraulics.

Pneumatic devises such as air casters, cable cylinders, rod cylinders, valves, regulators, air motors, and

rotary actuators have been helpful in solving problems that I have encountered in the theatre.

At each point on the earth there is a certain pressure, and this pressure varies with height from sea level and weather. This pressure is called atmospheric pressure.

When there is less than atmospheric pressure there is a vacuum differential. When pressure higher than atmospheric pressure is created it is called the working gauge pressure. This working pressure is identified by a unit of measurement called psi—pounds of pressure per square inch.

A compressor pulls in atmospheric air and compresses it to a positive pressure greater than the atmosphere. Compressors used for spray painting are considered low pressure—up to 60 psi. Industrial compressors used to drive power tools in shops and acti-

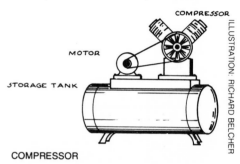

COMPRESSOR

ILLUSTRATION: RICHARD BELCHER

vate cylinders usually are designed for 125 psi to 200 psi. The other factor to consider in pneumatic power is "cfm", cubic feet per minute; that is the volume capabilities of the compressor.

If a storage tank is attached to the compressor it increases the air volume capacities, which will assist the compressor. Many pneumatic devices are used intermittently and storage tanks will keep the volume adequate for such uses. However, air motor, air drills, grinder, saws, and air casters require large quantities of cfm. A storage tank will give staying power for these devices but the compressor must be adequate to the device's usage if the device is to be used continuously.

One of my early discoveries was how "portable" pneumatic devices can be and how self-contained a system could be when a tank of gas was used instead of an air compressor.

Gases which are economical and safe for use as pneumatic power for the theatre are CO_2, nitrogen, and compressed air. Also, there are hydrocarbons in small aerosol containers. I have found CO_2 to be the most useful. It is readily available, inexpensive, and not flammable. It is packaged in various sized tanks from 5 pounds to 50 pounds, and is used by beverage manufacturers, in welding, and in fire extinguishers. The tank pressure is 900 psi, which is a lower pressure than a fully-charged nitrogen or compressed air tank.

CO_2 is sold by the pound in its liquid, concentrated state. As the pressure is removed from the tank, the liquid boils, producing a gas. There are two types of CO_2 tanks. One is designed to release gas, and the other is designed to release CO_2 liquid. CO_2 fire extinguishers are the most common liquid types and are called siphon tanks.

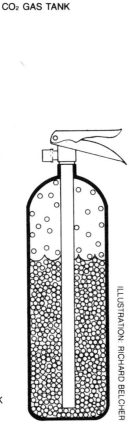

CO₂ GAS TANK

CO₂ LIQUID TANK

ILLUSTRATION: RICHARD BELCHER

The gas tank will retain 900 pounds of pressure until all the liquid has turned to gas; then the pressure will begin to fall. The tank must be weighed to determine the remaining liquid because it does not show on the primary gauge. The primary gauge will begin to drop once there is only gas

remaining in the tank. There is usually plenty of time to change tanks if you are operating the devices below 100 psi.

One problem with CO_2 gas occurs when more volume of gas is used than can boil off; then the tank, valves, regulators, and hoses will begin to freeze and obstruct the flow of gases. If CO_2 is being used to power air casters or large cable cylinders, this problem may arise. Heat lamps, heater tape cord, or a space heater directed to the valve will help solve this problem.

In the siphon type of cylinder, the gas of the CO_2 boil-off pushes the liquid to the outside through the stem. The same effect can be achieved with a gas CO_2 bottle turned upside down. The use of straight CO_2 liquid is effective to simulate steam from a train or to douse a hot poker in water.

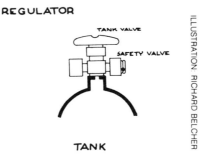

REGULATOR

TANK

ILLUSTRATION: RICHARD BELCHER

To make the CO_2 gas useful as pneumatic power, a CO_2 regulator is necessary. I would suggest that you have a regulator with two gauges. One gauge gives tank pressure and the other the regulated pressure, which usually is 0–150 psi. As a standard procedure, I suggest that you place a 1/4″ disconnect at the regulated pressure outlet. The connections on all CO_2 tanks, regardless of size, are the same, so that all regulators are interchangeable. There is a donut-shaped gasket that should be used to connect your regulator to prevent leaking at the tank connection. This gasket is usually attached to a full tank by a rubber bank or wire.

Very small tanks are available that can be used in special applications. From my experience, most contain liquids which boil off at about 60–80 psi. These are the propellants used in spray cans. These small tanks, or aerosol cans, are used to power air brushes, inflate tires, or blow air horns. There is more than one mounting for these types of tanks. My interest was to find the type of can and fitting that would easily adapt to pipe fittings.

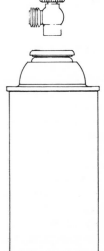

1/4″ PIPE FITTING

ILLUSTRATION: RICHARD BELCHER

In our theatre we do not have a compressor; therefore, we rely on bottle gases to power our pneumatic effects as well as to operate staple guns, nailers, spray painting equipment, and other pneumatic tools.

Future Lab Theatre articles will cover the basic elements of pneumatics, basic pneumatic working devices, and applications of pneumatics to solve specific technical theatre problems.

I would like to recommend the Womack Educational books on Fluid power for those who want to supplement the Lab Theatre information. Especially recommended are "Fluid Power Data Booklet" @ $.50, Industrial Fluid Power Volume 1 @ $7.90, and Industrial Fluid Power Volume 2 @ $6.80. These books are well illustrated, easily understood, inexpensive, and are found in many bookstores or can be purchased direct from Womack Educational Publication, 2010 Shea Road, Box 35027, Dallas, Texas, 75235.

Originally published in February 1981.

Pneumatic Fluid Power System Basics

Part 1: generator, circuitry, working device

Part 1: Generator, circuitry, and working devices

A pneumatic fluid power system is one that generates, transmits, and controls the application of power through the use of pressurized materials (gas and/or air) that are capable of flowing within an enclosed circuit. All components of the system are interconnected by hose and piping, which contains and carries the pressurized air similar to the way electrical wiring interconnects electrical power.

A pneumatic fluid power system has several desirable characteristics for application to theatre problems. Pneumatics are relatively inexpensive, flameproof, clean, and present no shock hazard. They respond quickly, and the functions of speed and direction are easily controlled. In addition, the power can be stored. Pneumatic systems are not affected by heat or lack of ventilation, and are low-noise, if exhaust can be plumbed away. The circuitry is simple, there is no vibration, and the systems are compact in size.

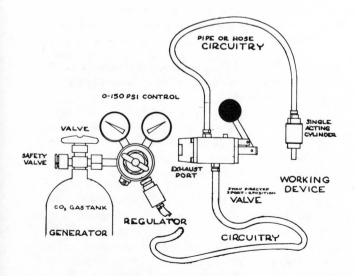

Six basic components are involved in a pneumatic system: 1) generator, 2) circuitry, 3) working device, 4) control valves, 5) control regulators, and 6) protective devices. The first three components are discussed in this issue. Control valves, con-

trol regulators, and protective devices follow in Part II. Before discussing each component, it is important to understand how these basic elements relate in a simple system. This simple circuit merely applies pressure to a single side of a piston and relieves the pressure through the exhaust port. There is no speed or direction control in this circuit. The regulator determines the pressure and force of the piston.

To operate any pneumatic device, there are always two factors that must be considered. Each device requires a certain amount of pressurized air (cfm) to function. Cfm determines speed of the device. The other factor is pressure per square inch (psi), which determines the force of the device.

Although a pneumatic system can be simple, it can also be made into very complex and sophisticated circuitry. There is an extremely wide range of components and component configurations available, but each of these devises would fall within the six categories mentioned. During the last two years, our shop at the Seattle Repertory Theatre has developed a wide inventory of working devices, valves, hoses, tubing, and gas tanks. Some items were found at surplus stores; others were purchased for specific applications. All items, however, make up an inventory of components that are used and reused, show after show. The major cost of any pneumatic system is the compressor. This is one reason that I use CO_2 gas, which I have found to be less expensive and more portable than compressors rented or purchased for use on stage. Also, CO_2 gas eliminates the problem of noises that the electric motor and compressor make.

1 Generator: The power agent, gas or air, compressed to a certain psi by means of compressors, pumps, blowers, and bottled gases.

Some types of compressors, such as rotary vane, blowers, and diaphram, are effective only in generating low pressure. The more common uses of industrial pressure power are piston, gear, and screw type, with piston type being the most common. The piston type of compressor has an extremely wide range of models available. It also has the flexibility of either lessening the piston stroke—to give more psi and less cfm—or lengthening the piston stroke, to give more cfm and less psi. The piston compressor works in the same manner as

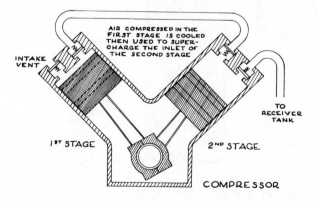

a hand pump or a bicycle pump. Powered compressors are driven usually by electric or gas engine. The rule of thumb is that for each drive of horse power (hp), the compressor normally delivers 4 cfm at 100 psi.

Compressing air also heats it. The higher the compression ratio, the hotter the air becomes. To prevent overheating of the air—if used to generate pressures beyond 75 psi—a piston compressor is usually a two or more "stage" compressor. Air is compressed in the first stage to 40 psi and in the second stage to 120 psi. The ratio is usually at 3:1 per stage. For the most common pressures of 0-125 psi, a two stage compressor will usually prove to be the most economical and efficient.

High cfm and low pressure (0—125 psi) compressors are usually rotary vane or screw type. When in use, these types of compressors usually run continuously. Storage tanks are not used.

2 Circuitry: The pipe, hoses, fittings, and tubing required to connect the system together.

Generally the port sizes of the device being used determines the circuitry size. The inside diameter of the circuitry determines the cfm capacity. The smaller the inside diameter of the circuit, the slower the air will move. Our shop has standardized our fittings to ¼" plastic tubing and hose and ½" hose. We also use two basic disconnects—one for ¼", another for ½". For liquid handling we use ⅜" hose and tubing with ⅜" self-closing disconnects. Air disconnects do not need to close off the plug or stem: only the feed pressure connectors (the coupler or body) need to check when disconnected. The disconnects, as well as all fittings, are restrictions that may slow the device functions below the speed desired. When more speed is required, we go to a larger inside diameter circuit or parallel circuit of existing size. If we were using four 12" or 15" air casters, the circuitry would probably be from a 1" or larger manifold with a ½" hose fed to each caster. There may be two CO_2 tanks in parallel feeding the manifold to acquire the volume required. For theatre use, hose and plastic tubing are usually more suitable than pipe and metal tubing.

At 100 psi, a ¼" hose will carry about 1 cfm and a ½" hose will carry 4 cfm. All pipe fittings used in air circuitry should have a sealant on the threads to prevent leaks. Our shop finds Teflon tape the easiest and most convenient technique.

Almost all pneumatic components have pipe thread ports. Many of the components can be connected conveniently by pipe fittings, but for moving pieces and temporary long runs, tubing and hose are quicker, easier to modify, lighter, and flexible. Almost any type of hose or tubing can be used to carry air. The only consideration is to make sure the hose or tubing will withstand the pressure you will be using. Most air hoses are rated for 200-plus working pressure. Most garden hoses are designed for 60 psi and are an inexpensive means of running a large volume of air at low pressure, such as a feed for air casters.

Our shop has standardized by using reusable swivel-type hose barb fittings, such as Parker Hannifin Low Pressure, Fast-Link, Push-Lock, V882 series fittings. This enables hoses to be disconnected from pipe fittings without the hose twisting or having to be removed from the barb. When the hose is inserted onto the fittings properly, there is no need for a clamp. These fittings are for hoses from ¼" to ¾" ID.

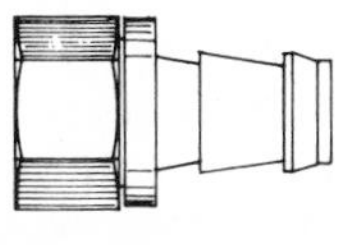

FEMALE PIPE - HOSE BARB

MALE THREAD - HOSE BARB

Pneumatic disconnects are the most convenient fittings to use when working with hoses. By pulling back the lock collar on the coupler, you can release the connection without tools. Unfortunately, there are several incompatible configurations of the disconnect in any one size. We have standardized to two disconnect sizes: Parker 20 series, ¼" body size, sleeve type, industrial interchange for ⅛", ¼", and ⅜" hoses and pipe fittings.

SLEEVE TYPE COUPLING

There are two parts of the disconnect: couplers or bodies (the female section) and plugs or stems (the male part of the connection). Each part of the disconnect is available with female or male pipe threads ⅛", ¼", and ⅜", and hose barb stems for ¼", ⁵/₁₆", or ⅜" hose. We have also standardized on a ½" body size for use with ⅜", ½", and ¾" hoses.

¼" ID plastic tubing is inexpensive and easy to work with if one is using fittings like Parker Poly-tite. The Poly-tite fittings can all be attached by hand and can be assembled and disassembled repeatedly. Poly-tite is a compact brass compression fitting. The body, nut, and sleeve are preassembled. An acetal resin sleeve holds the plastic in place beyond the bursting pressure of the tube. Assembly consists of sliding on the nut, then inserting the tube until it bottoms in the fitting, then tightening the nut finger. No tools are needed. This fitting is available from tubing to pipe fittings, male and female, ⅛", ¼", and ⅜", and also in tees, elbows, unions, and couplings.

COMPRESSION FITTING

If you use air devices in moving stage effects, the hoses need to be paged and dealt with as you would deal with electrical cable. Spring return hose reels are very effective in dealing with paging hoses. Care must be taken to prevent a kink or sharp bend in the hoses, which would restrict or prevent the air from traveling through.

3 Working Devices: Rod cylinders, cable cylinders, motor, air casters, telescoping cylinder, bellows cylinders, and rotary actuator.

The most common device is the cylinder that performs a rectilinear motion. When choosing a cylinder for a particular job, you must determine if it is to be single acting (push or pull, with or without spring returns) or double acting, the bore (diameter of the piston), stroke (length of moving the work), rod size, rod end, mounting, port-size, cushion, and material of barrel. Charts in the Womack Fluid data book and cylinder catalogs will assist in making these choices. Our shop has used rod, diaphragm, and cable cylinders that are ½" to 8" bore and have a stroke from 1" to 15'6".

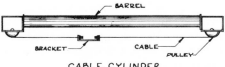

CABLE CYLINDER

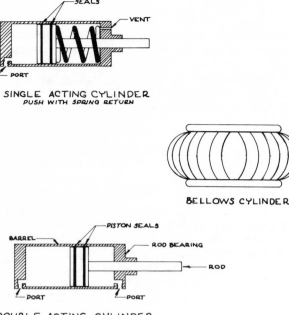

SINGLE ACTING CYLINDER
PUSH WITH SPRING RETURN

BELLOWS CYLINDER

DOUBLE ACTING CYLINDER

To determine the force capabilities of a cylinder, the piston area exposed to the fluid pressure is multiplied by the psi used. The bore size is the diameter of the piston. F = A x P.

The formula for the theoretical thrust is $\dfrac{P\pi D^2}{4}$. This represents the ideal possible force of the cylinder. When thrust or force is used to move an object, one should use the dynamic force ratio, which is 66% of the theoretical thrust. Dynamic thrust compensates for friction, inertia, loss in moving parts, and other factors.

The choice of a cylinder will be determined by the force required (bore based upon working psi), length of stroke, speed required, and whether the cylinder is to push, pull, or both. There are numerous basic mountings, the most common being flange, lug, clevis, or trunnion types. The rod usually is threaded and would accept a flange or clevis as well as threaded nuts.

Other pneumatic devices applicable to theatre uses are rotary actuators and air motors. The rotary actuator consists of a rack and pinion rotary action device driven by two cylinders, one on each side. Most rotary actuators will rotate 90°, 180°, or 360°. (See "Shop Talk," *Theatre Crafts* March/April 1979, pages 76-77, for more information on an application of rotary actuators.) Air motors make a slight putt-putt noise, even if the exhaust is plumbed away. We have used an air motor as a curtain pull for *The Glass Menagerie* and a driver for a film throwing device in *A History of the American Film*. Air casters or air bearings have solved several technical and scenic problems for me, and I continue to use them. Air casters demand some very particular conditions if they are to be effective. The floor surface must be crack-free, air tight, and level; the air supply or generator must produce a high quantity of air required to operate the devices.

Originally published in March 1981

Pneumatic Fluid Power System Basics

Part 2: Valves, regulation, protection devices

by Robert Scales

The first part of the basic element of pneumatic fluid power systems covered generator, circuitry, and working devices and appeared in the March 1981 issue of Theatre Crafts.

4 Control values: Control quantity and direction of air flow. Gate, ball, needle, spool, plate, and poppet type valves can be manually, electrically, and air pilot controlled to manipulate speed and direction of flow, to relieve excessive pressure, and to check direction of flow.

Valves are identified by their port size, number of ports, number of positions, detent or spring return, and function. Normally the ports of a valve will have the following function:

Port A or 1—inlet
Port B or 2—to cylinder port—Side 1
Port C or 3—exhaust for Port B
Port D or 4—to cylinder port—Side 2
Port E or 5—exhaust for Port D

A two port—two position valve would be an on/off valve and be indicated in two boxes as illustrated. It is also called a two way valve. The arrows inside the boxes indicate the direction of the flow. Each box represents on the possible positions. The two way valve symbol shows one position of the valve: Port A is open to Port B and the other position indicates that both ports are closed or blocked.

Diagrams of valves. The arrows within the boxes indicate direction of flow.

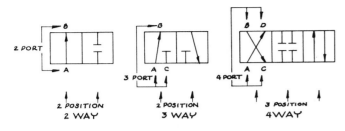

The three port—two position valve is mostly used for single acting cylinders and commonly called a three way valve. Four or five port, two and three positions valves are commonly used for controlling double acting cylinders and are called four way valves.

Plate and spool valves are the most common types of valves used for directional control. The plate valves are usually the least expensive and are manually controlled. Most electrically controlled directional valves are spool type and need at least 30 psi live pressure to provide pilot power to work the valves.

Manual valve

Solenoid (electrical) valve

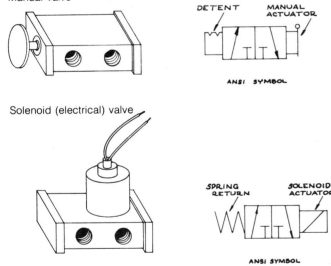

Valves which have a free flow in one direction and needle control check valve in the other direction are used for speed control. Speed controls for pneumatic devices are usually located on the exhaust side and regulate the escape of back pressure. Needle valves can be adjusted in a very gradual range and are useful for finite quantity control. The closer the speed control valves are to the cylinder, the smoother and more effective their control is.

Flow control valve

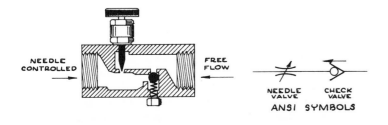

Flow control in circuit

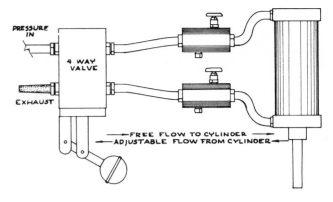

For on/off operation, the ball valve operates the quickest and the easiest to see whether it is open or closed. Poppet valves are usually used for electrical solenoid on/off operations.

Gate valve

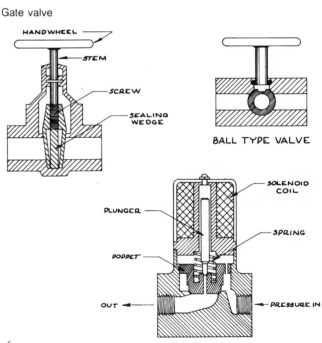

Electrically controlled poppet valve

5 Control regulation: Devices to control working pressure, psi. The regulator has a primary side which is the pressure of the tank of gas, the compressor output, or the line pressure of a system. And it has a secondary side, the regulated pressure, which is adjusted for the devices attached beyond the regulation. There are two basic types of regulators: relieving and non-relieving. The relieving regulator bleeds and lowers the pressure on the secondary side of the line as the pressure is lowered on the regulator. A non-relieving regulator affects only the input pressure as it is adjusted.

In order to monitor the adjustments of the regulator, a pressure meter or gauge is required; this would be placed in a port on the secondary side of the regulator. Regulators have various degrees of regulation, the most common being 0–30 psi, 0–60 psi, 0–125 psi, and 0–300 psi. To change the pressure capabilities of the regulator usually you merely need to exchange the pressure spring and gauge. Probably the most versatile for theatre, scene shop, and stage use is 0–125 psi.

Regulators come in a variety of sizes and configurations with various body shapes and adjustment knob handles. But the most common is a bell-like shape with a T adjusting handle. The miniature size regulator is usually available in 1/8″ through 1/4″, medium duty regulation in 1/8″ through 3/4″, and heavy duty regulation is available in 1/2″ to 1″. The sizes refer to the pipe openings of the ports of the regulator and the larger the size the higher the CFM capacity. The regulator works as it should only when it is properly connected in the flow of the circuit. An arrow usually is located on the device to show the way the air flow should be.

Regulator

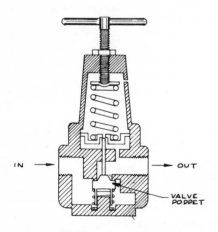

Usually there is a regulator for each function of the system. Spray painting, pneumatic tools, air casters, and clamping all require different pressures. For controlling a contained system (doing an onstage effect from a gas bottle) the regulator on the bottle is all the regulation that is required. Most spray painting pressures are less than 60 psi. Most air tools operate at 90 psi. Up-Right Scaffolding Air Lift operates at 120 psi. I try to keep all effects and working devices inside 0–100 psi working range but have used up to 150 psi on occasion.

6 Protection devices: Silencers, lubrication, filters, dryers, and gauges. These devices are also known as air preparation units or air system accessories. On a small, contained system that is driven by bottled gas, there is little need for these devices with the exception of a silencer. For the air system in the scene shop, a filter and lubricator will lessen the maintenance on the pneumatic tools.

In an air system the first device after the compressor should be a filter. This device captures liquids and large dirt particles by creating a cyclonic action that causes the undesirable elements to be thrown against the wall of the cup and fall into the "quiet zone" below the baffle to be drained off as the water builds up. The size of the filter is noted by the port size and should be as large as the size of output from the compressor. It is a good practice to have more than just one filter in the line. A filter just in front of each regulator in the system is another good location. This will capture rust, particles, and moisture that develop

in the line from the compressor to the working unit. The filter works properly only when the flow is in the right direction.

Filter

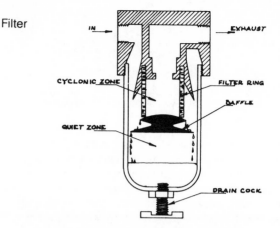

A lubricator is useful in keeping the pneumatics devices from rusting and keeping seals from drying out. It should be installed after the regulator and near the valves and working devices. The lubricator does cause the air to be a little dirty when it is exhausted. I have lubricated stage effects systems by dropping light weight oil into the disconnect stems and inlets rather than using a lubricator. The lubricator must be in a position so that it will not spill and must be attached with the right flow direction or it will not function properly. Most mist lubricators can be refilled while under pressure, and the mist is adjustable by a needle valve. Lubricators should not be used in spray painting systems.

Lubricator

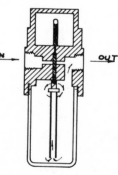

I have limited experience with dryers for compressed air. The only time I had a dryer on the line was when the air conditioning in the theatre used the same compressor and a dryer was necessary for operating that system's instruments. There are two basic types of dryers: chemical and refrigeration-type. Refrigeration-type dryers are expensive but require less maintenance than chemical dryers which must be attended and have chemicals changed or processed to maintain the drying abilities.

Pressure gauges are necessary throughout a pneumatics system in order to determine if there is pressure and to what degree. The meter is merely reading the pressure in the line to which it is attached. It is important to have a gauge at the compressor or tank which shows the psi that is available. Gauges are useful at all points where it is possible to adjust the pressure—that is at each regulator. A gauge is classified by its pipe thread size, edge or center mounting, its pressure scale, diameter of face of scale, and its functions, such as CO_2 gauge, oxygen gauge, acetyline, or air.

In Lab Theatre, we have covered the basic type of pneumatic hardware and circuitry. As you begin to use these basic elements of pneumatics, there are various considerations that you should keep in mind. One element of pneumatics which is often useful, but just as often annoying, is the softness of gas and air. The effect is manifest as spongy or cushion-like. Liquid-type fluid power is rigid and does not compress and expand as gas and air do. Air is not good to use when the load is being varied, such as a lift. When the load is removed, the lift would go up unless at the end of travel or pushed or pulled against a restraint. Also, if a load were placed on the lift, it would descend until the air had compressed adequately to match its weight in pressure. To prevent this spongy problem, air devices are usually designed to go through their full travel or to a stop. Pressure is maintained in the cylinder constantly to keep it stationary.

The following is a list of basic considerations:

1 Moisture should be controlled and removed from the system. Proper installation will help, but dryers are necessary on systems where precision equipment is in use, such as in the hospital or dentist's office. Also spray painting of oil-based paints may require a dryer.

2 Impurities should be filtered. This can be accomplished with filters on the intake of the compressor and in the pressurized line.

3 Lubrication of the lines and working units is necessary to prevent rust and drying out.

4 Leaks can cause loss of energy, noise, and excessive and unnecessary use of the compressor. Teflon tape or a pipe compound should be used on all pipe thread joints. Air or gas under pressure can escape through the smallest of spaces. If the compressor keeps coming on when no one is using the system, you can be sure you have a leak. In my experience, a slight leak in the system is almost unavoidable. There are often very minor leaks that can be detected in three ways: (1) if they can be heard, (2) if the compressor runs often without any devices being used, or (3) if the gas tank empties faster than it should.

5 There are three common ways of injuring yourself when using air power. (A) When a fitting comes loose under pressure, the end can whip around, causing damage; (B) When there is a break in the line or a fitting comes loose, the escaping air stirs up dust and debris that can get into your eyes, nose, and throat; and (C) When you are close to a break of a line under high pressure, 60 psi plug, the air may cause a burn. For your own safety, caution should be taken to make sure that all fittings are snugly attached and take care that kinks do not get in lines, tubing, and hoses. Care should be taken not to work on any systems that are under pressure. Before dismantling or changing fittings, be certain on/off valves have been closed, the system turned off, and the lines being altered have been drained of their pressure.

Originally published in May 1981

Hydro-Pneumatics

by Robert Scales

A principle relevant to the use of pressurized power applicable to the stage is pressure over fluid (hydro-pneumatics). Some ways of using this principle are in pumpless Hudson sprayers, in active, running water faucets, and for adjustable door closures.

Pumpless Hudson sprayers

The Hudson sprayer is a good example of the hydro-pneumatic principle. A Hudson sprayer consists of a tank in which liquid is pressurized. A hand pump creates air pressure on the liquid and this forces the liquid up a tube through a hose. With a control valve and spray nozzle, the liquid is sprayable.

Spray paint tanks operate in the same manner as the Hudson sprayer. Pressure is applied to the tank, and liquid is forced up a siphon tube and then through the hose to the spray gun.

With little difficulty, the Hudson pump sprayer can be replaced with a paint pressure tank. Cut the hose a short distance from the Hudson sprayer tank and attach the spray wand hose to the paint tank fluid output. If self-closing disconnects are placed on all hoses used for fluid, it enables any hose or spray nozzle which malfunctions or clogs to be easily replaced. Moreover, it enables any spray wand to connect to any paint or Hudson spray tank.

If the air input is a male disconnect stem, mounted with a one-way check valve or ball valve which closes the pressure in the tank, then the air line can be disconnected without the loss of tank pressure. Consequently, the paint tank can be moved about in the same manner as a Hudson type sprayer. To recharge the tank, merely plug in the air pressure line.

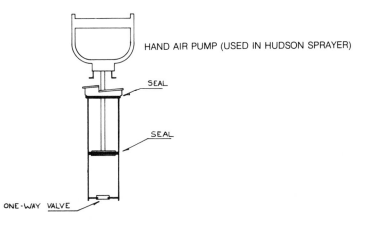

HAND AIR PUMP (USED IN HUDSON SPRAYER)

SEAL

SEAL

ONE-WAY VALVE

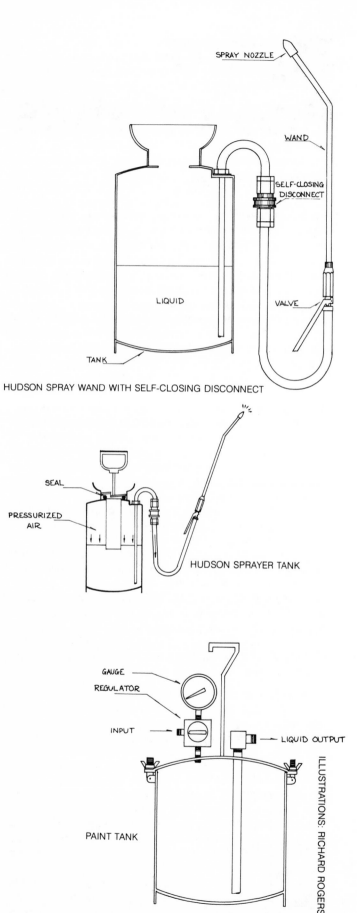

SPRAY NOZZLE

WAND

SELF-CLOSING DISCONNECT

LIQUID

VALVE

TANK

HUDSON SPRAY WAND WITH SELF-CLOSING DISCONNECT

SEAL

PRESSURIZED AIR

HUDSON SPRAYER TANK

GAUGE

REGULATOR

INPUT

LIQUID OUTPUT

PAINT TANK

ILLUSTRATIONS: RICHARD ROGERS

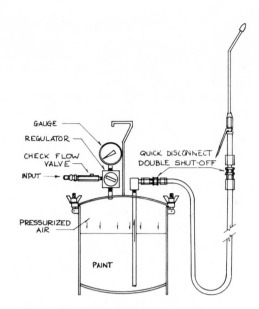

GAUGE

REGULATOR

CHECK FLOW VALVE

INPUT

QUICK DISCONNECT DOUBLE SHUT-OFF

PRESSURIZED AIR

PAINT

PAINT TANK WITH DISCONNECTS AND ONE-WAY CHECK VALVE

Disconnects used for fluids need to be kept clean. To clean out and drain the hose, a matching disconnect can be added to each end of the hose. Oil on the workings of the disconnect help keep it working properly; paint cleaner or solvent stored in the hoses help keep layers of dried paint from building up on the hose and fittings. The self-closing disconnects hold the cleaner or solvent in place.

When using a paint tank, the fluid hose may be as long as desired to minimize moving of the tank. If a clear plastic hose is used as a fluid carrying hose, then when the unit is cleaned it is easy to see when all the paint has been washed out. When using hot liquids or high pressure, be certain that the clear, plastic hose is strong enough not to expand or break.

With these modifications, a constant pressure can be selected by a regulator and the spray can be adjusted from mist to blobs of paint. If your shop is not equipped with an air compressor, bottled CO_2 or nitrogen can be used.

Philip Grayson, in "Solutions for painting and plumbing" (*Theatre Crafts,* May/June 1980), has suggested tapping the Hudson spray can tank and installing a valve core. I would suggest, however, tapping the tank, installing a one-way check valve or a ball valve, and then installing a male air disconnect stem. This would keep pressure on the tank at all times. Another alternative would be to disconnect the hose which would make the tank portable without the pressure escaping. The pump is also still functional if needed.

Running water faucets

I have often used the hydro-pneumatic principle when faucet water is needed on stage. Spray paint tanks come in a variety of sizes and one can be found to fit the available space and hold the required quantity of water. Any tank that can be made airtight, can be easily adapted to work. CO_2 is what we most commonly use for charging the water reservoir tanks. If space for a CO_2 tank is a problem, then small aerosol cans will provide adequate pressure; there is no noise, and the pressure is constant until the gas or water expires. When CO_2 is used, the

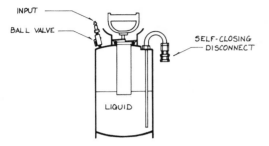

HUDSON SPRAYER WITH DISCONNECTS AND BALL VALVE

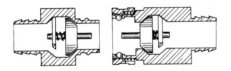

SELF-CLOSING DISCONNECTS

water will have a slightly carbonated taste. The reservoir water tank can be pre-charged with air or CO_2 and be identical in principle to the use of the Hudson sprayer.

The paint tank needs to be removable, so that it can be refilled. Disconnects make this convenient and should be on the liquid and pressure connections. To refill the tank, the pressure should be relieved first; then when the faucet is opened, the water in the hose will return to the tank—if the tank is located below the faucet. Self-closing disconnects should be used on the fluid hoses—to keep the fluid in the hoses and prevent spills. As the faucet is opened, if air has gotten into the water line, there will be noise and spurting of water. Pressure regulation will determine the force of the water coming out. The range of pressure required for a normal water flow is 10 psi to 40 psi. If paint tanks are used for the water reservoir in a stage faucet system, they must be clean. Or else a lining can be used to keep the water uncontaminated. All hoses and disconnects should be new. I prefer to use clear plastic hose for the fluid lines, so that the liquid in the line is visible.

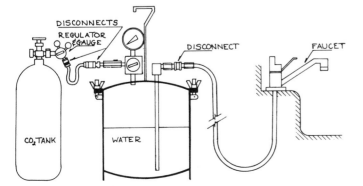

WATER FAUCETS ON STAGE.

Adjustable door closures

For Seattle Repertory Theatre's 1981 production of *Ah, Wilderness!* there were eight doors, each of which had to perform the following functions: 1) open and automatically close; 2) stay in the position; and 3) to be remotely controlled by a stagehand. The set consisted entirely of transparent walls and doors. All doors opened upstage. Only a 6″ baseboard was available to mask the devices.

The double-acting cylinder was used as the closure device. The cylinder was mounted on the back side of the transparent door and on the floor upstage of the door. The cylinder was connected to a four-way directional valve and pressurized to 24 psi, which was sufficient to push the doors shut and to pull the doors open. The cylinders were 1½″ bore, 6″ stroke. Four of the doors worked together on one four-way valve. A needle valve control in one direction, with full flow in the other direction, was installed to restrict the exhaust at the port of the cylinder used to pull open the door. Next, a piece of pipe was added to hold the amount of hydraulic jack oil required in the stroke which cushioned the door when it closed. After the pipe that held the oil was installed, a ¼″ plastic tubing was connected and circuited back to the four-way valve. The four-way valve had three positions:

1 Pressure on close side of cylinder, exhaust other side. This position was used as the door closure. When someone opened the door, the air would compress and the oil would be fully drawn into the other side of the cylinder. When the door was released, it closed automatically. The pressure on the close side of the cylinder would push the door back, and oil would flow back into the pipe reservoir, as regulated by the needle valve.

2 Center position of the valve. This placed both sides of the cylinder in exhaust. In this center position the door would stay at any position it was placed in. The piston created a minimal amount of friction—equivalent to using a paint brush attached as a drag on the door to hold it in position.

3 Pressure on the open side of the door, with exhaust on the close side of the door. This would open the door by remote control. The remote door closure is helpful in demonstrating the softness of air and how this is changed when oil is used to close the door with a smooth, controllable movement.

The amount of air or gas used to do this function is negligible. We used ¼″ plastic tubing and a 50 lb. CO_2 tank to control eight doors simultaneously. During the check outs, technical rehearsals, and the 40-performance schedule, the doors were opened and closed an equivalent of well over 1,000 valve movements. Only one 50 lb. CO_2 tank was used the entire time.

To prevent the doors from slamming shut and shaking the walls an oil cushion was necessary when closing the doors. No cushion was necessary when opening the doors because the open stop was set by the end of the cylinder travel and the doors did not need to touch or mate to the frame.

The amount of oil in the pipe reservoir can be varied to set the amount of cushion. Only the last inch of travel of the piston movement was cushioned. The limited cushion allowed the door to move quickly from full open to where the cushion starts to work, which slowed down the travel and cased the door into the door frame.

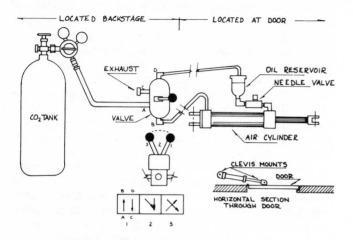

HYDRO-PNEUMATIC DOOR CLOSURE

Specialized parts and approximate cost

3/8" self-closing disconnects (a pair male stem and body)	$12.00
1/4" male stem disconnect	1.00
1/4" female body disconnect	3.00
1/4" one-way flow check valve	10.00
1/4" ball valve	7.00
1/4" free flow meter needle valve	10.00
1 1/2" bore, 6" stroke double acting cylinders	50.00
Four-way, three-position valve with detent and center exhaust both cylinder ports	40.00
Total	$133.00

Originally published in June 1981

The Remote Swivel Brake Caster

by Robert Scales

Remote swivel brake caster (RSB caster)

Problem: To provide a secure lock on a rolling scenic unit which will be moved on a raked, stage floor as part of a visible scene shift. The rolling unit will be moved into position by actors who must be able to easily place the unit on spike marks and activate an instantly responding brake that will hold the unit securely in place. *Enemy of the People,* Seattle Repertory Theatre (SRT), 1980.

Solution: To develop a remotely controlled brake for a free-wheeling swivel caster. When the brake is engaged, it would hold the caster in a fixed position regardless of the caster wheel position.

Design of device: To minimize mechanical complications, the brake device had to be a single unit that did not have to travel with the movement of the wheel or horn. The first problem was to find a common point where the caster wheel would always be, regardless of its moving position. There were two constant points which the wheel of the

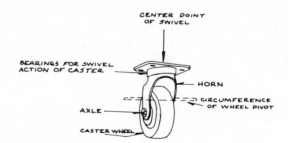

SWIVEL CASTER PARTS AND CONSTANT POINTS

caster maintains, regardless of position: 1) in the center of the pivot of the caster; and 2) the circumference of the wheel from the pivot of the caster horn. If a brake were installed at the center of the pivot, the device would need to extend above the mounting plate of the caster, and this would create problems in mounting the caster to the unit. I also wanted to have the locking device work in the same space in which the wheel operated to maintain as low a profile as possible.

Construction of swivel brake

For days I carried a Darnell 4″ swivel caster around with me, saying "there must be a way to do this." I constantly looked at the caster—studying its basic functions and exploring ways of braking the wheel.

Early in this project, I worked on braking the wheel at the circumference of the horn. First, I attempted to cut two lengths of pipe that would sleeve into each other. One

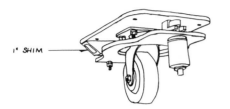

RSB CASTER UNIT PROTOTYPE

piece of pipe would be attached to the caster mounting plate, and the other would screw down to brake the wheel of the caster or screw up to free the wheel. The movement of the brake pipe ring would be guided by slanted lots in the sleeved pipe.

I never completed this prototype because I discovered a simpler method. Instead, I made a ¼″ plywood plate with a hole that had a slightly larger circumference than the circumference travel of the caster horn. After some experimentation with spacing in order to obtain leverage and working parameters of the piston, the wooden prototype was complete. It demonstrated that the idea would probably work.

The next step was to build a working model. The project was given to Michael Boulanger, our scene shop foreman, who made a ¼″ aluminum plate working unit. Aluminum was used because it is easily cut and because it would strengthen the unit.

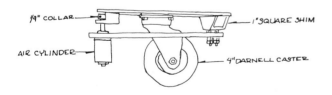

Although some of these parts were welded in the SRT model, welding is not necessary to create the device. Aluminum can be cut with the same tools and blades used to cut wood. The band saw is probably the best tool to cut the ¼″ aluminum plate into the desired shapes; however, a hand jigsaw or saber saw can also be used.

Pneumatic-controlled brake

Once the brake plate worked effectively as the stop mechanism for the wheel, the next concern was how to activate the brake plate. The original design made the device pneumatic-controlled. It consisted of 1″ bore, ⅝″ stroke, single acting spring cylinder. This cylinder was activated by CO_2 or through a small switch-type, 3-way valve hooked up to a small aerosol can.

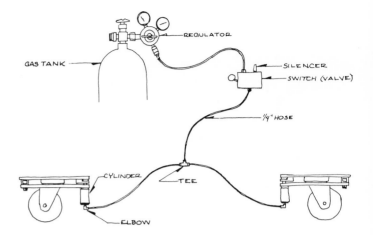

PNEUMATIC CONTROL CIRCUIT FOR RSB CASTERS

The control pressure used for this device was 40 psi. We used only two RSB casters per moving unit. This seemed enough to hold the moving unit in place, if the major weight was under the braking casters.

Hydraulic-controlled variation

For *Ah, Wilderness!*, SRT 1981 production, we had three RSB caster systems controlled by a simple hydraulic linkage device. All the furniture and scenic elements in *Ah, Wilderness* were on casters and shifted in view of the audience from scene to scene. Each caster unit had some brake mechanism to hold it in position when placed on spike marks for each scene. The hydraulic-controlled RSB casters were used on a couch, an overstuffed chair, and bed. The actors who were shifting the units moved a handle in one direction to free the valve; to lock the casters, the handle would be moved in the opposite direction.

The hydraulic-controlled RSB caster unit was identical to the pneumatic-controlled unit. The only differences in the control were: 1) the entire line was filled with jack oil, and 2) instead of a switch-type valve and pressure tank, a 1″ bore, 1½″ stroke double acting cylinder was used as a pump. A handle was devised to work as a lever and lock down the rod of the pump cylinder. When the pump cylinder pushed the oil into the 1″ bore, ⅝″ stroke cylinder that held the brake plate against the caster, a notch on the handle held the pump rod in position until freed. When the handle was released, to free the pump cylinder, a spring placed on the rod pushed the pump cylinder rod out, drawing oil out of the brake control cylinder and freeing the caster brake plate from the wheel.

The hydraulic-control has two major advantages over the pneumatic-control. First, it makes no noise, and second, there are no tanks to replace since the system is totally sealed. Maintenance, such as refilling the oil, is not necessary, if there are no leaks in the system. However, some leakage is to be expected around pockings and seals; therefore, a periodic check should be made to make certain the lines are full of oil.

Improvements of RSB device

The RSB device is workable in its present state, but there are several improvements, or at least changes, that can be

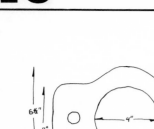

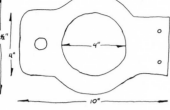

BRAKE PLATE

PARTS FOR SWIVEL BRAKE FOR CASTER

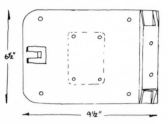

MOUNTING PLATE

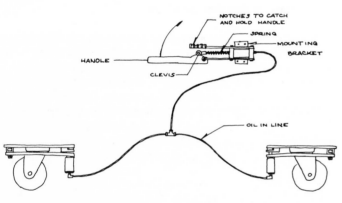

HYDRAULIC LINKAGE CONTROL CIRCUIT TO RSB CASTERS

made in the device to make it quiet and simpler. Some of the changes we are presently exploring are 1) a more positive hinge to minimize any rattling noise, 2) covering the posts with neoprene to prevent noise of metal-to-metal sounds, 3) use of a more compact cylinder to allow more clearance of mechanics when applying the brakes, 4) use of a closed system of linkage from the brake to the control that would be positive and not reliant on an air supply or any other form of diminishing power.

Parts and materials
The swivel brake unit
■ 4″ swivel caster with soft rubber tread over a hard rubber core wheel

■ ¼″ aluminum plate for base with hinge attachment holes for mounting the brake plate and holes for mounting the caster and a catch for the end of the piston

■ ¼″ aluminum plate with a circle cut that works as a brake plate against the caster wheel with holes for mounting to the hinge and for mounting the piston

The control of the brake unit
■ 1″ bore, ⅝″ stroke, single acting spring return pneumatic cylinder with a stop collar on the rod (P-100 Air Mite Micro model cylinder $10.00)

■ for pneumatic control: 3-way detented valve normally closed (31V Humphrey TAC toggle valve $10.00)

■ CO_2 tank and regulator or aersol can

■ or for hydraulic control: 1″ bore, 1½″ stroke double acting cylinder with spring return $15.00

Evaluation of device
The original four units have been used in several shows without a problem. The lock worked extremely well on the raked stage, ¾″ in 10″ rise. A safety cable was engaged on the unit to deal with the possibility of loss of air or accident in setting, but fortunately it was never required to catch the unit. We now have more than twelve RSB casters which were used on moving scenic and prop units for *Ah, Wilderness!* SRT, 1981. Other possibilities of this device could be to work as a lock pivot for a portable turn table, or jackknife pivot. At this point, we have made brakes only for 4″ Darnell swivel casters using a soft tread, hard core wheel. The idea may work on a smaller caster, but the piston would probably need to be mounted horizontally and have a mechanical linkage to the brake plate.

Originally published in October 1981

Pneumatics: Single Movement Effects

by Robert Scales

The problem: To make a bell located in a tree ring when an actor shoots at it from across the stage (*Penny For A Song*, Seattle Repertory Theatre, 1978).
The process: A 1″ bore, 1″ stroke, single-acting push cylinder with spring return was used to hit the bell on its upstage side. The bell was located on the railing of a platform. The platform, which held other signaling devices and a chair, was located about 12′ above the stage floor.

PENNY FOR A SONG

A plunger-type spring return, three-way spool valve activated the effect. When the gun fired, a second actor, who was on the platform playing a watchman sleeping in the chair, reacted with a start, hitting the valve with his hand. This rang the bell as if it had been hit by a bullet.

Two parts of the effect were particularly difficult to achieve: where and how to hit the bell so that the ring would not only be loud enough but also sound as if the bell had been hit by a bullet, and how to time the ring to correspond with the shot. We chose to use the second actor's reaction to the shot as the timing device, and that decision worked well. The actor's reflexes were very reliable. Even when the stage gun did not fire and the back-stage back-up gun was used, the actor was on cue.

After trying several locations for the piston—inside the bell and on the top of the bell—we determined that the best sound came when the lower lip of the bell was hit from the outside with a blow hard enough to swing the bell slightly. It was necessary to keep the clanger functioning because the actor had to ring the bell directly on several cues.

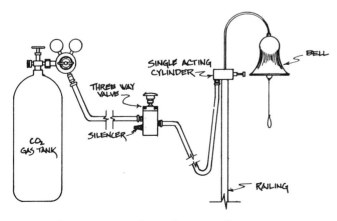

CIRCUIT FOR BELL RING BY GUNSHOT

Design of effect

The effect was a self-contained pneumatic system which was located entirely in the tree. A CO_2 tank located in the tree trunk (which was open in the back) provided the power. To achieve a fast, hard movement of the piston, 90psi was used. The stage crew would turn the tank on before each performance, making certain there was at least that much pressure. A 20-lb. CO_2 tank was used and lasted throughout the entire 40-performance run of the show. The device was always checked before each performance, to make sure that the piston and bell were aligned and that no obstruction had lodged in the tubing. We added a stop collar to the end of the cylinder to make sure it hit the edge of the bell. At the sound of the shot, the actor in the tree reacted by slapping his hands on the arm of the chair, hitting the valve handle with the palm of his hand. (Actually, the actor merely tapped the valve.) It released a shot of air, which caused the cylinder to push quickly against the bell and immediately retract. If the actor had held the valve down, the piston rod would have stayed next to the bell and deadened the ring. A silencer was placed on the exhaust of the valve.

Evaluation of the device

Pneumatics worked well for this system. It was self-contained, with no excessive wires or plumbing to ruin. It was also reliable. We could have used a solenoid and a momentary electrical switch, but that would have entailed an electrical feed from somewhere, a humming noise, and the inability to adjust the force of hitting the bell, which was possible by regulating the psi in the pneumatic system.

Parts of the system

CO_2 gas tank (cost of gas only)	$10.00*
CO_2 regulator	50.00
Three-way push spring return valve with ¼" ports	25.00
1" bore, 1" stroke, single acting push cylinder with spring return ¼" tubing, ¼" silencer, tubing fittings to pipe for connects to parts of all the devices	10.00
Total	**$105.00**

*Represents the only expended cost, since all other elements are reusable.

The problem: To create the effect of a hot poker being placed in a bucket of water (*The Taming of the Shrew*, Seattle Repertory Theatre, 1980).

The process: The setting included a barn, a blacksmith shop, haystack, hay loft, and ropes and pulleys for moving hay and actors. During the fight between the two sisters, Kate takes a hot poker from the forge and threatens to brand Bianca.

The poker was a wooden dowel with a vial of titanium tetrachloride mounted in one end. A skin of wax was used to close the vial. Kate would break the seal on the vial by poking it into a bed of nails concealed in the forge. Once the wax seal was broken, the end of the poker began to smoke, and Kate could brandish a seemingly hot poker at

THE TAMING OF THE SHREW

her sister. At the climax of the fight, the poker was returned to the forge and the hot end stuck into the water, producing hissing and bubbling sounds. It was a nice punctuation to Kate's actions.

A coffee can full of water was placed in the forge's water trough. A 5-lb. siphon-type CO_2 fire extinguisher was hidden in the forge under the glowing coals. After a futile search for an electrically operated valve that would deal with the 900psi liquid CO_2, we installed a 1" stroke, 1" bore, single-acting spring return cylinder to push down the handle and give a burst of CO_2 from the tank to the can of water.

The first time we activated the unit, we blew all the water out of the can. Needless to say, this was a bit excessive, so a low pressure hydraulic needle valve was added just beyond the fire extinguisher valve. This enabled a controllable burst of liquid to make the result credible and effective.

Design of the device

The entire set was placed on a raked floor, and the forge did not move during the production. This meant that hoses and wires could be run up through the floor and into the unit. We decided that the hiss of the poker would be done

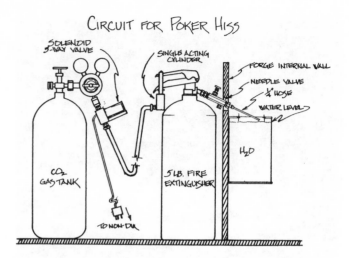

CIRCUIT FOR POKER HISS

by the electrician on a non-dim circuit. He was also controlling other effects in the forge, such as the glowing coals and a flicker device.

It was important to have an instant response to the poker hiss. Therefore, it was necessary to have the control device right at the forge—preferably in the forge. The use of an electrically controlled three-way valve also made the effect easy for the stage managers to cue and for the electrician at the switchboard to operate. Also hidden in the forge was a 5-lb. CO_2 gas cylinder, used to activate the piston cylinder. The piston cylinder pushed the handle of the siphon-type CO_2 fire extinguisher which caused the hiss and vapor when it was released into the water.

A small bracket was made to mount the piston cylinder on the fire extinguisher handle. This facilitated quick replacement of fire extinguishers when one became empty. Although we used only two bottles for over 50 performances, we were prepared in case there was a leak or if we needed to make a bottle change.

The only modification to the fire extinguisher was removing the nozzle and replacing it with a ¼" needle valve and a short piece of ¼" plastic tubing. (All fittings used in this project were ¼".) By placing the needle valve immediately after the fire extinguisher valve, it was possible to adjust

LOCATION OF POKER HISS MECHANISM IN THE FORGE

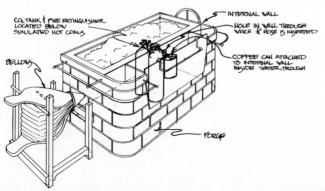

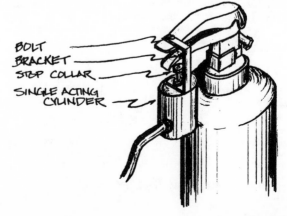

DETAIL OF CYLINDER ATTACHMENT TO FIRE EXTINGUISHER

the force of the CO_2 liquid. The needle valve was open only slightly for this effect.

The length of time that the electrically controlled valve was activated determined the length of the effect. We got the best effect when the valve was activated on the go of the cue, then immediately turned off. If we had used a momentary switch, it would have had to be held down for only a second.

When the fire extinguisher handle was activated, liquid flowed immediately into the pipe fitting and body of the needle valve. The needle valve restricted the flow, so that when the electrical control was disengaged the CO_2 liquid continued to come out for a short period. A 1″ long, ¼″ pipe nipple was used to connect the fire extinguisher to the ¼″ needle valve. Tighter control could have been achieved by using a reducing brush, a close ⅛″ nipple and a ⅛″ needle valve, which would have lessened the volume of storage in the pipe and valve cavities.

Evaluation of the device

Our only cost for this device was two small CO_2 fire extinguishers, which we have since refilled for use in the shop. All the other items were in stock. It is satisfying to be able to provide those little touches that are not really essential to the story but are helpful in creating the production's style and give actors an opportunity to play off the effect. And the effect fit well with Kate's character.

The effect was reliable. The bottles were weighed periodically as the run progressed to verify the amount of CO_2 they had. Periodic weighing allows the amount of usage to be determined. Bottles of CO_2 should also be checked on a regular basis for leaks or mechanical problems which may have developed.

CO_2 fire extinguishers are effective devices for creating steam effects, such as for radiator steam, a steam whistle, or a steam engine. The principle used in controlling the poker hiss device could easily be adapted to help achieve other effects utilizing CO_2 fire extinguishers.

Parts of the system

(These costs would have applied if we did not have a stock of pneumatic devices.)

CO_2 gas tank (cost of gas only)	$5.00*
CO_2 regulator	50.00
CO_2 fire extinguisher refill, per 5-lb. tank	5.00*
CO_2 fire extinguisher	30.00
Solenoid three-way valve	20.00
¼″ flow control valve	10.00
1″ bore, 1″ stroke, piston cylinder	10.00
¼″ plastic tubing, fittings, and silencer	10.00
Total	**$135.00**

*Represents the only expended cost, since all other elements are reusable.

Originally published in March 1982

Earthquakes

by Robert Scales

A History of the American Film offers numerous opportunities for interesting and unique effects, with the major effect being an earthquake. For the Seattle Repertory Theatre's production, in 1979, Jim Newton, the scenic designer, and the scene shop staff created a 90-second earthquake which completely rearranged the stage picture but allowed the set to be restored to pre-earthquake status in less than 30 minutes.

The general approach to the earthquake was to shake, tilt, and move all the scenic elements and to break apart specific elements of the set, as smoke swirled and lightweight debris rained down. The choreography of the scene destruction was synchronized with lighting and sound effects.

Most of the effects were achieved with pneumatic devices. We used our entire inventory of valves, cylinders, and air casters, as well as some new equipment. Many of the effects were controlled by the electrician by means of electrically operated valves. In addition to our regular six non-dim circuits, a special switchbox of 12 controllable circuits was used. All other scenic effects were managed by a fly on the rail and two stagehands behind the set at pneumatic control stations.

The set for this production consisted of black scrim walls with painted wallpaper in whites and grays, standing wall units, a balcony, orchestra boxes stage left and stage right with rails, a false proscenium in the center of the set, six doorways with curtains covering their entrances, and a three-tier seating unit complete with 20 theatre seats which rolled upstage and down. The earthquake functions were determined by three criteria:

- What would register with the audience as an effect;
- What effect was possible with the equipment we had in stock and could afford for the production; and
- What could be restored to pre-earthquake status within a 30 minute time period.

The final earthquake plot consisted of the following effects (with each step number, all effects of that number started simultaneously and continued throughout the earthquake effect):

Effect	Operator	Control device
1a—Theatre seats shake	Stage carpenter	Air valve–manual
1b—Stage right box wall shakes	Electrician	Momentary electric switch
1c—Stage left box wall and curtain shakes	Electrician	Momentary electric switch
1d—Smoke from back wall	Electrician	On/off switch

2a—Debris falls from flies	Fly	Counterweight line
2b—Film spews from projection	Stage carpenter	Air valve–manual
2c—Back and side walls of set shake	Stagehand A	Air valve–manual
2d—Smoke from projection windows	Electrician	On/off switch
2e—Wind to move smoke	Electrician	On/off switch
3a—Balcony rail falls	Electrician	Air valve–manual
3b—Downstage right curtain falls	Electrician	On/off switch
3c—Complete dump of debris	Fly	Counterweight lines
4—Stage left balcony curtain falls	Stage carpenter	Air valve–manual
5—Stage right balcony curtain falls	Stage carpenter	Air valve–manual
6—Projection booth explodes	Stage carpenter	Manual pull line
7—Masking falls revealing scrim walls	Fly	Counterweight lines
8—Stop all effects		

Devices and techniques

A wide variety of devices and techniques were used to create each step of the earthquake. One of the most interesting devices was Firestone's Airstroke Actuator, a bellows-type cylinder. I became acquainted with the Firestone Airstroke Actuator through a phone call with Duncan Mac-

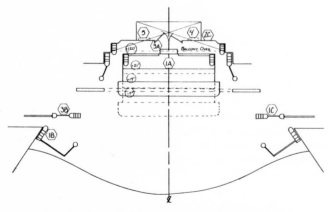

FLOOR PLAN PLOT OF EARTHQUAKE EFFECTS

Kenzie. When he described the device, it seemed to be the best solution for step 1a (theatre seats rise and shake).

The theatre seat platforms were framed in aluminum 1″ x 2″ rectangular tubing. The entire seating unit was bolted together to make a single unit. The seating unit was on straight casters, which enabled it to be moved up and downstage for various scenes. Four bellows-type cylinders were mounted under the unit on the aluminum framing. When the seat riser moved on the wheeled casters, the bellows' pistons were pulled in tight by a vacuum pump. Once the vacuum was complete a ball valve was closed to hold the vacuum, which held the bellows clear of the floor.

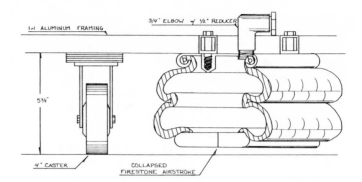

FIRESTONE AIRSTROKE MOUNTING TO SEATING WAGON

The bellows pistons used on this unit were Firestone Airstroke Actuators #21. We used a double convolution type, which gave a stroke long enough to lift the entire platform loaded with seven actors high enough to enable the unit to be bounced about.

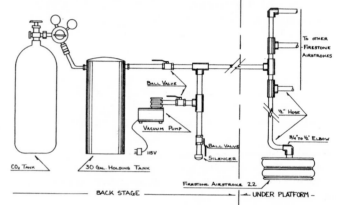

PLUMBING CIRCUITRY FOR CONTROLLING AIRSTROKE DEVICES

The port in the bellows piston was $3/4''$ pipe thread. This was reduced to a $1/2''$ hose feed. One 50-lb. CO_2 tank was used to inflate the four bellows pistons. For the earthquake effect the pistons were inflated to their complete lift. The pressure was kept low to make the bellows cylinder spongy. As actors moved about on the seating unit, the entire seating unit flexed and was very bouncy.

A reservoir tank has proved very helpful when using CO_2 bottled gas. The tank enables an adequate quantity of low pressure air to quickly inflate the bellows cylinders, without causing the CO_2 regulator to freeze. The tanks we have used for this purpose are 30-gallon tanks; one was a hot water tank and another was a tank used on a portable compressor. The tanks cost about $10 each, and were purchased according to weight from a scrap yard. One must be careful in bargain hunting for containers that will be put under pressure: we did a safety check on each of these tanks for a much higher pressure than we would use.

The Airstroke Actuator

Firestone Airstroke Actuators #21 cost about $90 each. Firestone Industrial Products Company (Firestone Boulevard, Noblesville, Indiana 46069) has prepared a pamphlet, phlet, "Actuate Isolate Ride," which gives detailed information on their actuators. Airstroke Actuators are made of reinforced rubber and metal, and are rubber bellows. They are furnished in single, double, and triple convolution types to cover a variety of force and stroke requirements. Metal closures, crimped over the ends, provide means of attachment and inflation. The metal endplates are furnished with $3/8''$ 16-thread blind holes for mounting, and with $1/4''$ NPT inflation fittings. The option of $3/4''$ NPT fittings for inflation is also available. I would recommend the $3/4''$ size, because this enables fast inflation and deflation. Some of the Airstroke Actuators' special features are:

- low initial costs, no air or fluid wasted because the actuators do not leak;
- there are no moving parts, no sliding seals, no rods, no pistons;
- less friction, because there are no moving parts;
- capable of considerable angularity, not requiring a clevis or mechanical linkage for attachment; and
- they are very compact.

We have used the Airstroke Actuator for tip jack devices and for lift devices for raising scenery to caster pallets for shifting.

Air bearings

Another interesting device was the Aero-Go air bearing. A dozen of these air bearings were used to shake the set's back and side walls. In order to accommodate the volume of air required for the air bearings, two 50-lb. CO_2 cylinders were hooked in parallel to a reservoir tank. The most satisfactory response of the air bearings resulted when the reservoir was charged to 100psi and a $1''$ orifice low-pressure regulator was used to turn on, regulate, and turn off the control of the air bearings.

I have accrued some experience with the use of air bearings over the last 14 years. Roger Cain, who was the layout carpenter for The Guthrie Theater in 1967, made me aware that air bearings existed. He knew of their use in television studios in California and helped me locate the manufacturer. I have continued to use air bearings but have become more selective about when to use them, as a result of learning where they best serve and, of course, where they are more trouble than they are worth. The air bearings used for the earthquake effect worked very well; I would have preferred, however, an air supply powerful enough to over-inflate the air bearings, which would have caused them to jump.

In order to keep the cost to a minimum for air bearings, I have made it a general practice to buy just the replacement bearing, without a load supporting frame. In the shop we have developed our own support system, which is less expensive and allows a lower profile for mounting the casters. (See *Theatre Crafts,* September 1977, for some operating information on air bearings.)

The effect in steps

Steps 1b and 1c—the downstage walls shake. This was activated by the electrician pushing momentary switches in an erratic timing.

The plumbing for the tipping walls was the same as for the single action effects described in lab theatre part six. The tipping wall units were hinged to the floor and pushed

and pulled in place by $8''$ stroke, $1\frac{1}{2}''$ bore double-acting pistons.

Step 1d—smoke begins to come through from two machines located upstage. The fog machines were remotely controlled electrically, with CO_2 tanks used as propellant of the fog juice and the electrician switching on the effect. The smoke machines were built using the same principle described in *Theatre Crafts,* January 1977.

Step 2a—debris begins to fall over the seating unit. A

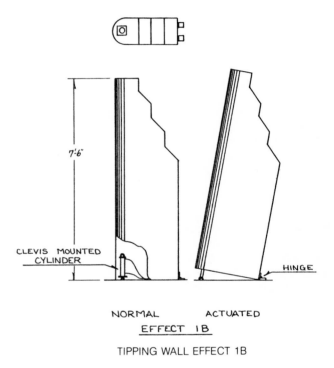

NORMAL   ACTUATED

EFFECT 1B

TIPPING WALL EFFECT 1B

$12'$ deep border, with a pipe stiffener in the bottom hem, was used as a trip bag, in which Styrofoam and rubber foam scraps, Ethafoam rod, rope, erosion cloth scraps, and corrugated cardboard scraps were placed. As the flyman lowered and manipulated the trip and hanging line sets, various pieces would tumble down between the wall of the set and the seating unit, which was in its downstage position.

Step 2b—35mm film stock begins to spew from the projection booth window. An air motor drove a double roller device that pinched the film between the roller—pulling it off its reel and pushing it out the window with force. The air motor speed was set by a needle valve on the exhaust side of the motor. A resistance was added to the film reel to keep the reel from unwinding the film faster than the pinch rollers were pulling it.

Step 2c—all set walls and the balcony begin to float and move in an erratic manner. Twelve Aero-Go air bearings were placed under the wall units. Four of the air bearings were $14''$ diameter, and these were located under the balcony in up center position. Six were $12''$, and these were employed three on either side under the side walls. All the wall flat units were hinged together. When the air bearings were inflated, a single stagehand was able to push and

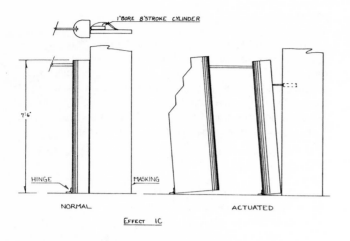

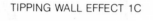

TIPPING WALL EFFECT 1C

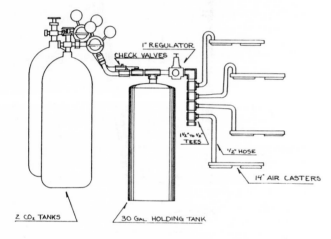

CIRCUITRY FOR AIR BEARINGS

pull on the stage right corner of the set walls and all the walls would move, shake, and vibrate.

Step 2d—the third smoke machine was turned on by the electrician, and smoke began to come through the windows of the projection booth.

Step 2e—a Mole-Richardson wind machine starts, causing the smoke to come out the projection booth windows.

Step 3a—the balcony rail falls over and dangles from restraining wire rope cables which predetermined the fall of the rail, a dramatic effect center stage. The activator was a single-control type of device: when the pins were retracted under air pressure, the railing was precut in an angle that caused it to slide forward and flip over. The railing was restrained at the bottom by cables, which caught it in an awkward looking angle in space.

Step 3b—curtains fall downstage. To do this, a single acting 1½″ bore, 2″ stroke with spring returns was activated by an electrically controlled valve, operated by the electrician. The curtain rod was a piece of tubing, which also had a wire rope attached to each end. When the piston pins were activated, the rods fell at a predetermined position.

Steps 4 and 5—the balcony curtains fall. These curtains were controlled by the stage carpenter, using manually controlled air valves, but otherwise operated in the same way as Step 3b.

Step 6—the projection booth falls apart. A stagehand pulled a cable connected upstage that pulled apart the projection booth wall. The booth was built of irregularly shaped blocks that were all cabled together, so it fell apart in a controlled manner.

Step 7—lowering all the masking, as flashing lights behind the walls revealed that the walls were scrim. At this point the stage was full of smoke and debris as well.

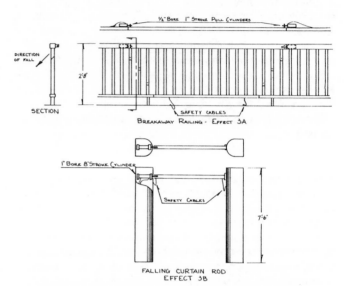

PIN RELEASE DEVICES FOR BALCONY RAIL AND CURTAINS

Problems

The plumbing for this project was not planned as well as it should have been. This made troubleshooting difficult. When tubing was neated up, staples had penetrated the lines, causing very small leaks, and there was no overall plan or drawing to trace what lines did what.

Because of the reliance on bottle gas and the need for so many tanks, the pre-show check required a lot of time. It was sometimes uncertain whether enough gas would be left in the tank for the effect. We needed either a good-size compressor or more accurate metering of tank level. In all, we used about thirty 50-lb. CO_2 tanks for approximately 40 performances, including rehearsals and previews.

Originally published in August/September 1982

Cable Cylinders

by Robert Scales

My first encounter with cable cylinders was over ten years ago, when we borrowed a 35′ stroke, 1½″ bore hydraulic cable cylinder from Bill Cruse, who at that time was with Hydrofloat. He lent us the cylinder, a power supply, and an electrically controlled proportional spool valve for a production of *Hough in Blazes*, designed by Robert Mitchell, at the Harold Prince Theatre in the Annenberg Center of Performing Arts, in Philadelphia.

The Harold Prince Theatre is a black box theatre about 80′ square. We used the cable cylinder to move a sound effects trolley wagon across the room, stopping it at various points in its travel. The cable cylinder was mounted under the elevated floor and track on which the trolley traveled. It was necessary to double purchase the system to allow the wagon to travel 70′ and also to increase its speed, which was useful in moving a wagon such a distance.

The cable cylinder solved this particular scenic problem, and this gave me the opportunity to explore its potentials. I have never used a hydraulic cable cylinder again, however. My experience has been primarily with pneumatic cable cylinders.

Pneumatic cable cylinders

While at the Stratford (Ontario, Canada) Festival Theatre, I purchased seven pneumatic cable cylinders; since I have been at the Seattle Rep, we have acquired three cable cylinders and put them to a variety of uses. In the United States I have used only cable cylinders manufactured by

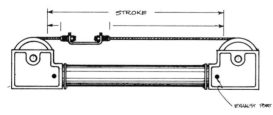

PNEUMATIC CABLE CYLINDER

STROKE

EXHAUST PORT

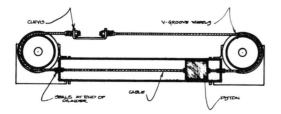

SECTION THROUGH CENTER

CLEVIS   V-GROOVE WHEEL

SEALS AT END OF CYLINDER   CABLE   PISTON

Tol-O-Matic. Another domestic manufacturer of cable cylinders is Cable-Trol. Two manufacturers in Canada are Martonair and Compair, which are both located in the Toronto area. Tol-O-Matic has a very complete information bulletin on cable cylinders, which is available upon request of the manufacturer.

Tol-O-Matic also makes a cylinder called Magneband, which is similar to the Swedish Origa rodless cylinder. I have not used cylinders, but I can readily see some advantages of the Magneband over the cable type. The primary improvement is that there is no cable stretch, and it has a very positive tracking. Cable cylinder cables will twist and stretch, which in some cases is an advantage but often creates problems.

Specifications

The cable cylinder is a very simple device in principle. A core piston with a cable attached is inserted into a tube that is sealed and capped at each end. The end seals enable the passage of the cable, which is a plastic-coated wire rope and provides ports to pressurize the tube causing the pistons to move. Also, at each end of a double acting cable cylinder there is a groove wheel for the run of the cables that are connected to each other by a bracket or clevis, which is the mechanical linkage to the work.

Cable cylinders are available in a diameter (bore) from ¾″ to 8″ and lengths from inches to 60′. The tube cylinder comes in brass, steel, or aluminum. I have used mostly steel, because it is less expensive. I would prefer aluminum, however, because it is less susceptible to rust. Adjustable cushions are extremely helpful and are supplied on all models except ¾″ and 1″. The cost of the cable cylinder is relative to its diameter and length. Two hundred dollars would be the approximate cost of a 5′ stroke, 1″ bore cylinder. A 12′ stroke, 4″ bore cylinder would be near $500. When you consider the equivalent cost of a variable speed electric controlled winch, the price is very reasonable.

Cable cylinders are also available for low pressure hydraulics. The following chart is Tol-O-Matic's cylinder forces at their respective psi:

FORCE AT VARIOUS PRESSURES

(Breakaway pressure is 6 to 10 psi; continuous pull is 2 psi on 2″ and larger)
(Low Breakaway 1.5–2 psi available on request.)

BORE	EFFECTIVE AREA	25psi	50psi	60psi	80psi	90psi	100psi	125psi	150psi
¾″	.435	10.9	21.8	26.1	34.8	39.2	43.5		
1″	.7785	19.5	38.9	46.7	62.3	70.1	77.9		
1½″	1.7395	43.5	87.0	104.4	139.2	156.6	174.0	217.4	260.9
1¾″	2.3777	59.4	118.9	142.7	190.2	214.0	237.8	297.2	356.7
2″	3.0925	77.3	154.6	185.6	247.4	278.3	309.2	386.6	463.9
2½″	4.8596	121.5	243.0	291.6	388.8	437.4	486.0	607.4	728.9
3″	6.9919	174.8	349.6	419.5	559.4	629.3	699.2	874.0	1048.8
4″	12.4897	312.2	624.5	749.4	999.2	1124.1	1249.0	1405.1	1873.5
6″	28.0780	702.0	1403.9	1684.7	2246.2	2527.0	2800	3510	4212
8″	49.8726	1246.8	2493.6	2992.4	3989.8	4488.5	4987	6234	7480
		150psi	200psi	250psi	300psi	350psi	400psi	450psi	500psi

One of the simplest functions to perform with cable cylinders is to open and close a sliding door or to open and close curtains. We have used the 5′ stroke, 1″ bore cable cylinder several times in various ways to deal with this function. At Seattle Rep in *Catsplay* we used a direct linkage; in *Ah,*

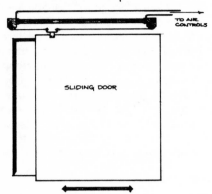

DIRECT LINKAGE

SLIDING DOOR

TO AIR CONTROLS

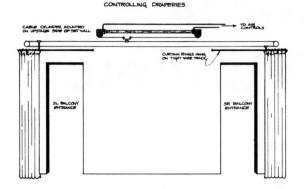

CONTROLLING DRAPERIES

Wilderness! it was attached to the continuous line for a sliding panel; and in *A History of the American Film* it pulled two sets of red, white, and blue flags into the balcony entrance. Pressures used for these effects ranged from 40 to 80psi.

Use in production

I have found cable cylinders extremely helpful in horizontal and vertical movement on a moving counterweight batten.

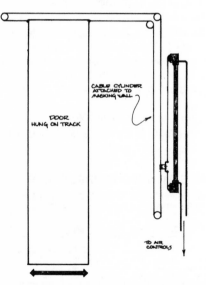

CABLE DRIVE LINKAGE

DOOR HUNG ON TRACK

CABLE CYLINDER ATTACHED TO MASKING WALL

TO AIR CONTROLS

The cable cylinder when mounted to an existing batten requires no additional space in the fly, and the air control hoses are easily paged in the same manner as one would page an electrical cable on a moving batten. Care must be taken to cradle the hose pick-ups to prevent the hose from crimping and restricting the air flow.

For a production of *Tintypes* the 5' stroke, 1" bore cable cylinder was mounted to the batten that lowered two industrial light fixtures into the scene. We attached the cable cylinder to the electrical cable of the socket of one of the two fixtures, so that on cue the light bulb would come down from the shade

and light, then return back into the light fixture. The pressure for this effect was 50psi.

For the Seattle Rep's production of *Saint Joan*, designed by Ming Cho Lee, the scene for the throne room consisted of three tapestries. One hung upstage parallel with the proscenium line, one hung stage left, and another hung stage right, perpendicular to the proscenium line. All scene shifts were part of the action of the play and visible to the audience. The tapestries that hung stage left and right were 8' high x 16' wide; the bottoms of the tapestries played about 12' above stage level. Because of other working scenery and lighting, it was necessary to store the side tapestries on an upstage

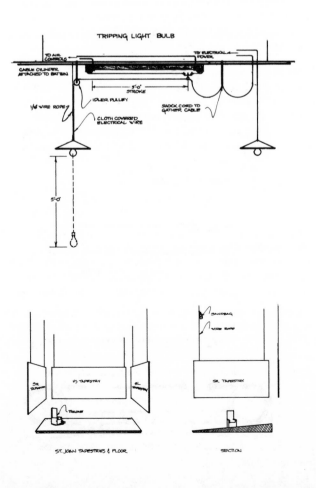

TRIPPING LIGHT BULB

ST. JOAN TAPESTRIES & FLOOR

SECTION

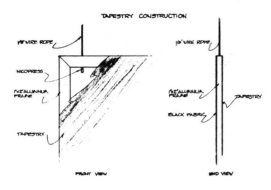

TAPESTRY CONSTRUCTION

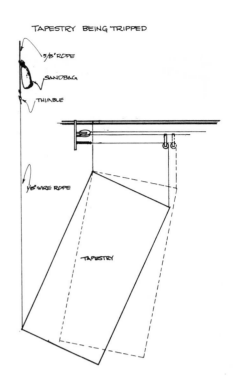

TAPESTRY BEING TRIPPED

batten and trip them into an up and downstage hang, using a downstage spot line.

To keep the tapestries in a stable position for flying in and out on the upstage batten, it was necessary to trip them in a way that would hold them level and parallel with the proscenium line, so they would not hang up on something in the crowded fly loft. A 12' stroke, 4" bore cable cylinder was used for the trip device after unsuccessful attempts were made using an adjacent counter weight batten—the variance in weight for the trip was too great for a strong fly to control confidently. The trip line only needed to travel 7', so it was necessary to make a very strong and stable stop on the cable

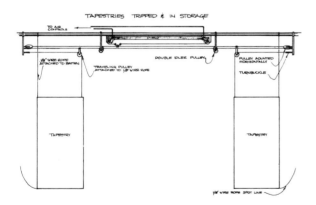

TAPESTRIES TRIPPED & IN STORAGE

cylinder to prevent it from pulling farther than required. The cable cylinder was mounted to the batten on which the tapestries were hung. When the tapestries came into view, the storage trip was released smoothly as the cable cylinder moved and the downstage trip line was pulled into trim.

The process was reversed when the tapestries flew out: the trip on the cable cylinder was activated as the batten began to fly out and the downstage pick-up line was released. The downstage pick-up made a loop, which remained above audience view but below the other battens that worked between it and the stored tapestries. The pressure to activate this effect was less than 40psi. The handling of the tapestries was very reliable in a crowded fly loft of 40 line sets, all being used. The weight of the cable cylinder on the storage line helped stabilize the batten, and there was very little swinging upstage and downstage.

The attachments on the tapestries were at three points—two on the upstage side and one on the downstage side. When the trip line, which was attached 1' from the bottom of the upstage side of the tapestry, was released totally, it ran exactly with the upstage hanging line so the two lines appeared as one. In fact, we determined the storage trip line by starting with the hang in its onstage position. Then a pulley on a cable track was used to pull the lower pick-up point onstage, which tripped the tapestries to storage positions. The hanging cables were suspended on brackets, to make all movement clear and direct from the cable cylinder. The downstage pick-up line required guides to keep from sagging on lighting instruments and other items in the fly loft. A bumper pipe was added on the downstage side of the adjacent electric pipe to hold the downstage trip line to a controlled path. The tapestries were painted muslin attached to a 1" x 2" aluminum frame by an industrial adhesive. To hang the tapestry frame we used 1/8" airplane cable. Black fabric was stretched over the back side of the tapestries.

Control valves

The type of control valve to use on cable cylinders depends on the type of work you want the cylinder to do. For most functions I have used a three-position, four-way valve with the center position exhausting both sides of the cylinder. This enables you to manually move the wagon, door, or drape when the valve is in the center. When the cable cylinder has to make several stops in its travel, however, it is best to keep pressure on both sides of the cylinder. This is so that the cylinder will not drift but will lock into position when it is stopped in its travel. The best valve for locking the cable cylinder is a three-position valve with five ports, which give a separate input pressure for each side of the cylinder. On each input there needs to be a one-way check valve to keep movement of air from one side of the cylinder to the other if a single air supply is used.

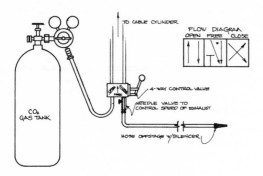

CIRCUITRY TO CONTROL CABLE CYLINDER WITH CENTER FREE

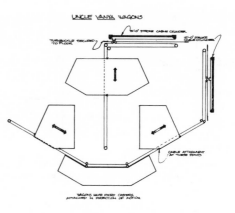

UNCLE VANYA WAGONS

Cable cylinders are good for moving devices in a straight line and for push-pull functions. At Seattle Rep we purchased the original cable cylinders for a production of *Uncle Vanya*, designed by Robert Dahlstrom. Technically, the set consisted of a bumper platform, the downstage fixed unit, two sets of wagons (one traveling upstage and downstage and a pair that, working together, came in diagonally to mate with the bumper platform), and a lot of hanging rope, on which interiors and exteriors were projected.

The upstage center wagon traveled 30' and the diagonal wagons traveled 24'. I chose to use 15' and 12' stroke cylinders and double purchase to move the wagons. The double purchase gave us a better speed, was less costly, and took up less space backstage. The cylinders were mounted to the floor, and we made a small caster unit to run on the floor

It was extremely difficult to dock the upstage center wagon softly. The wagon really could not travel a full 30', so the cable cylinder did not travel its full length. Therefore, the cylinder cushioning was lost in one direction. To solve this problem an 8' stroke rod piston cylinder was used as a shock absorber at the end of the travel. The extended rod cylinder was filled with oil; a needle valve restricted the flow of the oil out of the rod. We attached a reservoir to the cylinder and pressurized it with CO_2 to give an initial cushion to the cushion. The reservoir was placed above the cylinder, so that gravity would refill the cylinder with oil. (This type of shock absorber or cushion would be the same principle as described in the automatic door closure device in Lab Theatre, *Theatre Crafts* June/July 1981).

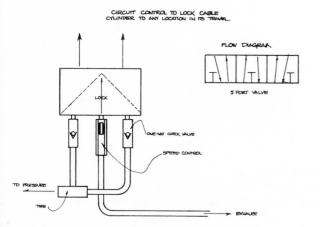

CIRCUIT CONTROL TO LOCK CABLE CYLINDER TO ANY LOCATION IN ITS TRAVEL

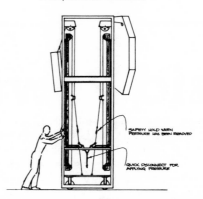

CABLE CYLINDER APPLICATION IN STAGE MOVEMENT INSTALLATION

and carry the double pulley on the cable clevis. The caster unit prevented the cables from twisting and kept the clevis from dragging on the floor. The caster unit also became the device to spike the floor for the position the cylinder needed for acceleration and for when it should be stopped.

The diagonal platforms worked exceptionally well. They traveled at the desired speed and cushioned in for stopping at each end. We used the full travel of the cable cylinders, and the cushion on the cylinder was adjusted as desired.

I have used cable cylinders a great deal in moving variable weight devices, such as raising and lowering a hot air balloon, sometimes with a person, sometimes without a person; raising and lowering stage elevators; and flying a set piece that is then unattached from the fly line. In some cases air pressure could be applied instead of iron weight for counter balancing. There are, however, numerous safety factors that you must consider to use this principle extensively. I have used air pressure for counterweight to a great degree in the devices for clearing the Stratford Festival stage of its stage balcony unit. Six cable cylinders, all 10' stroke, were used to fold up the platforms, steps, and trap covers.

Winches would be the conventional adjunct to this type of mechanical advantage in the theatre. I have difficulty with winches: the cable spools when there is no load; they are slow and noisy; and they lack a cushioned start and stop. We did use two small electric winches in the Stratford balcony changeover plan. They were quiet, but there were problems with spooling and they were too slow.

When using the cable cylinder to lift, a safety lock is easily employed to hold the load at the raised position if pressure is lost. Some of the Stratford balcony functions have a safety hold. The hold is a snap on the end of a restraining cable that clamps into an eye on the clevis of the cable cylinder, enabling the cylinder to be disengaged from pressure and the raised load to stop in its top position.

The cable cylinder is a versatile mechanical advantage device that is simple to use in a linear action effect and can be mounted easily on the floor, the wall, the grid, or a batten. Noise is minimal if the exhaust is plumbed offstage. Direction and variable speed are easy to control with use of valves.

Resources
Tol-O-Matic
1028 South Third Street
Minneapolis, MN 55415
(612) 335-6605

Greenco Corporation
PO Box 1035
Dearborn, MI 48121
(313) 582-5650

Originally published in August/September 1983

Fluid Power

by Robert Scales

Regardless of your fascination with fluid power—hydraulics and pneumatics—and interest in using it to solve technical problems, you must always weigh its value, advantages, and disadvantages over mechanical and electrical devices. Fluid power is not always the best solution for a problem but, if you are familiar with its capabilities and workings, it can be more useful, simpler, and less costly than other power sources for solving particular technical problems.

In the theatre, most technical personnel know the relationships among wattage, amperage, and voltage—and know how and why to use what wire, fuse, connector, and fixtures. If you are to use fluid power the basics need to be known. The right selection and application of pipe, hoses, valves, regulators, actuators, and so forth should be made in full consideration of the relationships of CFM (cubic force per minute), psi, and mechanical force required.

Safety rules
1 Understand the basic principle and be familiar with components of the system.
2 Use only the pressure required to achieve the effect. (If this rule is applied, an obstruction, overload, or added friction would result in stalling until the problem had been corrected.)
3 The pressure in the system should never exceed the pressure of the lowest rated component used.
4 Always secure all tanks in an upright position using small welding gas tank trucks for handling CO_2 bottles has proved useful onstage and in the shop.
5 Never work on a system that is under pressure.
6 Test all circuitry for accuracy with low pressure before the load is attached.
7 Be certain that all interface to the fluid power system is adequate in strength.
8 Use common sense.

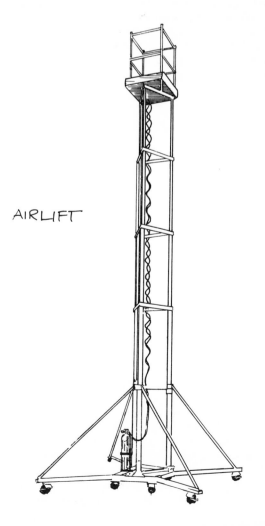

AIRLIFT

Many fluid power suppliers have personnel in the company who have some training in fluid power systems application and are helpful in the design and selection of components. This assistance is usually free—in hope that the client will then buy equipment from the company giving the advice. Some fluid power manufacturers give short term seminars for a small fee, which usually includes the cost of literature, a catalogue, demonstration materials, meals, and lodging. I took a three-day course from Martinoir (Canada) and found it very useful. Other than my experience in fluid power application, this is my only source of instruction. Most of the participants in these seminars are engineers and salesmen for distributors.

The use of fluid power has revolutionized several industries. It has made automation of heavy machinery practical. It has made our lives safer with power brakes and power steering. It offers compactness to high power. It provides quiet and safe, stage elevator power. It will be interesting to see what affect it will have on the theatre. Will Vertilift become successful? Was Hydrofloat before its time? Will the theatre technician know any more about fluid power in ten years than he knows now?

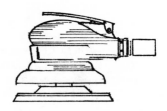

AIR POWERED
HANDTOOLS

GAS BOTTLE
ON 2-WHEEL
CART

Air powered tools

Although this Lab Theatre series has focused on fluid power, I find pneumatics easier to use than hydraulics because of its simplicity, portability, and cost.

Air powered hand tools are generally more compact, lighter, less expensive and need less maintenance than electric tools. Some tools, such as power nailers and staplers, are almost exclusively air powered.

My experience has been that once air tools are introduced into the scene shop the staff will prefer them over electric

tools. Air tools are lighter, smoother and cooler running, and, because they are smaller, more comfortable to grip.

Our scene shop at Seattle has more air powered tools than we can use at one time. Each tool requires a certain CFM. The total consumption of air at any one moment cannot exceed the capabilities of the compressor and reservoir. When an air system is overloaded, the result is inadequate pressure and CFM (cubic force per minute) to operate the tool(s) connected to the sytem. Insufficient air pressure and CFM are not necessarily harmful to the tool, but the tool will not function properly, and the compressor will have to work beyond its designed air volume. Repeated overloads cause the com-

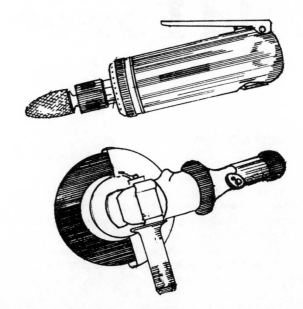

pressor to overwork, which may result in overheating of the compressor and/or compressor motor.

For air tools to function at maximum efficiency, a constant line pressure of 90 to 100 psi is required. Each air tool requires a specific quantity of air CFM to operate. If air use lowers the psi to less than 90, the air tool will begin to lose efficiency; it will stall if the pressure goes much below 70 psi. Some air tools, such as a pneumatic hot glue gun and spray painting equipment, operate at lower pressures. Be certain to set the appropriate operating pressure before plugging in any pneumatic tool under pressure.

The following chart list air power tools useful in a scene shop, along with their operating pressures and air consumption. Much of the information for this chart is from the W. W. Grainger, Inc., catalogue. Grainger has sales offices and warehouses in almost every state; its central office is at 5959 W. Howard Street, Chicago, Illinois 60648 (312) 647-8900.

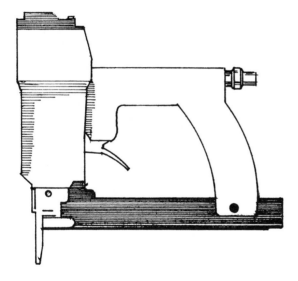

Estimated air requirement

*CFM requirements based on use 25% of the time. All other CFM calculated on full time use.

*Drill 1/16–3/8″	6.3
*Screw driver #2–#6	3.0
*Screw driver #8–#10	6.0
*Nutsetter to 3/8″	6.0
Die grinder–small	3.8
Die grinder–med.	5.0
Filing/sawing small	3.0
Jigsaw	5.0
Air hammer/scaler	3.0
Circular saw 8″	3.0
Sander 5″ orbital	8.8
Occelating med. duty sander	20.0
Small stapler/nailer @60 staples	0.12
Med. stapler/nailer @60 staples	0.3
Lrg. stapler/nailer @60 staples	0.8
Touch up spray paint	3.5
Texture sprayer	19.0
Blow guns–small orifice	5.0
Blow guns–lrg. orfice	20.0
Air Caster 12″ 25psi 1000lb	10.0
Air Caster 15″ 25psi 2000lb	10.0
Air Caster 21″ 25psi 4000lb	10.0
2″ bore cylinder per 12″	0.0218
4″ bore cylinder per 12″	0.087

Compressor and bottle gas

The tools with the least amount of air consumption are staplers and the nailer. Therefore, several can be used simultaneously without a large compressor. The rule of thumb is: for every horse power of the compressor there is a delivery of 4 CFM. It would be possible to run any of the tools listed in the chart with a 5HP compressor; the total CFM draw, however, could be no greater than 20 CFM at any one time.

My recommendation would be to purchase at least a 5HP or 7.5HP compressor. I have purchased compressors of 10HP, 15HP, 20HP, and 25HP. The 25HP can deliver 100 CFM, which is probably adequate for almost all theatrical application except extensive uses of air casters. The choice of a compressor is often determined by available funds. You should also consider that the compressor needs adequate, clean, and soundproofed (in relation to the stage) space.

When using bottle gas, calculate the potential CFM usage of the tool or device to determine the consumption requirement. For each pound of CO_2, use the factor of 6.1 to determine CFM. A 20 lb. CO_2 tank would deliver 122 CF and a 50 lb. CO_2 tank would deliver 305 CF.

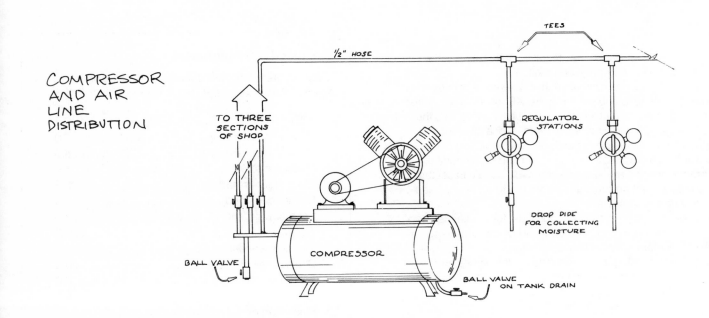

COMPRESSOR
AND AIR
LINE
DISTRIBUTION

Care needs to be taken to make certain the pipe and hoses from the compressor or bottle gas maintain adequate CFM for the tool or device to function properly. To keep pressure drop to a minimum, the following air line sizes should be used:

Air CFM	ID pipe and hose
1–5	½″
6–25	¾″
26–59	1″
60–100	1½″

The Seattle Repertory Theatre's shop air distribution uses ½″ hose. We have three feeds from the compressor. Each feed can be cut off separately if any problem occurs in any section. And if an adjustment is needed, the entire system is not turned off. Moisture is the major problem with air powered tools. We have taken very simple precautions to prevent moisture build-up. When the air lines are taken up from the compressor to the ceiling, the drop allows moisture to drain easily.

One of the most common pneumatically controlled devices in many theatres is Upright Scaffolding's air lift, which consists of a platform elevated by three telescoping air cylinders. It is extremely useful in hanging and focusing lights. For the last ten years, I have used this device for almost all stage work that exceeds 16′ and have found it reliable, compact, light-weight, and versatile for stage use. The air lift is a good example of applying pneumatics to solve a specific problem.

Originally published in November/December 1983

BIOGRAPHICAL INDEX

Bryan H. Ackler, formerly a theatre technican at Vassar College and a faculty member at the University of Maine, Orono, is now in the design department at Electro-Controls, Salt Lake City, Utah.

William Anderson, formerly technical director and lighting designer at Louisiana State University, is now a consultant with N.D. Traylor and Associates in Louisiana.

Keith Arnett, formerly sound engineer at the McCarter Theatre, is now customer service manager and theatre amplifications specialist at Audiotronics in Memphis, Tennessee.

Barry L. Bailey, formerly a set designer at University of South Carolina, is now a principal in Bailey Designs in Malden, Massachusetts.

James R. Bakkom, formerly the Guthrie Theatre property master, is now a freelance designer.

Peter Bendevski is on the production staff of the George Street Playhouse, New Brunswick, New Jersey.

Stancil Campbell, formerly a scene designer at University of North Carolina, Greensboro, is now a visiting professor of design in the Drama and Fine Arts Department at the University of Alberta, Edmonton, Canada.

Richard H. Chapman was a student at Humboldt State University.

John Chenault has served as technical director at Jersey City State College.

Thomas J. Corbett, formerly technical director at the University of California, Santa Cruz, and the University of Washington, is now with Paoletti-Lewitz in San Francisco.

Pete Davis has served as technical director for the Pacific Conservatory of the Performing Arts in Santa Monica, California, and production supervisor at the Denver Center for the Performing Arts.

Richard W. Durst is a scenic designer and chairman of the Department of Theatre at the University of Minnesota, Duluth.

Allan Fanjoy is technical director at the University of Delaware.

James Fay is a technical director, designer, and associate professor of speech at the University of Missouri, St. Louis.

William Daniel File, formerly associate professor of technical theatre at Northern Michigan University, is now a designer and technical director at the University of North Carolina, Greensboro.

Mark Freij is scene shop supervisor at the Center for the Arts, State University of New York/Purchase.

Leo Gambacorta is a freelance designer and member of the Theatre Department faculty at John Jay College in New York City.

David Glenn, formerly a designer/technical director at Playmakers Repertory Company, Paul Green Theatre, University of North Carolina, is now a technical director with Arena Stage in Washington, D.C.

Phillip Grayson is technical director at James Madison University in Virginia.

A. Evan Haag was a student at Stanford University who went on to become a technical director in community theatres in Rochester, New York.

Delbert L. Hall is a designer and technical director at LaGrange College in Georgia.

Michael Hottois, formerly production designer at the University of Louisville, is now associate professor of scenic and lighting design.

Russell Houchen was a PhD student in theatre and engineering at the University of Florida.

John T. Howard, Jr., is the technical director of the Laboratory Theatre at Mount Holyoke College.

Karen Huffman was a freelance designer.

Daniel Koetting, formerly technical director of the Theatre and Film Department at Hunter College in New York City, is now chairman of the department.

Wayne Kramer is associate professor of theatre and co-Dean of the School of Humanities and Arts at Hampshire College in Amherst, Massachusetts.

Everett Littlefield is senior scene technician in the Department of Theatre Arts at UCLA.

William Lord is a theatre consultant and teaches technical theatre at North Central High School in Indianapolis.

R.J. Loyd was the technical director/touring lighting designer for the Dayton Ballet company.

Michael Ludwick has served as technical director at Northwest Missouri State University.

R. Duncan Mackenzie, formerly technical director at the Oregon Shakespeare Festival, is now a project consultant with George Thomas Howard in Los Angeles.

William Miller has served as technical director at the State University of New York/Plattsburg.

Gregg Olsson is a graduate of the University of Washington School of Drama.

Leon Pike is a professor at Lewis and Clark College in Portland, Oregon.

Karl T. Pope is a professor in the Department of Theatre and Cinematic Arts at Brigham Young University in Utah.

John Priest and Pierre Cayard are technical director and head of scenic construction, respectively, with the San Francisco Opera.

Charles Purchase has served as technical director for the American Festival Ballet.

Patrick Reed was an MFA candidate and assistant technical director at Southern Illinois State University at Carbondale.

Charles L. Riccillo is a scenographer and instructor of theatre at Christopher Newport College in Virginia.

Terry Sateren has served as technical production director of the Guthrie Theatre.

Robert Scales is technical production director for the Seattle Repertory Theatre.

David Sealy has headed a company that provided instruction and services for fine arts application of computer techniques.

Richard Slabaugh has been a designer and technical director at Washington State University.

Raynette Halvorsen Smith has been an assistant professor of drama at San Diego State University.

Mike Stair has been a theatre arts faculty member at Dordt College, in Sioux Center, Iowa.

Jeffrey Sultan has worked in technical production at Stanford University and various other theatres across the country.

Michael Glenn Ward has been an assistant professor of architecture at North Dakota State University, and a freelance designer and technical director at theatres in Florida and Idaho.

Carey Wong, formerly resident designer for the Portland Opera, is now a freelance designer based in Portland.